Elements of Basic-Plus Programming

WILSON T. PRICE

Merritt College
Oakland, California

Holt, Rinehart and Winston

NEW YORK   CHICAGO   SAN FRANCISCO

PHILADELPHIA   MONTREAL   TORONTO   LONDON

SYDNEY   TOKYO   MEXICO CITY

RIO DE JANEIRO   MADRID

Library of Congress Cataloging in Publication Data

Price, Wilson T.
  Elements of Basic-plus programming.

  Includes index.
  1. BASIC-PLUS (Computer program language)
I. Title.
QA76.73.B36P75   001.64'24   82–6081
ISBN 0-03-060148-7   AACR2

Printed in the United States of America
Published simultaneously in Canada

  3 4 5   016   9 8 7 6 5

CBS COLLEGE PUBLISHING
Holt, Rinehart and Winston
The Dryden Press
Saunders College Publishing

Contents

APPENDIXES

Preface

As the title suggests, this text was written around Basic-Plus as implemented on the Digital Equipment PDP 11 computer. It was written for students who will be taking their first course in computer programming. However, it includes both basic and advanced topics. It can be used for a one-semester, comprehensive beginning course or for a two-quarter sequence (beginning and advanced). A primary consideration in its original design was to focus on the use of Basic language as a tool for students from a variety of disciplines whether they be in data processing, computer science, general business, the humanities, or whatever. To this end, a relatively low mathematical level is incorporated into the book. For instance, sample programs involve such operations as computing the average of a data set, bringing a simple inventory up-to-date, checking the validity of input data, and processing a data array. However, techniques and programming problems are included which will be challenging to the mathematically oriented student. Some of the important features of this book are:

1. Each new topic is introduced through and oriented around a simple example. Each example is described in detail, its implications are discussed, it is solved, and important features of the solution are discussed. The progression is always from the concrete to the abstract.

2. As a rule, example programs are kept short with primary focus on the topic being introduced. For the beginning student, it is felt that the value of an example program or sequence in illustrating a concept is inversely proportional to the amount of code which is extraneous to that particular concept.

3. In all examples, modularization of programs is emphasized. This is especially important to the beginning student when covering advanced topics where example programs necessarily become much larger than earlier examples. Not only does modularization provide examples for the student which are easy to follow but it illustrates programming techniques which are critical to writing good, easy to maintain and readable programs.

4. Emphasis is placed on using structured techniques and minimizing use of the GOTO statement. Since Basic-Plus does not include a true block IF-THEN-ELSE, this concept is simulated to maintain good structured techniques.

5. Each chapter includes "mind-jogger" exercises within the chapter with answers

at the end of the chapter. The intent is to provide a reinforcement vehicle for important concepts. In many cases these exercises relate the significant point(s) concerning an example program and give the student a better insight into some of the fine points. The student should be urged to complete each exercise as it is encountered and then refer to the answer to be certain of comprehending it.

6. Extensive coverage is included for RSTS/E file handling. Random file processing using virtual arrays and record (block) I/0 is illustrated with comprehensive examples. A special set of programming problems and projects is included following Chapter 17. Some of them represent fairly sophisticated file applications which will keep an advanced student busy for quite a while.

7. The book contains seven appendixes which include reserved words; the ASCII character set; summaries of BASIC-PLUS commands, statements, functions, and error messages; and sample errors together with their diagnosis.

Concerning the topical organization of this book, the detailed table of contents speaks for itself. However, some important points may not be evident from the list of contents.

First, Chapter 1 uses a subset of the language which allows the student to write a complete, meaningful program from the beginning. Many of the topics presented in this chapter (in some cases the approach is "do it because it works") are expanded in later chapters.

Second, the "core" content of the book (for use in a single programming course) is Chapters 1 through 9, 12, and 13. These cover the basic concepts that should be found in any Basic course. The remaining chapters describe advanced concepts which might be used on a pick and choose basis in a first course, or they could form the basis for an advanced course.

Acknowledgments

For many years I was a product of IBM batch processing. I was "born" to IBM (1960), nursed on their methods, and "matured into IBM adulthood" over the next 15 years. Then several years ago I came to the realization that the remarks—no, blasphemy—which some of my associates were making concerning the existence of other computers (than IBM) were really true. That began my "affair" with the DEC PDP 11 computer. During my initiation, I received some pretty good lumps but, by and large, I have come away with a healthy respect of "other" equipment. What is the point of this dialogue? The point is that I grew together with my students during this learning experience (which is *still* going on). So it is to my students that I must first express my appreciation. I thank them for their patience, for their ideas, for their stimulation, and for everything else that may be difficult to verbalize.

As part of our bid specification in acquiring our 11/70, we had included an extensive benchmark. Ted Sorbin, who was a DEC systems engineer at the time, was assigned to this project. In addition to being a super guy, Ted is one of the most knowledgeable RSTS people with whom I have had the pleasure to work. His thoughts and ideas were most helpful in getting me off the ground. In addition, an outstanding internal DEC publication which he did on string handling and random file processing gave me my insight and provided the basis for the corresponding topics in this book. Thank you Ted.

In addition, Robert Wilson (California State University at Long Beach) provided many valuable ideas and insights. Numerous others have influenced this book through their ideas, observations and comments. These include Bruce Beattie, Richard Bidleman, George Grill, Jack Olson, Peter Simas, Norman Sandak, and Robert van Keuren. They have my sincere appreciation and thanks.

I must not omit Kathy Kain who has done superb typing and proofing work for me on several projects including this one. Thank you, Kathy. (I bury my head in the sand regarding the fact that she will eventually go on to other things and I will be faced with finding a replacement.)

Finally, I wish to thank users of my books who have taken their valuable time to send me their reactions, observations, and critical remarks; many of them are reflected in this book. I will sincerely appreciate any and all comments about this book. They may be sent to me at Merritt College, 12500 Campus Drive, Oakland, CA 94619.

Wilson T. Price

Introduction

BASIC CONCEPTS OF PROGRAMMING

A Story of Success

To gain a little insight into the world of the computer, let us consider the story of a very bright college student who had a strong dislike for conventional "work." When faced with the prospect of financing his college education, he decided to do so by playing the horses—a means of earning an income that he considered infinitely superior to pumping gas or washing dishes. Since his hobby had long been horse racing, he had an extensive file of information on the horses that generally raced at the local tracks. This file consisted of a set of 5 × 7 cards, one for each horse. Each card showed the past record of the horse (including best running times), information on how well the horse did under various weather conditions, and so on.

The information file was the key to the student's success. Prior to each weekend, he would select from his file the record of each horse running that weekend. Armed with this stack of cards, a summary form, a pencil, his brilliant mind, and his system, he would sit down to work (Figure 1). His system consisted of a series of calculations that gave each horse a performance score between 0 and 100. Past experience had shown that the horse with the highest score in each race was usually the winner.

The procedure the student followed was simple:

1. Take the next card from the set of data cards.
2. Calculate the HPS (Horse Performance Score) for that horse.†
3. Record the horse's name and score on the summary form.
4. Go back to step 1 and repeat the sequence for the next horse.

The summary form then provided the student with all of the information he would need at the track that weekend.

Figure 1
A human computer system

---

†What is involved in this step? We can assume that many detailed calculations are required. Since the formula was a closely guarded secret, only the student knew what the exact procedures were.

By the time the student finished college, the horse racing project had become drudgery. Capitalizing on his vast (by now) programming experience, he obtained a highly paid position as a computer programmer, and lived happily ever after.

Horse Racing and Computer Programming

What does all of that have to do with computer programming? To answer, let us consider the following.

First, it illustrates a data processing application. "Data processing" is a very common term, which can be defined as the processing of raw data (information) to obtain useful results. In the story the raw data was supplied by the 5×7 cards, the calculations comprised the processing, and the summary sheet represented the useful results.

Second, the set of 5×7 cards consisted of the same components as data to be used by a computer. The student had a *file* of *data*. This file consisted of a set of *related records*. Each record contained several *pieces of information* about that horse. In data processing terminology each piece of information is called a *field*. The notions of file, field, and record are illustrated for the horse racing example in Figure 2(a). It is important to recognize that data to be used by a computer contains the same three components: files, records, and fields. For example, a file of employee payroll records that a company uses to pay its employees is illustrated in Figure 2(b). As with the horse racing example, you can see that the file consists of a set of related records (employee master records). Each record contains information about one specific element of the file (one employee). The information on each record is divided into fields. Each field contains one piece of information about the employee: the Name field contains the employee's name, the Pay Rate field contains the employee's pay rate, and so on. Most data going into or coming out of a computer consists of files, records, and fields.

Third, the sequence of steps carried out by the student in processing his data is very similar to the manner in which a computer operates. That is, one performs a sequence of steps (such as the following).

1. Read next record.
2. Calculate the HPS.
3. Record the results.
4. Return to step 1.

Now you might wonder about how to calculate HPS (step 2). Is the computer so smart that it knows what to do without being told in detail? The answer is NO! Just as we cannot do the horse racing calculation without being told exactly what has to be done, so the computer cannot do any desired calculation without being told exactly what to do. The computer is capable of some amazing things. But it has no intelligence and no judgment, and so it cannot decide what has to be done. This brings us to the First Law of Programming:

> *If you want the computer to do a particular thing, you must tell it in exacting detail to do that particular thing.*

Figure 2
Files, records, and fields

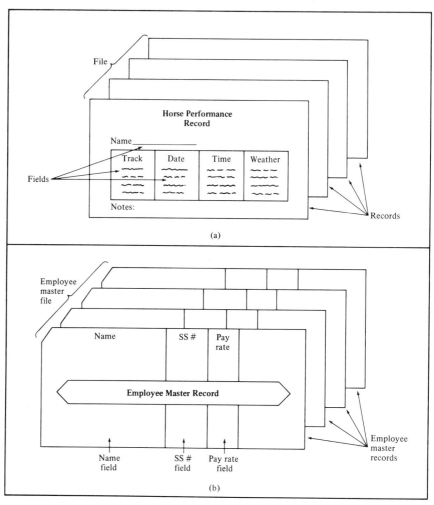

Horse Performance Record

Name

Track	Date	Time	Weather

Notes:

(a)

Employee master file

Name	SS #	Pay rate

Employee Master Record

Name field   SS # field   Pay rate field

Employee master records

(b)

The corollary of the First Law can be stated as:

If you don't tell it, it won't do it.

The second corollary is:

The computer will do what you tell it to do, even if you don't mean it.

For most people, learning to program means learning to be precise.

Writing Computer Programs

If you accept the fact that you must tell the computer exactly what to do, you are probably wondering "how" to do it. Let us consider this question in two parts: (1)

How do you figure out what you want the computer to do? (2) Once you have figured out what you want it to do, how do you tell it to do it? That *how* is what this book is all about—to learn the answers to these questions. Basically there is a very simple procedure to follow in writing any computer program.

1. *Define the desired results.* Analyze the problem to see what useful results, or output, are required. Decide on exactly what information the computer is to output.

2. *Examine the input data.* Does the data contain everything that you need to produce the desired output? If the needed data is not there in exactly the desired form, can you combine some of the input fields to produce the desired output? If the answer to one of these questions is yes, you can go ahead. However, if the answer to both questions is no, you do not have the necessary input data to produce the desired output.

3. Devise an overall plan (sometimes called an *algorithm*) for converting the input data into the desired output. A number of techniques are commonly used for this purpose, including structured flowcharts (described in a later section) and pseudocode.

4. Express the solution in a language that the computer can understand. This is called "coding the program"; this book involves coding programs in the Basic language.

Many students dislike the preliminary work of clearly defining and solving the problem. They prefer to get right on to the coding. However, these students usually find, as the problems become more complicated, that the program cannot be coded until the solution algorithm has been developed. The flowchart is a convenient way to express the algorithm. This brings us to the Second Law of Programming:

The longer you spend on defining your output and developing your overall solution, the faster the programming task will go.

The corollary to the Second Law is:

Resist the urge to code!

TECHNIQUES OF PROGRAM SOLUTION

Modular Design of Programs

For many years *good* programmers have tended to view the solution of a programming problem as the process of breaking a problem down into its component parts and then proceeding. Within the past several years the value of this approach in producing programs that are easy to read and modify has become clearly evident. The result has led to a clear recognition of the value of *modular design* of programs. A program module is commonly defined as a segment of a program that performs a particular function. For instance, on a very small scale, the horse performance sequence can be considered as consisting of three modules: data input, computations, and output of results. In a computer program the input module might consist not only of getting the next record, but also checking to ensure that the data is within certain predefined limits (data validation). On the other hand, if the computation module is a very sizable task, it might be broken down into logical submodules. This process is normally continued until all modules are of a manageable size. Then each module (beginning from the top) can be programmed and tested independently of the others. This approach has proved highly effective in producing easily coded and maintained programs.

Although these concepts are important to bear in mind, the need for them is not too obvious to the beginner. The reason for this is that beginners generally encounter relatively small and simple programs in their struggle with the rules of the language involved. The concept of modularization should always be borne in mind.

Structured Programming

One inevitable result of poor program planning is a program that is virtually impossible to follow. This commonly results from excessive jumping around within the program to patch up earlier omissions. Within recent years the technique called *structured programming* has come into wide use. This approach to programming involves three basic logic structures:

1. *Simple sequence*—progression from one operation or group of operations to the next successive one.
2. *Selection*—selection of one of two or more operations or group of operations to be performed, depending upon a particular test condition.
3. *Repetition* or *looping*—repeated execution of one or more operations until a given condition is satisfied.

Although Basic-Plus was not designed as a structured language, many of the structured programming principles can be utilized in writing Basic programs. The nature of these three logical structures and their application to Basic-Plus are described in Chapter 4.

The Use of Flowcharts

A flowchart is a pictorial representation of the logic of a program solution. With the advent of modern programming techniques, the use of flowcharts has seen some criticism. However, flowcharts, when used in conjunction with modular techniques and structured principles, can be very valuable. That approach is used in this book.

For the sake of standardizing, differently shaped symbols will be used to represent different program functions. The flowchart symbols used in this book are summarized in Figure 3.

COMPUTER HARDWARE

A computer is a tool that can be used to process information and obtain results. Computers do not themselves solve problems; we do. We write programs of instructions telling the computer what to do. Then it will accept information (*data*); perform required operations on that data; and provide the results we need. Every computer system consists of two fundamental components: *hardware* and *software*.

Figure 3
Flowchart symbols

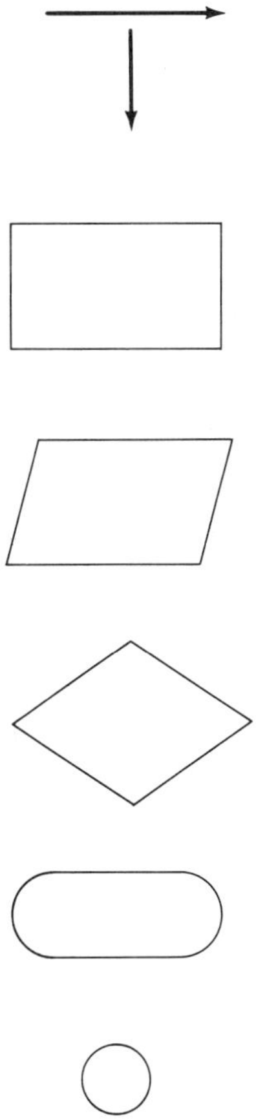

The *flow direction symbol* represents the direction of processing flow, which is generally from top to bottom and left to right. To avoid confusion, flowlines are often drawn with an arrowhead at the point of entry of a symbol. Whenever possible, crossing of flowlines should be avoided.

The *processing symbol* is used to show general processing functions not represented by other symbols. These functions are generally those that contain the actual information-processing operations of the program. In the case of Basic, this is primarily arithmetic.

The *input/output symbol* is used to denote any function of an input/output device in the program. Both input and output are common to the computer terminal or, as we shall learn, to computer files.

The *decision symbol* is used to indicate a point in a program at which a decision is made to take one of two or more alternative courses of action. This symbol represents the selection structure.

The *termination symbol* represents any point at which a program originates or terminates. With normal program operation, such points are at the start and completion of the program.

One other symbol that will be of use is the *connector symbol*. Whenever a program becomes sufficiently complex that the number and direction of flowlines is confusing, it is frequently useful to utilize the connector symbol. This symbol represents an entry from, or an exit to, another part of the flowchart. It is also used to indicate a "juncture" point in the selection structure.

Hardware is the physical portion of the computer system. For use within this book we consider the basic components of the computer to be those illustrated in Figure 4. Following is a brief description of these components.

Input/Output

As the name implies, *input* units allow us to enter data into the computer for processing. A wide variety of devices are used for input, including machines that read data from punched cards, magnetically encoded checks, and even handwritten documents.

Results of the machine computations are made available to us through *output* devices. These include printers that print full lines, and even pages, at a time, video display units, and audio devices.

Most systems that use Basic are designed around *terminals* that perform both input and output. Information is entered into the computer via a typewriter-style keyboard. Some terminals print the results on paper much as an ordinary typewriter does (called *hard copy* devices). Cathode-ray-tube (CRT) terminals display the results on a television-like screen (called *soft copy*).

Processor

The processor is the computer's "electronic control center." Here instructions are carried out for bringing information into the system, performing computations, making decisions, and producing results.

Internal Memory

Internal memory is used for temporarily holding programs of instructions and data that are currently being operated upon. The memory of any computer is a highly organized storage area. Each "cell" of memory has its own individual address and can be referred to by a program. Fortunately, the Basic programmer need not be concerned with details of memory and memory addressing since this task is handled automatically by the system.

Figure 4
Schematic diagram
of a computer
system

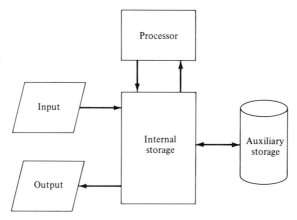

Auxiliary Storage

Where internal memory retains programs and data that are currently in use, auxiliary storage is used for long-term retention of both programs and sets of data. Auxiliary storage can best be thought of as equivalent to a large file cabinet capable of storing huge quantities of information. As a rule the capacities of auxiliary storage devices are many times those of internal memory units.

The words "memory" and "storage" are often used interchangeably. However, in this book *memory* will refer exclusively to internal "working" memory (which is commonly considered part of the processor, or *central processing unit*, as it is often called).

COMPUTER SOFTWARE

The Operating System

The term *software* is used to describe programs of instructions that make the computer work. On a broad basis, software is divided into two general types: user-written programs (such as those we shall write in using this book) and operating system programs. Our programs will describe the data we want the machine to process, the operations to be performed on that data, and the results we wish to receive. The operating system programs are really a basic component of the overall computer system itself. It is these programs that supervise the operations of the computer and ensure that various tasks are carried out properly.

The key to the operating system and most modern computers is the *supervisor* program (sometimes called a *monitor* or *executive* program). The supervisor remains in memory at all times and maintains control, directly or indirectly, while the computer is in use (see Figure 5). In addition, the operating system consists of programs for performing such chores as automatically maintaining records and keeping track of what is stored in auxiliary storage (the libraries). The overall nature of the supervisor as it relates to the computer is illustrated in Figure 6.

Timesharing

Through the use of operating systems and special hardware features of the modern computer, the total amount of useful work performed (throughput) has been greatly increased over earlier systems. One widely used technique for serving multiple users at the same time is called *timesharing*.

Generally speaking, timesharing refers to the allocation of computer resources in a time-dependent fashion to several programs simultaneously in mem-

Figure 5
The supervisor in memory

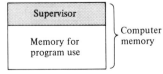

Figure 6
Animated repre-
sentation of an
operating system

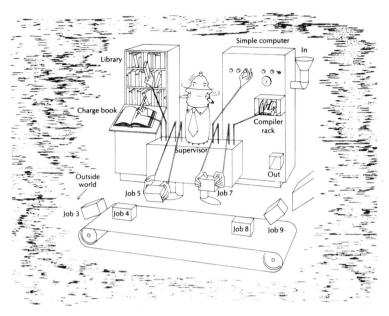

ory. The principal notion of a timesharing system is to provide a large number of users with direct access to the computer to solve their individual problems. The user thus has the ability to "converse" directly with the computer for problem solving (hence the term *conversational* or *interactive* computing). In timesharing the basic consideration is, in a sense, to maximize efficiency of each computer user and keep the user busy.

Figure 7
Time-sharing
environment

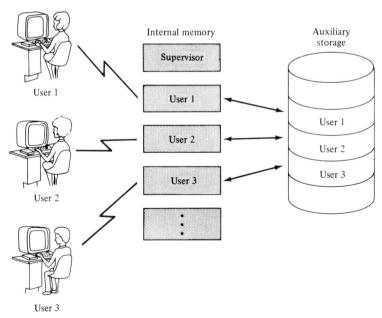

Figure 7 illustrates the notion of a timeshared system. Each user has a communications terminal, a portion of memory, and auxiliary storage. In timesharing the processor time is divided among the users on a scheduled basis. Each program will be allocated its "slice" of the processor time (commonly measured in fractions of a second) based on some predetermined scheduling basis, beginning with the first program and proceeding through the last. Upon completing the cycle, it is begun again so that an individual user scarcely realizes that someone else is also using the computer.

It is these timesharing features that are characteristic of the Digital Equipment PDP 11 computer. The interactive programming language designed for use with this computer is Basic-Plus, the subject of this book.

A Subset of Basic

FUNDAMENTAL PRINCIPLES OF BASIC

A Bookstore Inventory

Let us assume that we work for a bookstore with a large stock of books, and that keeping a check on the number of each title in stock has become a problem. In view of the fact that the bookstore management is very backward regarding modern inventory techniques using the computer, we decide to prepare a simple demonstration program to show what can be done. Before we can do the programming job, we must first figure out what results we want from the computer, and then determine whether the necessary data is available. After some digging we decide simply to calculate the number of copies on hand at the end of each month. To be complete, we formally define the job as follows.

Example 1-1 Prepare a program to calculate the number of copies of each book in the inventory given the following information for each title.

Book identification number
Inventory balance at beginning of month
Copies received during the month
Copies sold during the month
Copies lost or destroyed during the month

The printed results must include appropriate headings and the following information for each book processed.

A line count
Book identification number
Inventory balance at beginning of month
Updated inventory balance

We can see that the operations are relatively simple; the sequence involves reading a data record, performing the calculations, and then printing a line. The process is to be repeated for each book in the inventory. The calculations are:

New balance = old balance + copies received
                    − copies sold − copies lost and destroyed

In view of the fact that this program is to be used to demonstrate simple inventory processing to the bookstore manager, we decide to utilize a few typical records from the inventory file. The following data will be incorporated into the test case.

Table 1-1
Test Data for
Example 1-1

BOOK NUMBER	OLD BALANCE	COPIES RECEIVED	COPIES SOLD	COPIES LOST
4451	453	150	313	2
4892	512	0	186	4
5118	82	500	160	1
6881	0	201	0	0
7144	147	180	60	1

Expected results from the computer processing run are shown in Figure 1-1.

Overall Logic of the Problem

The overall sequence of steps involved in this problem can be summarized as:

1. Print headings.
2. Read data for next book.
3. Perform calculations.
4. Print the results.
5. Return to step 2.

A common practice in programming is to represent *logic* of the program in the form of a *flowchart*. The flowchart of Figure 1-2 illustrates the basic repetitious nature of Example 1-1—that is, a sequence that is executed repeatedly. We should note that this flowchart shows no end to the processing: Technically it is called an *infinite loop* and is considered bad practice. Ending the processing in an "orderly" way is considered later.

A Program—Example 1-1

A program of instructions to perform this task is shown in Figure 1-3. The similarity to ordinary English and algebra make the function of this program and of individual statements intuitively apparent. By comparing the program statements with what we know of the problem requirements and the flowchart of Figure 1-2, we can surmise the following.

```
READ B,O,R,S,L                     Read input data

LET N = O + R - S - L              Calculate new balance

PRINT C,B,O,N                      Print results

GO TO 410                          Branch to read next data set
```

Figure 1-1
Expected output
from inventory run

LINE NUMBER	BOOK NUMBER	OLD BALANCE	NEW BALANCE
1	4451	453	288
2	4892	512	322
3	5118	82	421
4	6881	0	201
5	7144	147	266

One feature of the Basic language is that each program statement begins with a verb that directs the computer to carry out some action. This characteristic and many other important concepts of Basic are illustrated by the program of Figure 1-3. The important features that it will reveal are:

1. Line or statement numbers in Basic
2. Remarks in the Basic program
3. Basic constants and variables
4. Basic expressions
5. Input and output capabilities
6. The LET statement
7. The transfer statement
8. The END statement

In the following sections of this chapter we study each of these features and relate them to the fundamental principles of Basic.

Figure 1-2
Flowchart for
Example 1-1

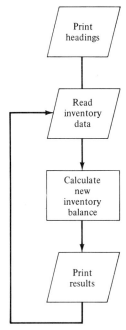

16 A SUBSET OF BASIC

Figure 1-3

Updating an inventory—Example 1-1

```
100     REM   EXAMPLE 1-1
110     REM   PROGRAM TO UPDATE AN INVENTORY
120     REM   INPUT QUANTITIES AND NAMES ARE:
130     REM     B - BOOK NUMBER
140     REM     O - OLD BALANCE
150     REM     R - COPIES RECEIVED
160     REM     S - COPIES SOLD
170     REM     L - COPIES LOST AND DESTROYED
180     REM   CALCULATED QUANTITIES AND NAMES ARE:
190     REM     C - LINE COUNT
200     REM     N - NEW BALANCE
300     REM
310     REM   PRINT THE HEADINGS
320       PRINT 'LINE', 'BOOK', 'OLD', 'NEW'
330       PRINT 'NUMBER', 'NUMBER', 'BALANCE', 'BALANCE'
340       PRINT
400     REM
410     REM   BEGINNING OF PROCESSING LOOP
420       READ B, O, R, S, L
430       LET N = O + R - S - L
440       LET C = C + 1
450       PRINT C, B, O, N
460       GO TO 410
            •
            •
            •
            •
32767   END
```

Note: Although the program of instructions is complete, more statements are required here to make this program fully operational. These are included in Fig. 1-7.

Line Numbers

Each line we see in the program of Figure 1-3 is called a *statement* and has a *statement number,* commonly called a *line number,* associated with it. Whenever we write a program in Basic, we must assign a unique line number to each line we enter into the computer. Furthermore, these line numbers must be selected so that they fall in the order in which we want the computer to consider each statement. In this example each line number is 10 greater than the preceding line. Incrementing line numbers by 10 is a common practice since it allows space to insert additional statements later if a program must be changed. In general these numbers may be chosen by the programmer; in Figure 1-3 they could have been 50, 100, 150, and so on. The only restriction is size. The largest number that can be used in Basic-Plus is 32767.

Remarks in Basic

By placing REM at the beginning of a statement, the entire line may be used by the programmer for descriptive comments. Although the remarks line is ignored by Basic during the running of the program, it will be printed or displayed with the program. The remarks included in this program adequately describe the purpose of the program. *The value of using extensive remarks in a program cannot be overemphasized.* Programmers commonly find that they must modify or expand an extensive program after completing it and progressing to another job. Even though they have written it themselves, much of the program can be very confusing unless remarks are used liberally.

In addition, Basic-Plus allows use of the exclamation mark (!) to signal a remark as shown in Figure 1-4. Here we should note that everything following the exclamation mark on lines 430 and 440 is treated as a remark, but the statement preceding it is not affected.

Exercises **1-1** Which types of statement entries in a Basic program do not require line numbers?

1-2 How is a descriptive remark indicated in a Basic program?

Variables

Upon inspecting the program statements in Figure 1-3, we see input, calculations, and output. Together with descriptive remarks, statement 420 almost explains itself:

```
420    READ B,O,R,S,L
```

That is, we are directing the computer to read data into memory for the *variables* B, O, R, S, and L (book number, old balance, and so on).

The term *variable* has much the same meaning in Basic as in algebra; it is a symbolic name given to a quantity that may change in value during the running of a program. Each variable in a program will be assigned by the Basic system to some internal memory area into which a number may be stored. In Figure 1-3 we see the following variable names to represent the designated quantities.

VARIABLE	FIELD
B	Book identification number
O	Old inventory balance
R	Number received
S	Number sold
L	Number lost
C	Line count
N	New inventory

Figure 1-4
Using the exclamation mark to indicate a remark

```
100      !     EXAMPLE 1-1
110      !     PROGRAM TO UPDATE AN INVENTORY
120      !     INPUT QUANTITIES AND NAMES ARE:
         .
         .
         .
420      READ B, O, R, S, L
430      LET N = O + R - S - L    !  CALCULATE NEW BALANCE
440      LET C = C + 1            !     AND LINE COUNT
450      PRINT C, B, O, N
         .
         .
         .
```

Although, in this example program, each variable is represented by a single letter, variable names are not, in general, so restricted. Earlier versions of Basic-Plus operated in the so-called **NO EXTEND** mode, in which names were restricted to one letter or one letter followed by one digit. However, currently available versions operate in the **EXTEND** mode, in which names may consist of one letter, or one letter followed by up to 29 letters and/or digits as well as imbedded periods. On the other hand, certain words such as **LET, READ**, and **PRINT** are called *reserved words* and cannot be used as variable names. Appendix I contains a list of reserved words. The following are examples of valid and invalid choices for variable names.

NO EXTEND Mode

VALID	INVALID	
A	2N	Letter must be first
Z	JR	May not be two letters
B3	X25	Only one letter and one digit allowed
N9	6	Cannot be a single digit
B8	C+	Only letters and digits allowed

EXTEND Mode

VALID	INVALID	
JR	2N	Letter must be first
OLD.BALANCE	7	Cannot be a single digit
A	WORK#	Only letters, digits, and periods allowed
BB	LET	Reserved word
COUNT	HOLD A	Spaces not allowed within a name

When selecting names for program variables, the name chosen should always describe the quantity it represents. For instance, Figure 1-5 is a revised version of statements 420–450 from Figure 1-3 using longer variable names. Note how well these names document the program.

Variables in Memory

Each variable used in a program will cause the Basic system to reserve one memory area into which a number may be stored. Thus the program of Figure 1-3 would require seven memory areas, one for each of the variables used. Each such memory area may contain one number at any given time. However, we can easily change the contents of a memory area by placing a new number in it, either by bringing in a new data value through an input operation or by performing a

Figure 1-5
Long variable
names in the
EXTEND mode

```
420    READ BOOK, OLD.BAL, RECEIVED, SOLD, LOST
430    LET NEW.BAL = OLD.BAL + RECEIVED - SOLD - LOST
440    LET LINE.COUNT = LINE.COUNT + 1
450    PRINT LINE.COUNT, BOOK, OLD.BAL, NEW.BAL
460    GO TO 420
```

calculation. Prior to execution of any program the Basic system sets all numeric variables to zero. Then execution of the program places values in them as needed. For instance, let us consider the first data set for which this program is written:

Book number	4451
Old balance	453
Copies received	150
Copies sold	313
Copies lost	2

The contents of the assigned memory areas would appear as shown in Figure 1-6.

Exercises **1-3** Which of the following variable names are invalid? Answer this for both NO EXTEND mode and EXTEND mode.

B	73	READ	SD
Q1298	4C	R4	WORK 3

1-4 What value is stored in each variable of a Basic program prior to execution of the program?

INPUT/OUTPUT OPERATIONS

The DATA Statement

Throughout this book emphasis is focused on the processing of data files. The simple program of Example 1-1 involves the processing of an inventory data file. Needless to say, each time the processing run is made, the data stored in the inventory file will be different. In a disk-oriented computer system the output of a run would probably be a printed report and an updated inventory file. In a tape-oriented computer system it would be the report and a new inventory file with updated data. It is important to recognize that a data file and a program to process the file are usually two separate entities and are stored separately.

However, the Basic language has a feature that allows data for a program to be included as part of the program itself. Although this is not practical for most actual applications, it is very convenient for the beginner learning Basic. It involves a special statement called the DATA statement. As we see in the

Figure 1-6

Memory contents

Initial contents	0	0	0	0	0	0	0
	B	O	R	S	L	N	C

After reading first record	4451	453	150	313	2	0	0
	B	O	R	S	L	N	C

After performing calculations	4451	453	150	313	2	288	1
	B	O	R	S	L	N	C

expanded program in Figure 1-7, the **DATA** statements are included following the program instructions. As with all Basic statements, the **DATA** statement is preceded by a line number. The keyword **DATA** is then followed by a list of quantities representing the input data to be processed. For example, by comparing the test data from Table 1-1 we see that the fields listed in each **DATA** statement represent the inventory information for one book. Adjacent fields in a **DATA** statement need only be separated by a comma. If it helps to make the program more readable, one or more blank spaces may be inserted whenever appropriate. When the program, including all **DATA** statements, is brought into memory for a run, the fields from each **DATA** statement are placed, in order, into a *data pool,* one field after the other. Upon execution of the program, these fields will be available for processing.

Figure 1-7

DATA statements in a program

```
100     REM   EXAMPLE 1-1
110     REM   PROGRAM TO UPDATE AN INVENTORY
120     REM   INPUT QUANTITIES AND NAMES ARE:
130     REM     B - BOOK NUMBER
140     REM     O - OLD BALANCE
150     REM     R - COPIES RECEIVED
160     REM     S - COPIES SOLD
170     REM     L - COPIES LOST AND DESTROYED
180     REM   CALCULATED QUANTITIES AND NAMES ARE:
190     REM     C - LINE COUNT
200     REM     N - NEW BALANCE
300     REM
310     REM   PRINT THE HEADINGS
320        PRINT "LINE", "BOOK", "OLD", "NEW"
330        PRINT "NUMBER", "NUMBER", "BALANCE", "BALANCE"
340        PRINT
400     REM
410     REM   BEGINNING OF PROCESSING LOOP
420        READ B, O, R, S, L
430        LET N = O + R - S - L
440        LET C = C + 1
450        PRINT C, B, O, N
460        GO TO 410
800     REM
810     REM     ** INPUT DATA **
820        DATA 4451, 453, 150, 313, 2
830        DATA 4892, 512,   0, 186, 4
840        DATA 5118,  82, 500, 160, 1
850        DATA 6881,   0, 201,   0, 0
860        DATA 7144, 147, 180,  60, 1
32767   END
```

The READ Statement

Data stored in the data pool is made available to the program for processing by the READ statement; for example:

```
420    READ B, O, R, S, L
```

This statement will cause the computer to bring the next five fields of data from the data pool into memory, placing the first in the memory area reserved for B, the second in the area reserved for O, and so on. Execution of this statement a second time will cause the next five fields to be brought into storage. This procedure is illustrated in Figure 1-8. Each time the READ statement is executed in a program, a new set of data values will be brought into the program. If a READ is executed and no more data remains, the program will automatically be terminated. Thus, using the example data for the program of Figure 1-7, after the fifth (and final) line has been printed the sixth attempt to read will cause execution of the program to be terminated.

Exercise 1-5 Following is a READ statement and sequence of DATA statements. What will be read into the listed variables with each execution of the READ?

```
150 READ A,B
  .
  .
  .
200 GO TO 150
210 DATA 25,13
220 DATA 281,16,37,48,122
230 DATA 53
240 END
```

String Variables

Example 1-1 involves numeric data; for instance, the book is identified by its "Book Number." What if it is necessary to identify it by its title instead? It is important to remember that all of the preceding descriptions of variables have actually related to numeric quantities. In actual practice most programs do read and process nonnumeric data as well as numeric data. In a loose sense, data can be considered in two broad categories: that upon which arithmetic can be performed and that upon which arithmetic will not be performed. For instance, an employee pay rate will be multiplied by hours worked. On the other hand, the employee

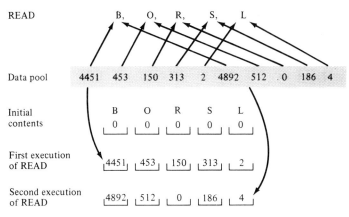

Figure 1-8
Reading data from the data pool

name or even the employee Social Security *number* will not be involved in any arithmetic operations. Thus the latter is commonly referred to as *string data.* String data can be read into a program in exactly the same way as numeric data. However, it is imperative that the system "know" that a particular variable will contain string data. In Basic, *string variables* are defined in exactly the same way as numeric variables, except they are indicated as such by adding the character $ at the end of the name. The following are some examples.

NUMERIC VARIABLES	STRING VARIABLES
B	B$
BOOKNUM	BOOKNAME$
C3	C3$
WORK.FIELD	WORK.FIELD$

Any data quantity read into a numeric variable must be a valid numeric quantity. On the other hand, a string data quantity may include letters, digits, and special characters. In other words, virtually anything can be validly processed as a string variable. For instance, consider the following READ and DATA statements.

```
READ EMPLOYEE$, VAR$, D$, SSN$, N$
    .
    .
    .
DATA "ALICE JONES", X, 3/29/84, 521-99-1234, 783
```

The following string values would be read into the variables.

VARIABLE	VALUE
EMPLOYEE$	ALICE JONES
VAR$	X
D$	3/29/84
SSN$	521-99-1234
N$	783

The PRINT Statement

The results of running the program of Figure 1-7 are repeated in Figure 1-9. As we can see, the statement

```
450    PRINT C, B, O, N
```

will cause the current values in storage areas reserved for the variables C, B, O, and N to be printed. Since this statement will be repeated as long as there is data, we see one line of output for each DATA statement (book record) in the program.

Whenever a variable name is listed in a PRINT statement, the current value of that variable will be printed. In contrast, fixed descriptive information (such as the headings) can also be printed. For instance,

```
320    PRINT "LINE", "BOOK", "OLD", "NEW"
```

causes the first line of the heading to be printed. In other words, anything included in quotes will be printed exactly as quoted. Furthermore, quoted quantities and variable values can both be printed with the same PRINT statement. For instance, an example output from

Figure 1-9
Sample output for Example 1-1

LINE NUMBER	BOOK NUMBER	OLD BALANCE	NEW BALANCE	
				Headings printed by lines 320 and 330.
				Blank line printed by line 340.
1	4451	453	288	
2	4892	512	322	Detail lines printed by
3	5118	82	421	repeated execution of
4	6881	0	201	line 450.
5	7144	147	266	
?Out of data at line 420				Error line printed by system indicating that the READ statement could find no more DATA.

```
980    PRINT "BOOK NUMBER",B
```

might be

```
BOOK NUMBER    4451
```

We should note that Basic-Plus allows the use of both the ordinary, double quote and the single quote. Thus the following statements 320 and 325 are equivalent.

```
320    PRINT "LINE", "BOOK", "OLD", "NEW"

325    PRINT 'LINE', 'BOOK', 'OLD', 'NEW'
```

Whenever a PRINT statement is included with nothing in its *list,* it results in a blank line (see Figure 1-9). This is very convenient for improving the readability of program output.

When the PRINT statement is used as it is here, the output will be printed according to a predetermined fixed format. In this respect we can think of the terminal as a typewriter with preset tab stops at positions 1, 16, 31, 46, and 61. Thus the value for C in statement 450 will be printed beginning at position 1. The comma separating C and B causes the terminal to tab over to position 16 where the value of B will be printed, and so on. Each output field will be left-justified beginning with the corresponding tab position. (This is in contrast to normal data processing procedures in which numeric fields are right-justified and alpha-numeric fields are left-justified.) However, Basic includes other provisions for output to enhance the appearance of printed results.

Exercise 1-6 The following PRINT statement is executed.

```
400    PRINT N2, N4, N6
```

Where will each field be printed on the page?

Use of the Semicolon

It is possible to override the automatic tabbing operation by separating the variables in the list by semicolons. An example PRINT statement and its corresponding output are shown in Figure 1-10. Because of the manner in which printing works, the semicolon provides us with an interesting (and useful) capability. That is, a semicolon after the last field will cause the cursor (or printing element) to maintain its current position for the next PRINT. Thus the following PRINT statements produce the output of Figure 1-10.

```
600      PRINT A;
610      PRINT B;C


700      PRINT A;B;
710      PRINT C
```

Figure 1-10

Printing using the semicolon

Assume that A, B, and C contain
A   1593
B   −3.69
C   25.82

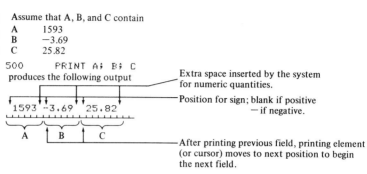

The TAB Function

Positioning of output is improved by combining use of the semicolon with the **TAB** function. The typical terminal has 80 printing positions or columns (some have 132). These are numbered 0 through 79; thus the first column would be identified by the system as position 0, the second as 1, and so on. By using the **TAB** function we can specify in which column we wish a field to begin. This is illustrated in the two examples of Figure 1-11.

Figure 1-11

Using the TAB function

Assume the values of A, B, and C are
A   1593
B   −3.69
C   25.82

(a)

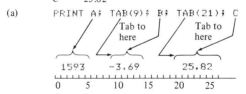

(b)

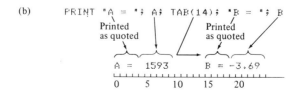

Exercise 1-7 The following variables in a program have the values indicated.

$$X \quad -381 \qquad Y \quad 49.768 \qquad Z \quad 1.934$$

Show how they will be printed by each of the following PRINT statements.

(a) `100    PRINT X;Y;Z`

(b) `200    PRINT TAB(6);X;TAB(14);Z`

(c) `300    PRINT "X IS: ";X;TAB(15);"Z IS: ";Z`

OTHER PROGRAM STATEMENTS

Arithmetic Operations

Computation with the computer in Basic involves (1) performing arithmetic operations on two or more quantities from memory, and (2) saving the result in a preassigned area of memory. For example, if we assume that the length and width of a rectangle have been read into storage, then the following LET statement would calculate the perimeter and store it in PERIM.

```
LET PERIM = 2 * (LEN + WIDTH)
```

Let us first direct our attention to the so-called *expression* located to the right of the equal sign. In Basic the term *expression* carries much the same meaning as it does in algebra. In a nutshell, an arithmetic expression is any collection of variables and constants related by *arithmetic operators*. The five common operator symbols are

addition	+
subtraction	−
multiplication	*
division	/
raising to a power	^ or **

Note that the first three symbols are identical to ordinary arithmetic; the asterisk (*) is used to denote multiplication. Since Basic requires that each operation be explicitly indicated, the computer form will appear slightly different from the equivalent alegbra form, as further illustrated by the following.

DESCRIPTION	ALGEBRA	COMPUTER LANGUAGE
Simple interest	$P + Prt$	P + P*R*T
Simple discount	$\dfrac{P}{1 - dt}$	P/(1 - D*T)
Resistance of parallel circuit	$\dfrac{R_1 + R_2}{R_1 R_2}$	(R1 + R2)/(R1*R2)

Whereas in algebra multiplication is commonly implied (for instance 2*w* means 2 times *w*), in programming languages the multiplication must be indicated by the operation symbol.

   In general the rules for performing the arithmetic operations (that is, *evaluating* an expression) are much the same for evaluating an algebraic expression. That is,

1. All expressions within parentheses are evaluated first.
2. Raising to a power (exponentiation) is next.
3. Multiplications and divisions are then performed.
4. Additions and subtractions are performed last.

The rule of performing multiplication and division operations before addition and subtraction is commonly referred to as the *hierarchy of operations*. As a simple illustration of this hierarchy rule, let us evaluate the expression:

A + B * C

given that values for A, B, and C are 25, 3, and 16 respectively.

      25 + 3 * 16
      25 + 48
      73

With a hierarchy of operations, there are no ambiguities because the multiplication is performed *before* the addition.

   The use of spaces in forming expressions is strictly up to the programmer. That is, spaces may be inserted for the purpose of clarity—note that the preceding interest and discount forms use spaces on each side of the addition and subtraction operators but not around the multiplication and division operators. This is done solely to clarify (to the programmer) the grouping of the various elements of the expression.

Exercise 1-8 Given the values A = 6, B = 22, and C = 2, evaluate each of the following:
   (a) A+B/C
   (b) 2*A+B/C
   (c) 2*(A+B)/C

The LET Statement

As we saw earlier, the LET has much the same form as the ordinary equation in algebra.

```
LET PERIM = 2*(LENGTH + WIDTH)
```

However, the equal sign as used in Basic has a far different meaning than in algebra. In Basic the equal sign says:

1. Using the currently stored data values, evaluate the expression to the right of the equal sign.

2. Place the result in the storage area indicated by the variable on the left.

Most versions of Basic currently in use, including Basic-Plus, allow the LET statement to be written with or without the word LET. Thus statement 430 of Figure 1-7 could have been written in either of the following ways.

```
430    LET N = 0 + R - S - L

430    N = 0 + R - S - L
```

Example programs in chapters that follow omit the word LET.

Incrementing a Quantity

The important distinction between the algebra equation and the Basic LET statement is clearly demonstrated by the second LET statement (statement 440) used in the program of Figure 1-6:

```
440    LET C = C + 1
```

This statement characterizes the difference between the equal sign as used in algebra and in Basic. In algebra the equation

$$x = x + 1$$

is never true, regardless of the value assigned to x; it is a contradiction. In Basic the statement

```
C = C + 1
```

is quite valid and very useful. Remember, the equal sign says, "Evaluate the expression on the right and assign that value to the variable on the left." Initially the value in C will be 0. Execution of the statement will cause the expression

C + 1 to be evaluated as 0 + 1, or 1. Then the result, 1, will be stored back in C, replacing the previous value of 0. Continuing, if we assume that the fourth record has been processed and execution has proceeded to the **GO TO** statement, the value of C will be 4. Upon executing the loop once more (processing the fifth record), C + 1 will be evaluated as 5, with the result being stored back into C replacing the previous value of 4. The overall result, as we see, is that C serves as a simple accumulator being incremented by 1 each time through the loop.

The GO TO Statement

In the program of Figure 1-7 it is necessary to return to the **READ** statement after a given set of data has been processed. This is accomplished with the **GO TO** statement, as used in the program of Figure 1-7 and repeated here.

```
420    READ B, O, R, S, L
         .
         .
         .
460    GO TO 420
```

This statement interrupts the sequential execution of statements and specifies the number of the next statement to be executed; in this case it causes a branch to statement 420. The designated instruction may be anywhere in the program; that is, we can direct the computer to branch back to an earlier statement or to skip ahead to a later statement, whichever is required in the program.

Basic-Plus (as do most versions of Basic) allows **GO TO** to be written either as two words or as a single word. Thus the following are equivalent.

```
460    GO TO 420

460    GOTO 420
```

The END Statement

Every program must include an **END** statement, which has a line number larger than that of any other statement in the program. All programs in this book use 32767 (the largest allowable line number) for the **END**. This is not mandatory, but it is a good practice that prevents the error of numbering a statement in the program that is larger than the **END** statement. In Figure 1-7 the sole purpose of the **END** is to indicate to the Basic processor that no more statements follow. We should be aware that during execution of this program the **END** statement does not play any role. That is, the **READ** statement (420) is executed first, followed by the **LET**s and the **PRINT**. Then control is returned to the **READ** by the **GO TO** statement (460). This loop is repeated until there is no more input data, at which time execution is terminated.

On the other hand, the **END** can also be used to terminate execution of a program. For instance, Figure 1-7 is modified in Figure 1-12 to process one data record. In this case the **END** serves both to signify no more statements in the

Figure 1-12

Using the END to terminate processing

```
100      !    THIS PROGRAM PROCESSES ONE DATA
110      !    RECORD THEN TERMINATES ON THE
120      !    END STATEMENT
130      !
200           DATA 4451, 453, 150, 313, 2
210           READ B, O, R, S, L
220           LET N = O + R - S - L
230           PRINT B, O, N
32767         END
```

program to the Basic processor and to terminate processing after the printing operation.

Exercise 1-9 What would occur in the program of Figure 1-7 if statement 460 were accidentally written as follows?

(a) 460 GO TO 430   (b) 460 GO TO 450

Answers to Preceding Exercises

1-1 All Basic program statement entries must have line numbers.

1-2 A descriptive remark is indicated by entering REM or an exclamation mark following the line number. In Basic-Plus it is also possible to follow any statement with an exclamation mark and then a descriptive remark.

1-3 NO EXTEND
73—does not start with letter
READ—too long (and reserved word)
SD—letter not followed by a digit
Q1298—too long
4C—first character not a letter
WORK 3—too long
EXTEND
73—does not start with a letter
READ—reserved word
4C—does not start with a letter
WORK 3—no spaces allowed

1-4 All Basic variables contain zero prior to execution.

1-5 This exercise illustrates an important feature of the DATA statement: that is, fields are taken from the DATA statement to form the DATA pool without any reference to the "record" concept with which we are familiar. Values read into A and B are as follows:

EXECUTION OF READ	A	B
First	25	13
Second	281	16
Third	37	48
Fourth	122	53

1-6 The value for **N2** will begin in printing position 1. The value for **N4** will begin in printing position 16. The value for **N6** will begin in printing position 31.

1-7

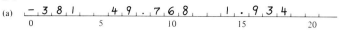

(a)
```
    - 3 8 1       4 9 . 7 6 8       1 . 9 3 4
    0         5           10          15          20
```

(b)
```
                    - 3 8 1               1 . 9 3 4
    0         5           10          15
```

(c)
```
    X   I S :    - 3 8 1              Z   I S :     1 . 9 3 4
    0         5           10          15          20          25
```

1-8 (a) 17;   (b) 23;   (c) 28

1-9 (a)   Only the first record would be read and calculations would be made continuously for the same data set. For the sample input values, the output would be

1	4451	453	288
2	4451	453	288
3	4451	453	288
.	.	.	.
.	.	.	.
.	.	.	.

Note that the line counter would change.

(b)   No new calculations would be made, and the first line would be continuously repeated:

1	4451	453	288
1	4451	453	288
1	4451	453	288
.	.	.	.
.	.	.	.
.	.	.	.

Programming Problems

1-1 Each DATA statement includes the following employee payroll information:

Employee number
Hours worked
Pay rate
Deductions

Write a program that will calculate the net pay for each employee as follows:

Net pay = Hours × Rate – Deductions

Print each of the input quantities and the calculated net pay.

1-2 An instructor keeps student exam information in the computer. Assume that for each student there is a DATA statement with the following information.

Student name
First hour exam
Second hour exam

Third hour exam
Final exam

Write a program to calculate the total points earned as the sum of the three hour exam scores and twice the final exam score. Then calculate the average by dividing the sum by 5. Print the student name, total points, and average.

1-3 A stock market investor keeps a record of all stocks that have been purchased and then resold. Assume that for each stock there is a DATA statement with the following information.

Stock ID number
Number of shares of stock
Purchase price per share
Sale price per share
Total commission paid to broker

Write a program to calculate the profit (or loss) for each stock. Print the stock ID number, number of shares, and profit.

1-4 The total resistance (R) of an electric circuit with three elements in parallel can be calculated from the individual resistances of the elements (1, 2, and 3) by the following formula.

$$\frac{1}{R} = \frac{1}{R_1} + \frac{1}{R_2} + \frac{1}{R_3}$$

Each DATA statement contains the following.

Circuit number:
R_1
R_2
R_3

For each data set, calculate the total resistance. Print this value and the input quantities.

1-5 The linear system

$$a_1x + b_1y = c_1$$
$$a_2x + b_2y = c_2$$

when solved for x and y assumes the form

$$x = \frac{b_2c_1 - b_1c_2}{a_1b_2 - a_2b_1}$$

$$y = \frac{a_1c_2 - a_2c_1}{a_1b_2 - a_2b_1}$$

Each DATA statement contains values (in order) for a_1, b_1, c_1, a_2, b_2, and c_2. Write a program to compute x and y for each data set. Output for each data set should include:

First line—input data
Second line—values of x and y
Third line—blank

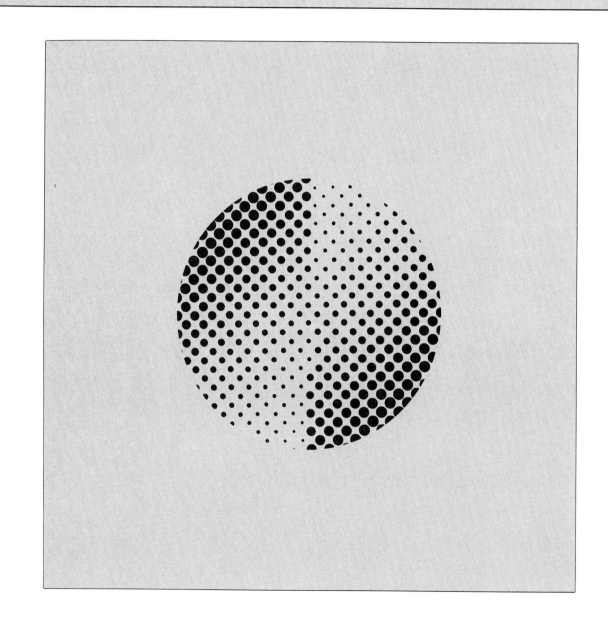

2

Entering and Running Programs

ACCESSING THE SYSTEM

The Terminal Keyboard

In using an interactive language such as Basic, the user "converses" with the computer via a terminal. The terminal may be a hard copy device or it may be a CRT. In either case input to the computer is via a typewriter-style keyboard such as that shown in Figure 2-1. As information is entered through the keyboard, it is transmitted to the computer and also printed by the terminal (hard copy units) or displayed on the screen (CRTs). We should note that in Figure 2-1 special attention is called to certain keys. These will be referred to throughout this chapter.

In this book certain symbols and conventions are used to illustrate interaction with the computer.

CONVENTION	MEANING
Password	Unshaded computer printout is information printed by the computer.
RUN	Shaded computer printout is information that is typed from the keyboard by the user.
ⓒⓡ	Indicates the Carriage Return key, which must be depressed upon typing information into the computer.
^	The *circumflex* is commonly used to indicate depression of the CONTROL key while another key is struck. For instance, $^\wedge$C means to hold down the control key and concurrently depress the letter C. Note that this has nothing to do with the circumflex key (found on the 6 key of the keyboard). It is simply the way in which the system shows at the terminal that a control sequence has been entered.

Log-on

On a timesharing system in which many users have access to the computer, some method is needed to maintain order. For instance, you would not be very happy if you spent several hours working on a program and someone else wiped it out. Timesharing systems resolve this problem by assigning each user a separate account and an individual password for access to that account. An account "owner" who wishes to use the account must follow an exact procedure for logging on. The process is illustrated and described in Figure 2-2.

Log-off

After the end of a session with the computer, the user must *log off* the system. Figure 2-3 illustrates the process of logging off. Upon typing BYE, the system

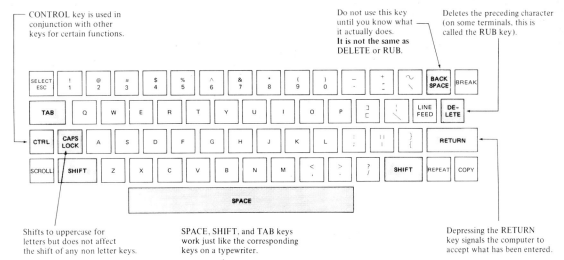

CONTROL key is used in conjunction with other keys for certain functions.

Do not use this key until you know what it actually does. **It is not the same as DELETE or RUB.**

Deletes the preceding character (on some terminals, this is called the RUB key).

Shifts to uppercase for letters but does not affect the shift of any non letter keys.

SPACE, SHIFT, and TAB keys work just like the corresponding keys on a typewriter.

Depressing the RETURN key signals the computer to accept what has been entered.

Figure 2-1 Typical terminal keyboard

responds with a request for confirmation. In Figure 2-3 Y (for Yes) was typed so the session was terminated with a short summary of the activity. Had the user changed his/her mind, then a response of N (for No) would have caused the system to ignore the BYE and return a Ready prompt.

Controlling the System—Commands

As we have seen in Chapter 1, using the computer to do a job for us involves first figuring out the solution to the problem, then writing a detailed program telling the computer what to do. The program of Example 1-1, as do all programs in this book, consists of a series of statements, or instructions, telling the computer what

Figure 2-2

The log-on procedure

Turn terminal on.

```
^C                Control C clears anything which might cause a problem.
HELLO (cr)

RSTS V7.0-07 MERCOMPFAC-PCCD   Job 12   KBO   26-Apr-81   15:41
Account# 59,7 (cr)
Password:       (cr)           Enter password (will not be displayed).



 SW BASICS (cr)        Enter the Basic control system.

Ready
```

Figure 2-3

Logging off

```
BYE (cr)
Confirm: Y (cr)     Y means "Yes", let me terminate."
Saved all disk files; 64 blocks in use, 936 free
Job 12 User 59,7 logged off KBO at 26-Apr-81 15:42
System RSTS V7.0-07 MERCOMPFAC-PCCD
Run time was 1.4 seconds
Elapsed time was 1 minute
Good afternoon
```

to do in processing our data. Once the program is completed, then it may be entered into the computer and run. This involves our sitting at a terminal and interacting with the computer. As described in the Introduction, the computer is always under control of a monitor (supervisor) program. It is with this monitor that we interact. With any timesharing system there are numerous tasks that we might carry out. For instance, we may wish to enter a NEW program, or modify an OLD program, or RUN a program just entered. The action we desire to take is indicated to the monitor by means of *commands*. It is very important to recognize the distinction between statements and commands. Briefly, programs are made up of statements that tell the computer the operations to carry out in solving our problem. We use the commands to tell the monitor what we want to do with the program. PRINT, LET, and READ are statement forms. NEW, OLD, and RUN are commands that we will be using in controlling the system.

ENTERING AND CORRECTING A PROGRAM

Creating a New Program

Assuming that we have already logged on to the system, the command NEW is used to indicate that we wish to enter a new program. Use of this command is illustrated in Figure 2-4. Here the procedure involves typing the command NEW (followed by (cr)). Then we must key in the name we wish the system to give this program. The name may consist of 1 to 6 letters or digits. For instance, A5, INVEN, and PROB3 are all valid as program (file) names. (We should note that the command NEW can be followed by a space and the program name.) From there, the program is keyed in with a carriage return following each statement.

Figure 2-4
Creating a new
program—the NEW
command

```
NEW
New file name--INVEN
Ready
100      REM  EXAMPLE 1-1
          .
          .

410      REM  BEGINNING OF PROCESSING LOOP
420         READ B, O, R, S, L
430         LET N = O + R - S - L
440         LET C = C + 1
450         PRINT C, B, O, N
460         GO TO 410
```
———— Indent statements to show that they
         are all part of the processing loop.

```
32767  END
```
——— Note: The TAB key is used before the
         statement to align the statements
         cleanly.

It is of utmost importance to recognize that the computer does not perform the operations required by the program as the program is entered. That is, after the entering task of Figure 2-4 is finished, no calculations of B or anything else have been performed. The program is first typed into the computer and then, when completely entered, it can be run by a separate command.

Inserting and Deleting Lines

One of the useful features of Basic relates to the fact that the system always keeps statements in order according to line numbers. For instance, let us assume that we left out statement 440 when keying in the program. Upon noticing our error we could simply key in the omitted statement as shown in Figure 2-5. The system would automatically place the statement in its proper position, as shown in the illustration.

In writing a program we sometimes forget a statement and only realize our omission after the program has been entered. This presents no problem because the statement can be inserted later between two existing line numbers as shown in Figure 2-6. Now we see the value of incrementing line numbers by 10.

Perhaps we need to delete a statement from a program. This is easily done simply by typing the line number alone, and then hitting the return key. Figure 2-7 illustrates a very subtle error. Statement 430 has been misnumbered as 4330 and will end up some place other than where it belongs. The remedy as shown in Figure 2-7 involves deleting the incorrect line and adding the correct one.

Errors and Error Correction

Try as we might to eliminate them, errors will always creep into a program. In general they can be classified in two broad categories: syntax errors and logic errors. The Basic language consists of a very concise set of rules for writing statements. Any statement that does not follow those rules is said to have a *syntax* error. For instance, consider

```
440    PRINT C, B, O, N
450    GO TO 210
```

Figure 2-5

Inserting a statement

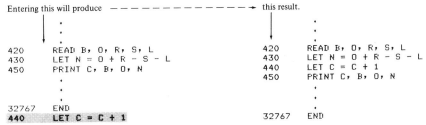

Note: The system will automatically insert statement 440 in its proper place (between 430 and 450) regardless of when it is entered.

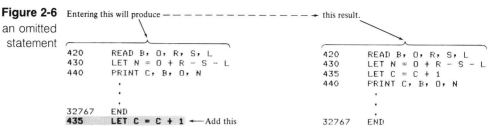

Figure 2-6
Inserting an omitted statement

Entering this will produce ─ ─ ─ ─ ─ ─ ─ ─ ─ ─ ─ ─ → this result.

```
420        READ B, O, R, S, L              420        READ B, O, R, S, L
430        LET N = O + R - S - L           430        LET N = O + R - S - L
440        PRINT C, B, O, N                435        LET C = C + 1
             .                             440        PRINT C, B, O, N
             .                                          .
             .                                          .
32767      END                                          .
435        LET C = C + 1 ◄──Add this       32767      END
```

Note: Line 435 will be inserted between lines 430 and 440 regardless of when it is typed in.

entered incorrectly as

```
450     PRIMT C, B, O, N
460     RETURN TO 210
```

In statement 450 **PRINT** is misspelled; the system, knowing the "rules" for writing statements, will respond with an error indication as soon as the statement is entered. Similarly, statement 460 should be **GO TO**; we must use the exact forms defined in the language, not our own variations. The sequence of events of

Figure 2-7
Deleting and inserting a statement

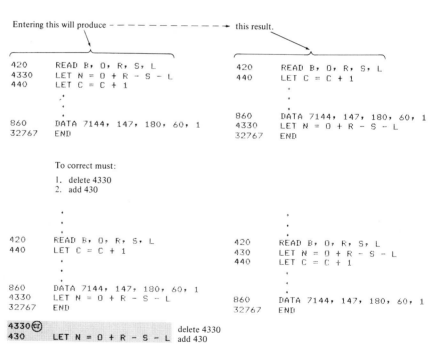

Entering this will produce ─ ─ ─ ─ ─ ─ ─ ─ ─ ─ → this result.

```
420        READ B, O, R, S, L              420        READ B, O, R, S, L
4330       LET N = O + R - S - L           440        LET C = C + 1
440        LET C = C + 1                                .
             .                                          .
             .                             860        DATA 7144, 147, 180, 60, 1
             .                             4330       LET N = O + R - S - L
860        DATA 7144, 147, 180, 60, 1      32767      END
32767      END
```

To correct must:
1. delete 4330
2. add 430

```
             .                                          .
             .                                          .
             .                                          .
420        READ B, O, R, S, L              420        READ B, O, R, S, L
440        LET C = C + 1                   430        LET N = O + R - S - L
             .                             440        LET C = C + 1
             .                                          .
860        DATA 7144, 147, 180, 60, 1                   .
4330       LET N = O + R - S - L           860        DATA 7144, 147, 180, 60, 1
32767      END                             32767      END
4330 (cr)                                  delete 4330
430        LET N = O + R - S - L           add 430
```

Note: Typing a line number with no statement (4330 in this example) deletes any statement with that line number.

Figure 2-8

Syntax error
messages

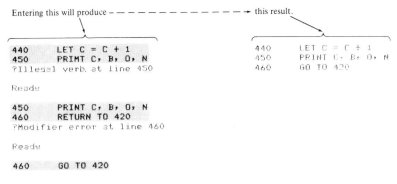

Note: The system inspects each statement for syntax errors
as it is entered; if it is incorrect, a description error
message is printed. If the line is re-entered, the new
one will replace the previous one with the same
number.

entering and correcting these errors is illustrated in Figure 2-8. In some operating
environments the immediate diagnostic ability illustrated by Figure 2-8 is disabled. In such a case statements are inspected and appropriate error messages
given at a later time. The reader should consult the system manager or instructor
for these details.

As a rule the system is very helpful in detecting syntax errors. However, logic
errors are a completely different story. For instance, if in the inventory problem we
accidentally added the copies sold instead of subtracting them, we would have

```
430   'LET N = 0 + R + S - L
```

rather than the correct

```
430   LET N = 0 + R - S - L
```

Here we have an error in our *logic* and the system has no way of recognizing what
we mean. It would be up to us to check everything carefully and reenter a corrected
version of the statement.

Listing a Program

When we are making corrections to a program, what we see typed at the terminal
or printed on the screen often is confusing. For example, after making the
corrections shown in Figure 2-7 (lower left), it is usually convenient to see the
program as it actually exists (lower right). This is easily done using the command
LIST. That is, typing LIST (followed by cr) will cause the latest form of the
program on which we are working to be printed (or displayed) on the terminal.

RUNNING A PROGRAM

Once the program has been entered, we may run it using the RUN command as illustrated in Figure 2-9. When program execution is complete, the system returns to the Ready state to await our next command. The line immediately following the RUN command in Figure 2-9 consists of the program name, the time, and the date; it is called the *header line*. It can be omitted by typing RUNNH (RUN, No Header) instead of RUN.

Sometimes logic errors will request the computer to do something that is impossible (such as divide a number by zero). When this happens the computer prints an error message and usually terminates the program. For example, let us assume that we accidentally entered alphabetic data in one of the DATA statements. Upon running the program, we would get the results shown in Figure 2-10.

SAVING PROGRAMS

Temporary and Permanent Program Storage

Whenever the user signs on to an account, a temporary work area is set up within the computer's internal memory. This temporary area initially is empty. As a program (or anything else, for that matter) is entered, it is held in this temporary portion of memory. When the session is terminated (by logging off) everything in that temporary area is lost. It is somewhat analogous to "borrowing" the use of a desk. When we first sit down, the desk top is clean. When we leave, someone comes in and cleans it by discarding everything that is there. In other words, the

Figure 2-9
Running a program—the RUN command

Assuming that the program has just been entered, it can be run as follows:

1. RUN (CR)

INVEN 11:27		01-Jan-84	
LINE NUMBER	BOOK NUMBER	OLD BALANCE	NEW BALANCE
1	4451	453	288
2	4892	512	322
3	5118	82	421
4	6881	0	201
5	7144	147	266

2. (brace around rows 1-5)

3. ?Out of data at line 420

4. Ready

Note: 1. The command RUN causes execution of the program just entered.

2. The above is the output (results) from the PRINT statement.

3. Execution continues until there is no more data.

4. The system is ready and waiting for the next task.

Figure 2-10

Termination of a
program by an error

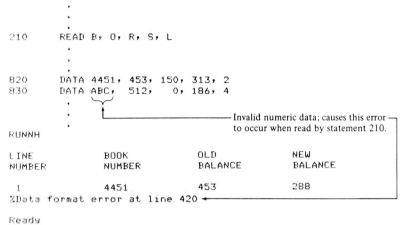

```
       .
       .
       .
210       READ B, O, R, S, L
       .
       .
       .
820       DATA 4451, 453, 150, 313, 2
830       DATA ABC,  512,   0, 186, 4
       .
       .
RUNNH
```

Invalid numeric data; causes this error
to occur when read by statement 210.

```
LINE              BOOK          OLD           NEW
NUMBER            NUMBER        BALANCE       BALANCE

  1               4451          453           288
%Data format error at line 420

Ready
```

desk top is a work and temporary storage area. Now let us carry this example one step further and assume that we have been provided a file cabinet for permanent storage of any work that we wish to save. This concept is illustrated in Figure 2-11. Anything we wish to keep must be placed in the file cabinet before we leave, or else it will be lost. If we must work on it at a later time, we can obtain it from the file and continue.

This is exactly the situation that exists in a timesharing system. Referring to Figure 4 of the Introduction, the work space of internal memory corresponds to the

Figure 2-11

The concept of temporary and permanent storage areas

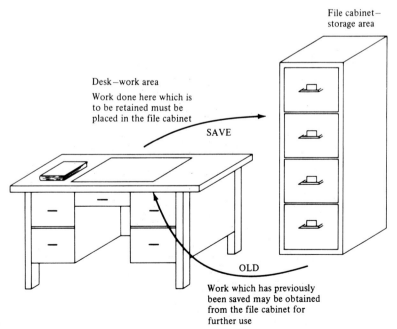

File cabinet—
storage area

Desk—work area

Work done here which is
to be retained must be
placed in the file cabinet

SAVE

OLD

Work which has previously
been saved may be obtained
from the file cabinet for
further use

Figure 2-12

Getting a catalog
listing of an
account—the CAT
command

```
CAT (cr)
CUBE    .BAS      1        60      23-Mar-81  23-Mar-81  08:13
PROB3   .BAS      3        60      23-Mar-81  23-Mar-81  08:20
SALE    .BAS      3        60      23-Mar-81  23-Mar-81  08:20
MEAN    .BAS      6        60      23-Mar-81  23-Mar-81  08:25

Ready
```

desk top and the disk storage corresponds to the file cabinet. If we wish to know what we have stored in the computer file, we simply type in the command CAT and the system gives us a list as shown in Figure 2-12. Here we see that four programs MEAN, PROB3, SALE, and CUBE are stored on the disk under this account. We should note that each name is followed by .BAS. This is called the *extension* and is the method used by the system to distinguish Basic programs from other types of files that may be stored.

The SAVE and UNSAVE Commands

After we enter a new program, one of the first things we should do is save it on disk. Most programmers have had the aggravating experience of entering and correcting a large program and then forgetting to save it before signing off. A typical timesharing session is shown in Figure 2-13. Here a new program (INVEN) is entered, saved (using the SAVE command), and run.

To delete a program that no longer is needed, the UNSAVE command is used. The "before and after" catalog listings show that these changes have indeed been made.

The RENAME and REPLACE Commands

Occasionally the user will select a program name that has already been used for another program. For instance, what would happen if we were to enter

NEW MEAN

and then enter a new program? (From Figure 2-13 we see that there already is a program by this name stored in the account.) The answer is that nothing would happen until we tried to save the program. Then the system would tell us that there is already a program by that name in the file—in others words, it protects us against our own carelessness. Two ways of handling this are shown in Figure 2-14. In (a), upon being informed of this error, the name of the current program (MEAN) is changed to MEAN2 by using the RENAME command. Then it is saved. In (b) the command REPLACE is used, which causes the program stored on disk by the name MEAN to be deleted and the new one stored in its place. In other words, in this instance,

Figure 2-13

Using the SAVE and
UNSAVE commands

```
NEW                            ⎫  Identify to the system that a new program
New file name--INVEN           ⎬  (to be named INVEN) will be entered.
                               ⎭
Ready

100     REM EXAMPLE 1-1  ⎫
  .                      |
  .                      |
  .                      ⎬  Enter the program.
420     READ B,O,R,S,L   |
  .                      |
  .                      |
  .                      |
32767   END              ⎭
CAT ◄──────────────────────── Obtain a listing of the account contents.
CUBE  .BAS    1      60    23-Mar-81  23-Mar-81  08:13  ⎫ Note: The program INVEN is in
PROB3 .BAS    3      60    23-Mar-81  23-Mar-81  08:20  |       the working area and not
SALE  .BAS    3      60    23-Mar-81  23-Mar-81  08:20  |       in the user's file.
MEAN  .BAS    6      60    23-Mar-81  23-Mar-81  08:25  ⎭
Ready

SAVE     Save the program INVEN which is presently in the work area.
'
Ready

UNSAVE SALE    Delete the program SALE currently stored in the account.

Ready

CAT
INVEN .BAS    1      60    26-Apr-81  26-Apr-81  15:53   INVEN has been added
CUBE  .BAS    1      60    23-Mar-81  23-Mar-81  08:13
PROB3 .BAS    3      60    23-Mar-81  23-Mar-81  08:20   ─── SALE is gone.
MEAN  .BAS    6      60    23-Mar-81  23-Mar-81  08:25

Ready

RUN ◄──────── Causes the program previously entered (INVEN) to be run.
  .
  .
  .
```

$$
\left.\begin{array}{l}
\text{UNSAVE MEAN} \\
\text{SAVE}
\end{array}\right\} \quad \text{are equivalent to} \quad \textbf{REPLACE}
$$

Care should be taken, of course, to ensure that a desired program is not accidentally lost through the **REPLACE** statement.

The OLD Command

With a timesharing system it is common practice to work on a program over the course of several sessions at the terminal. For instance, we might have sufficient time today only to enter a program, and we intend to return tomorrow to test it and make necessary corrections. Obviously we must save the program upon completing the entry. When we wish to retrieve it from disk storage at a later date, we must use the command **OLD**. This command causes the system to get the selected program from disk and load it into memory so that we may continue just as if we had never left. For instance, let us assume that we entered and saved **INVEN** during a previous session. Upon checking a program *listing* (printout of the program) we discover that the **READ** statement (420) is incorrect. Upon signing

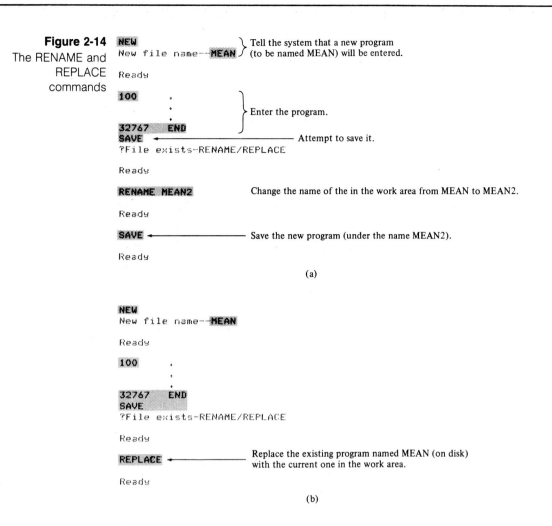

Figure 2-14
The RENAME and REPLACE commands

```
NEW                         ⎱  Tell the system that a new program
New file name---MEAN        ⎰  (to be named MEAN) will be entered.

Ready

100          .
             .     ⎱
             .     ⎰  Enter the program.
32767   END
SAVE     ◄────────────────── Attempt to save it.
?File exists-RENAME/REPLACE

Ready

RENAME MEAN2                  Change the name of the in the work area from MEAN to MEAN2.

Ready

SAVE ◄──────────────── Save the new program (under the name MEAN2).

Ready
```

(a)

```
NEW
New file name---MEAN

Ready

100          .
             .
             .
32767   END
SAVE
?File exists-RENAME/REPLACE

Ready

REPLACE ◄──────────    Replace the existing program named MEAN (on disk)
                       with the current one in the work area.

Ready
```

(b)

into our account, the correction procedure would be as shown in Figure 2-15. After the program has been corrected and saved, it may be run as if it had just been entered.

> NOTE: Do not forget to **REPLACE** a corrected program before proceeding with other operations!!!

SUMMARY OF COMMANDS

Interaction with the system can be speeded up in many cases by combining instructions. This is illustrated by the following examples.

SHORT FORM	IS EQUIVALENT TO
HELLO 50,99	HELLO
	Account #50,99
NEW INVEN	NEW
	New file name—INVEN
OLD INVEN	OLD
	Old file name—INVEN

Following is a summary (in alphabetical order) of the commands used in this chapter.

CAT   Lists the names of programs stored in the user's library.

LIST   Lists the program that is currently in the working area of memory.

Figure 2-15
Using the OLD
command

```
OLD
Old file name--INVEN                     Get the program previously SAVEd.
Ready

LIST
INVEN    12:43           03-Jan-81  ⎫
100      REM   EXAMPLE 1-1           ⎪
          .                         ⎪
          .                         ⎪
          .                         ⎪
420      READ O, R, S, L ◄── Statement  ⎬  Verify that this is
430      LET N = O + R - S - L     in error    the correct program.
440      LET C = C + 1              ⎪
450      PRINT C, B, O, N           ⎪
460      GO TO 410                  ⎪
          .                         ⎪
          .                         ⎪
          .                         ⎪
32767    END                        ⎭

Ready

420      READ B, O, R, S, L         Enter the corrected statement 420.
LIST
INVEN    12:43          ·03-Jan-81  ⎫
100      REM   EXAMPLE 1-1          ⎪
          .                         ⎪
          .                         ⎪
          .                         ⎪
420      READ B, O, R, S, L         ⎬  Verify that the correction
430      LET N = O + R - S - L      ⎪   has been entered properly.
440      LET C = C + 1              ⎪
450      PRINT C, B, O, N           ⎪
460      GO TO 410                  ⎪
          .                         ⎪
          .                         ⎪
          .                         ⎪
32767    END                        ⎭

Ready

REPLACE                            Replace the old copy with
                                   this corrected one.
Ready
```

NEW	Clears the work area of memory and prepares for the entry of a new program.
OLD	Makes a copy of a selected program stored in the library and places it in the memory work area.
RENAME	Changes the name of the program currently in the memory work area (*not* a program in the library). Must include the new program name.
REPLACE	Stores a copy of the program currently in the memory work area in the disk library. If another program is already stored under the same name, it will be deleted.
RUN	Runs the program currently in the memory work area; if a program name is also specified, first loads the program from the library and then runs it.
SAVE	Stores a copy of the program currently in the memory work area in the disk library.
UNSAVE	Deletes the named program from the library.

TERMINATING PROCESSING

Concept of a Trailer Value

In Example 1-1 processing continues until there is no more data, at which time an error occurs in attempting to read further. As a general rule, this is a poor way to terminate a program. For instance, in this example we might desire to total the number of books sold and, after processing the last record, to print this value. This means that some method is required for knowing when the last data set has been read. Broadly speaking, there are two ways of accomplishing this. One of them, which is used with data files, involves an automatic "end-of-data" indicator detection technique. This is a somewhat advanced topic and is covered in a later chapter. The other involves using a special data value terminating the data set for which the program can search. For instance, let us assume that the book identification number of Example 1-1 will always be less than 9999. Then our data set, together with a *trailer record,* might appear as shown in Figure 2-16. Note that the

Figure 2-16
A trailer record

```
810     REM    ** INPUT DATA **
820          DATA 4451,  453,  150,  313,  2
830          DATA 4892,  512,    0,  186,  4
840          DATA 5118,   82,  500,  160,  1
850          DATA 6881,    0,  201,    0,  0
860          DATA 7144,  147,  180,   60,  1
870          DATA 9999,    0,    0,    0,  0 ←─ Trailer record; does *not* contain
                                                  data to process.
```

trailer does *not* contain information on a book. However, since the READ statement includes five variables in its list, the DATA statement must provide a total of five values. Hence meaningless zeros are included. Now the program, upon reading each record, must test the book number to see if it is 9999. If it is, then whatever action is required can be taken before terminating the program.

Detecting the Trailer Value

To illustrate the concept of loop termination, let us consider a minor expansion of Example 1-1.

Example 2-1 The data set of Example 1-1 includes a 9999 trailer record as illustrated in Figure 2-16. Upon detecting this record, print the message

PROCESSING COMPLETE

and then terminate execution of the program.

This program, as is the case with most programs, may be considered to consist of three overall components or *modules*: initialization, processing, and termination operations. These are illustrated in the broad flowchart of Figure 2-17a. Although this example is relatively simple and brief, the beginner should become accustomed to breaking each programming problem down into its basic components. The details of what is to be done are illustrated in the expanded flowchart of Figure 2-17b.

The obvious distinction between this flowchart and that of Figure 1-2 is the test performed on the book identification number. In Basic this is done with the IF statement, which, in its simplest form, is little more than a "conditional GO TO." That is, execution will GO TO the specified statement if a particular condition is true; otherwise it simply continues to the next sequential statement. In line 430 of the program in Figure 2-18 we see use of the IF statement. Although there is much to be said about the IF, a detailed description of it and its use is left to Chapter 4. For our current needs, we simply interpret this statement as it reads. That is, "If the value of B is equal to 9999, then GO TO statement 490." If not, then simply continue on to the next statement (440 in this case) as if nothing had happened. In other words, processing continues as in the program of Figure 1-7 as long as the book number is not 9999. However, upon detecting the 9999 value, control jumps to statement 490, whereby the final message is printed and processing is terminated. This is illustrated in Figure 2-19.

The STOP Statement

Line 530 is a STOP statement that terminated execution of the program when encountered. Technically speaking, it is not required here since the DATA statements are *nonexecutable*. Thus upon completing statement 520 the DATA statements would be skipped and execution would continue to the END (statement

Figure 2-17
A flowchart for
Example 2-1

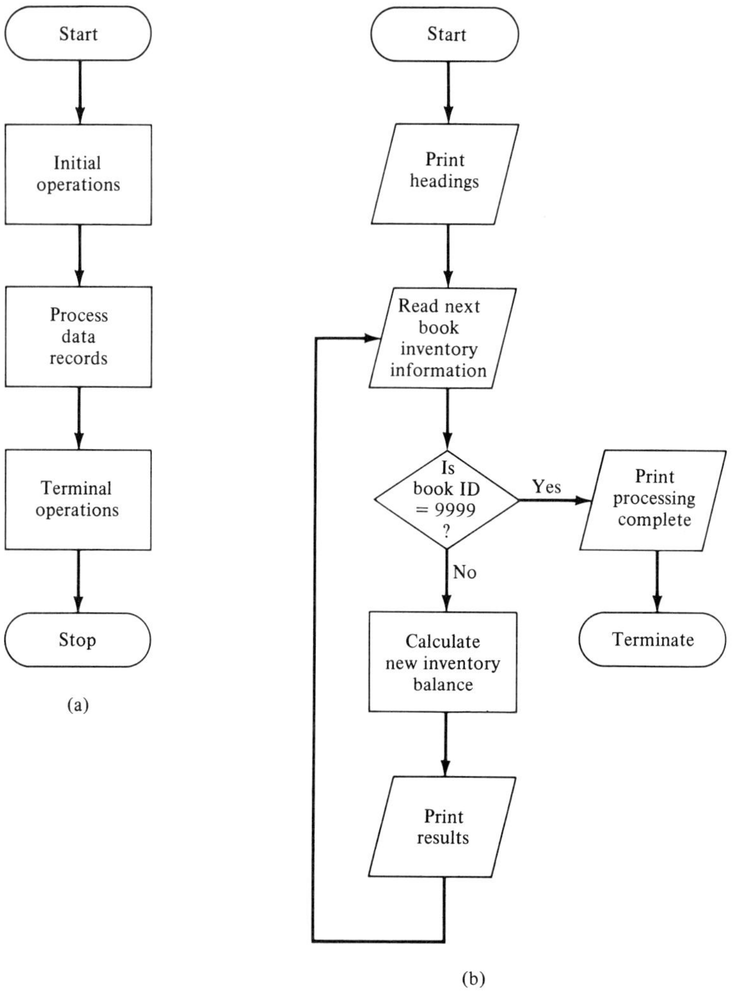

(a)

(b)

32767). However, inclusion of the **STOP** in this case clearly illustrates what will occur. Furthermore, the **STOP** is sometimes used temporarily to halt execution of a program since it is possible to continue processing after a **STOP** merely by typing in **CONT** (for continue).

Exercise 2-1 What would occur in the program of Figure 2-1 if line 870 were accidentally numbered 810?

Detecting a String Trailer Value

Now it remains to include a string trailer that may be used to terminate processing for Example 2-1. Again the concept involves selecting a value that will never occur in any of the actual data values. The program segment of Figure 2-20 uses

Figure 2-18

Terminating a
loop—Example 2-1

```
100  !    EXAMPLE 2-1
110  !    PROGRAM TO UPDATE AN INVENTORY
120  !    INPUT QUANTITIES AND NAMES ARE:
130  !       B - BOOK NUMBER
140  !       O - OLD BALANCE
150  !       R - COPIES RECEIVED
160  !       S - COPIES SOLD
170  !       L - COPIES LOST AND DESTROYED
180  !    CALCULATED QUANTITIES AND NAMES ARE:
190  !       C - LINE COUNT
200  !       N - NEW BALANCE
300  !
310  !  PRINT THE HEADINGS (INITIALIZATION)
320       PRINT 'LINE', 'BOOK', 'OLD', 'NEW'
330       PRINT 'NUMBER', 'NUMBER', 'BALANCE', 'BALANCE'
340       PRINT
400  !
410  !  BEGINNING OF PROCESSING LOOP
420       READ B, O, R, S, L
430       IF B=9999 THEN GO TO 490
440       N = O + R - S - L
450       C = C + 1
460       PRINT C, B, O, N
470       GO TO 410
480  !
490  !  PRINT MESSAGE & TERMINATE
500       PRINT
510       PRINT
520       PRINT 'PROCESSING COMPLETE'
530       STOP
800  !
810  !  ** INPUT DATA **
820       DATA 4451, 453, 150, 313, 2
830       DATA 4892, 512,   0, 186, 4
840       DATA 5118,  82, 500, 160, 1
850       DATA 6881,   0, 201,   0, 0
860       DATA 7144, 147, 180,  60, 1
870       DATA 9999,   0,   0,   0, 0
32767    END
```

the letters EOF (which stand for End Of File) as the trailer. Of particular importance to us here is the IF statement:

```
430    IF BOOK$ = "EOF" THEN GO TO 490
```

We should note that the test value (EOF) is enclosed within quotes. These quotes ensure that the system will recognize the quantity as a string and not attempt to interpret it as a numeric variable. During processing of the data records on lines

Figure 2-19

Execution of the
simple IF

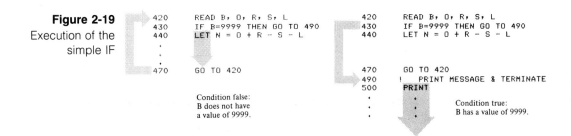

Figure 2-20

Using a string
variable for an
end-of-file test

```
400     !
410     !      BEGINNING OF PROCESSING LOOP
420            READ BOOK$, O, R, S, L
430            IF BOOK$="EOF" THEN GO TO 490
440            N = O + R - S - L
450            C = C + 1
460            PRINT C, BOOK$, O, N
470            GO TO 410
480   !
490   !   PRINT MESSAGE & TERMINATE
500          PRINT
510          PRINT
520          PRINT "PROCESSING COMPLETE"
530          STOP
800   !
810   !   ** INPUT DATA **
820          DATA "INTRO TO DP", 453, 150, 313, 2
830          DATA "SOCIOLOGY"   , 512,   0, 186, 4
840          DATA "ADVANCED TRIG",  82, 500, 160, 1
850          DATA "BASIC"        ,   0, 201,   0, 0
860          DATA "PHYS SCI"     , 147, 180,  60, 1
870          DATA "EOF"          ,   0,   0,   0, 0
32767   END
```

820 through 860, the value read into **BOOK$** will be different from EOF (the test value) so processing will continue. However, upon processing line 870 the test condition will be true and execution will branch to statement 490. In other words, this version of the program functions in exactly the same way as that of Figure 2-18, which operates on the book number.

Exercise 2-2 What would occur in the program of Figure 2-20 if the programmer accidentally used EOD (standing for End Of Data) instead of EOF in line 430?

Answers to Preceding Exercises

2-1 The sequence of statements would be arranged by the system as follows:

```
      .
      .
      .
800   !
810   DATA 9999,    0,     0,     0, 0
820   DATA 4451,  453,   150,   313, 2
      .
      .
      .
```

Upon reading the first data set the 9999 trailer would be detected and execution would proceed to the termination portion of the program. The only output would be the PROCESSING COMPLETE message.

2-2 Upon reading the data set at line 870, the string quantity stored in **BOOK$** (EOF) would be compared with EOD. Since they are not equal, the trailer record would be processed and printed as if it were an actual data record. Then processing would return to the **READ** statement and immediately be terminated on an error condition (no more data). The PROCESSING COMPLETE message would not be printed.

In all of the programs that follow, include appropriate descriptive headings.

2-1 Each **DATA** statement includes the following employee payroll information:

> Employee number
> Regular hours worked
> Overtime hours worked
> Pay rate
> Deductions

The data set is followed by a trailer record with 9999 punched for the employee number field.

Write a program that will calculate net pay for each employee. Overtime pay is to be calculated at 1.5 times the regular rate. Add overtime pay to regular pay, then subtract the deductions. For output, print appropriate headings and, for each employee, the employee number, regular pay, overtime pay, and total pay. After processing the last employee, print NO MORE EMPLOYEES.

2-2 This problem is identical to 2-1, except that the employee number field is replaced by the employee name. The trailer record includes EOF in this field.

2-3 This problem is identical to 2-1, except that the terminating message should indicate how many employees were processed. For example, the message might be

NUMBER OF EMPLOYEES PROCESSED: 23

Here the value 23 will come from a counter that must be included in the program.

2-4 Modify Problem 1-3 to include a trailer record with a stock number of 9999. Upon detecting the trailer, print the number of stock records processed and the total profit.

2-5 An engineering company keeps a record of the number of failures that occur during each test series. Each **DATA** statement includes two fields: the test number and the number of failures for the entire set of tests. The last **DATA** statement includes a trailer value of 999 for the test number. For this problem it will be necessary to count the number of test records (refer to line 440 of Figure 1-7) and to accumulate the data values. Accumulation is handled in much the same way as the counter.

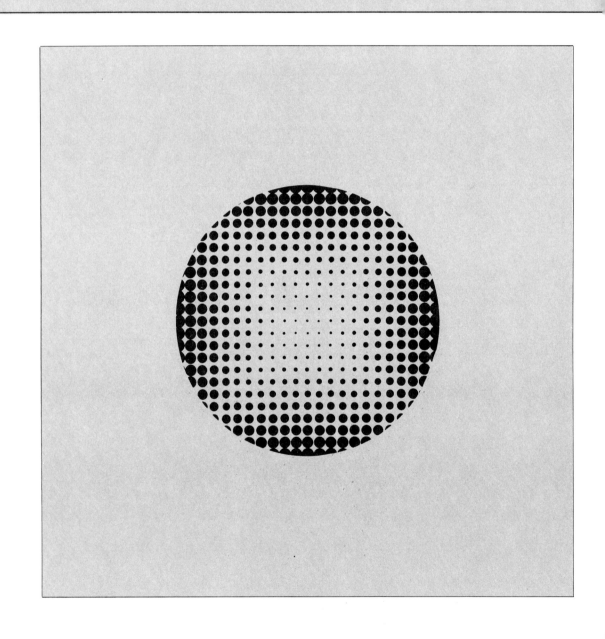

3

Sequential Files

THE INPUT STATEMENT

Transactional and Batch Processing

Although the DATA statement is a simple way of providing data for a program, it is not very practical for real applications. If we think about it for a moment, we recognize that an actual inventory system involves inventory data that is continually changing. Since the data using DATA statements is imbedded right in the program, changing the inventory quantities would involve "modifying" the program with each processing run. In the real world two different situations actually exist. In some applications data is entered into the computer through a keyboard on an interactive basis, the processing is carried out, and the results are displayed immediately. An airline reservation system in which a clerk makes your reservations through a terminal and the computer confirms it while you stand there is a perfect example. This is commonly referred to as *transactional* and *online processing* and is well suited to Basic.

At the other extreme, many applications are well suited to accumulating a series of transactions, storing them in a computer file, and then running them all at once. A payroll system is a good example. Hours worked are accumulated during the week and at the end of the week wages are calculated and checks printed. This is commonly referred to as *batch processing*.

In online processing data input to the program is via direct communication between the computer and user. In batch processing data to be processed is stored in a form somewhat like that of the DATA statements but in a computer data file that is entirely separate from the program. This chapter deals with both interactive input and input/output using files.

A Simple Interactive Program

To illustrate the nature of interactive processing, let us consider the following example.

Example 3-1 A program is required that will accept two numbers from the keyboard, and then calculate and print their sum, difference, and product.

In referring to Figure 3-1 we see that the INPUT statement has the same form as the READ. The difference between the two is that the READ gets data from DATA statements but the INPUT causes the computer to stop and await data from the keyboard. Whenever an INPUT statement of this type is encountered, the computer displays a question mark (?) prompt and awaits input from the keyboard. Figure 3-2 is a typical interactive session with this program. Note that by using a semicolon following the prompt message (line 310), the question mark generated by the PRINT remains on the same line as the prompt NUMBERS. Actually it is possible to include a message preceding the variable list of an INPUT statement. In other words,

```
310    INPUT "NUMBERS"; A,B
```

and

```
310    PRINT "NUMBERS";
320    INPUT A,B
```

are equivalent.

Since this program is an infinite loop (it will always return to the INPUT statement), some means is necessary for terminating execution.

Figure 3-1

Interactive comput-
ing—Example 3-1

```
100 !                EXAMPLE 3-1
110 !             INTERACTIVE COMPUTATION
120 !    THIS PROGRAM DEMOSTRATES INTERACTIVE COMPUTING.
130 !    THE USER ENTERS TWO NUMBERS FROM THE KEYBOARD AND THE
140 !    COMPUTER PRINTS THE SUM, DIFFERENCE AND THE PRODUCT.
150 !
200 !    INITIAL SEQUENCE
210        PRINT "THIS PROGRAM CALCULATES THE SUM, DIFFERENCE AND PRODUCT"
220        PRINT "OF TWO NUMBERS ENTERED FROM THE KEYBOARD."
230        PRINT "TWO NUMBERS SEPARATED BY COMMAS ARE TO BE ENTERED"
240        PRINT "IN RESPONSE TO THE PROMPT."
250        PRINT
260        PRINT
300 !    PROCESSING LOOP
310        PRINT "NUMBERS";
320        INPUT A, B
330        SUM = A + B
340        DIFF = A - B
350        PROD = A*B
360        PRINT
370        PRINT "A = "; A; TAB(15); "B = "; B
380        PRINT
390        PRINT "A+B = "; SUM
400        PRINT "A-B = "; DIFF
410        PRINT "A*B = "; PROD
420        PRINT
430        PRINT
440    GO TO 300
32767  END
```

Initialization block

Processing loop

Figure 3-2

Interaction on the
terminal—Example
3-1

```
THIS PROGRAM CALCULATES THE SUM, DIFFERENCE AND PRODUCT
OF TWO NUMBERS ENTERED FROM THE KEYBOARD.
TWO NUMBERS SEPARATED BY COMMAS ARE TO BE ENTERED
IN RESPONSE TO THE PROMPT.

NUMBERS? 210,60

A =   210        B =   60

A+B =   270
A-B =   150
A*B =   12600

NUMBERS? 28,-13

A = 28           B = -13

A+B =   15
A-B =   41
A*B = -364
   .
   .
   .
and so on
```

Figure 3-3

Terminating
processing

```
300  !   PROCESSING LOOP
310          INPUT "NUMBERS"; A, B

410          PRINT "A*B = "; PROD
420          PRINT
430          PRINT
440          INPUT "DO YOU WISH TO CONTINUE (YES OR NO)"; Q$
450          IF Q$="YES" THEN GO TO 300
500  !   TERMINATE PROCESSING
510          PRINT "PROCESSING COMPLETE"
32767    END
```

Terminating an Interactive Program

The process of terminating an interactive program involves the same basic principles as described in Chapter 2. That is, the user may enter a "never occurring" value as a trailer for which the program tests. Another approach is to query the user; this is used in the program segment of Figure 3-3. In this case, after processing each set of numbers, the computer asks if the user wishes to continue. Entering "YES" will cause the program to repeat; "NO" produces an unequal condition and causes the program to terminate.

Exercise 3-1 What is the difference between the basic form of the INPUT statement considered in this chapter and the READ statement?

3-2 What will occur if the user enters MAYBE in response to the yes–no question of line 450 in Figure 3-3?

BASIC CONCEPTS OF FILES

The File-Name and Extension

One of the most important topics in all of programming is that of files. Everything stored on disk storage is stored as a *file*. (In simple terms, a file is defined as a set of related records.) This means, technically speaking, that each Basic program stored in an account is a file. In any timesharing system a wide variety of types of files will be stored. For instance, a given user might have Basic program files, Fortran program files, special system files, data files, and so on.

In Basic-Plus files are identified by a file-name and an extension that must conform to the following restrictions.

File-names are 6 letters or digits (or less).
Extensions are 3 letters or digits (or less).
A period is used to separate the file-name and extension.

In referring to the directory listing of Figure 2-13 we see that Basic programs have the extension BAS (for example, CUBE.BAS and MEAN.BAS). When the NEW and OLD commands are used, the Basic system automatically adds the .BAS to the designated file-name. For all other files the user must specify the file-name *and* the extension. For standardization certain types of files have predetermined extensions (for example, Basic programs use BAS). Otherwise selection of the extension is up to the user; for instance:

INVEN.DAT   A data file for an inventory control system
STOCK.OUT   A report output file for a stock market summary program

The Nature of Sequential Files

A *sequential file* is one in which information must be processed in the order in which it is stored in the file. In other words, prior to processing the 20th record the 19 preceding it must be read. As a general rule sequential files are processed by beginning with the first record and proceeding, record by record, until the entire file has been processed. The end of a sequential file is usually marked by some type of indicator or special record to indicate the end of the file.

In contrast to sequential files, Basic-Plus also provides *random files*. A random file allows access to records in whatever order they are needed. For instance, the 20th record could be the first (or only) record processed in a given run. Random files are described in Chapters 15 and 17.

A File Processing Example

Many example programs in the remainder of this book will use input data files and will write the results to output files. Such output files can then be printed on a separate printer.

To illustrate file processing, let us consider the following minor variation of Example 2-1.

Example 3-2 The inventory control program of Example 2-1 is to be modified to process data stored in an input file named INVEN.DAT. Each record of this file contains the book title, old inventory balance, copies received, copies sold, and copies lost. Following the last data record is the trailer with EOF in place of the book title. A new file named INVEN.OUT is to be created and all calculated results are written to this file.

A complete program to perform these operations using input and output files is shown in Figure 3-4.

Figure 3-4

A program to process input and output files

```
100 !              EXAMPLE 3-2
110 !       PROGRAM TO UPDATE AN INVENTORY
120 !    INPUT QUANTITIES AND NAMES ARE:
130 !       BOOK$ - BOOK TITLE
140 !       O - OLD BALANCE
150 !       R - COPIES RECEIVED
160 !       S - COPIES SOLD
170 !       L - COPIES LOST AND DESTROYED
180 !    CALCULATED QUANTITIES AND NAMES ARE:
190 !       C - LINE COUNT
200 !       N - NEW BALANCE
300 !
310 !    OPEN FILES
320         OPEN "INVEN.DAT" FOR INPUT AS FILE #1
330         OPEN "INVEN.OUT" FOR OUTPUT AS FILE #2
340 !
410 !    PRINT THE HEADINGS
420         PRINT #2, "LINE", "BOOK", "OLD", "NEW"
430         PRINT #2, "NUMBER", "TITLE", "BALANCE", "BALANCE"
440         PRINT #2
450 !    BEGINNING OF PROCESSING LOOP
460         INPUT #1, BOOK$, O, R, S, L
470         IF BOOK$="EOF" THEN GO TO 530
480         LET N = O + R - S - L
490         LET C = C + 1
500         PRINT #2, C, BOOK$, O, N
510         GO TO 450
520 !
530 !    PRINT MESSAGE & TERMINATE
540         PRINT #2
550         PRINT #2
560         PRINT #2, "PROCESSING COMPLETE"
570         CLOSE #1, #2
32767   END
```

Exercise 3-3 Indicate which of the following would be invalid for use as a file-name and give the reason for each.

W2.BAS	TEST.3
W2.BASIC	SET.1.2
DATABANK.A4	7.FLE

PREPARING A FILE FOR USE

The OPEN Statement

Since files are stored separately and are completely independent of the program, each program must designate the files to be used. This is done with the OPEN statement, which names the file to be processed, designates operations to be performed, and opens a "communication channel" between the program and the file. Each file to be processed in a program must include its own OPEN statement. The OPENs from the program of Figure 3-4 are illustrated in Figure 3-5.

Figure 3-5
The OPEN state-
ment

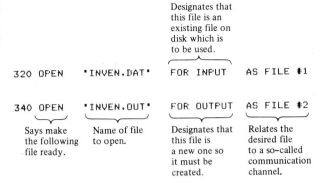

```
                                 Designates that
                                 this file is an
                                 existing file on
                                 disk which is
                                 to be used.

   320 OPEN    "INVEN.DAT"    FOR INPUT    AS FILE #1

   340 OPEN    "INVEN.OUT"    FOR OUTPUT   AS FILE #2

   Says make     Name of file    Designates that    Relates the
   the following to open.         this file is       desired file
   file ready.                    a new one so       to a so–called
                                  it must be         communication
                                  created.           channel.
```

Opening for Input

When an existing file is to be opened the option **FOR INPUT** should be used. The system searches its directory for the named file and, upon finding it, makes it ready for use. However, if there is no such file, the **OPEN** operation will fail and an error will be generated. Line 320 of Figure 3-5 designates the input data file INVEN.DAT as the input file in this example.

With the "programming tools" we have considered thus far, an open failure will automatically cause termination of the program. Thus the user should take care to ensure that the file-name and extension are spelled properly.

Opening for Output

Most timesharing computer systems include a high-speed printer for printing program results (output). Although it is possible to set up a system to allow printing directly to the printer, that is not usually done. The reason simply relates to efficiency: The printer must serve many users. As a result most programs create a new file (an *output* file), and then write all program output to that file. Other capabilities are normally provided for automatically sending completed output files to the printer for fast and efficient printing.

The **OPEN** statement in Figure 3-4 (and 3-5) uses the option **FOR OUTPUT**. When this statement is executed, the new file name (INVEN.OUT in this case) is entered into the system directory and space is reserved for the file. At this point it will be empty as nothing has been written to it. If there is already a file with this name, it will be deleted and the new one created as if the old one had never existed. It is important to realize that no warning is given. A careless programmer can easily lose a file in this way.

Opening Without INPUT or OUTPUT

Although minimal use will be made of it in this book, it is possible to open a file using the following form.

```
200    OPEN "ABC.XYZ" AS FILE #2
```

This form, without FOR INPUT or FOR OUTPUT, causes the system to search for an existing data file (ABC.XYZ in this case). If found, it will be opened as if the FOR INPUT option had been used. If no file ABC.XYZ exists, then one will be created and opened as if the FOR OUTPUT option had been used.

Exercise 3-4 A program is to open a file TEST.DAT to serve as the input data file. A lazy programmer does an open without the FOR INPUT option, assuming that the program, upon finding the file, will open it for input regardless. What is the flaw in this thinking?

Designating a Channel

The data file names with which we deal in a program (for example, INVEN.DAT) are related to files that are *external* to the program. That is, they are separate, independent entities. One of the functions of the OPEN is to link an external file to an internal (within the program) communication *channel*. The AS FILE portion of the OPEN (see Figure 3-5) defines this internal channel. Thus in Figure 3-5 INVEN.DAT is associated with channel #1 and INVEN.OUT is associated with channel #2. Basic-Plus allows the use of 12 channels, numbered #1 through #12. Thus the OPEN statements could have been:

```
320     OPEN "INVEN.DAT" FOR INPUT AS FILE #9

330     OPEN "INVEN.OUT" FOR OUTPUT AS FILE #4
```

However, the channel number defined in the OPEN must be used for all program references to the designated file.

Obviously, if a channel number is selected for a particular file in a program, that same number must not be used concurrently for another file.

CLOSING A FILE

All files that are opened in a program should be closed before terminating execution of the program. If an output file is left open at the end of a program, then part of the output will probably be lost. Each OPEN statement must specify the external file name, the channel number, and normally INPUT or OUTPUT. Furthermore, each OPEN can be used to open only one file. On the other hand, the CLOSE must designate only the channel number, and can be used to close one or more files. In other words, the following statement 800 is equivalent to 900 and 910.

```
800     CLOSE #1 , #2


900     CLOSE #1
910     CLOSE #2
```

FILE INPUT AND OUTPUT

General Form of File Input and Output Statements

As we have already learned, the INPUT and PRINT statements allow input and output operations at the terminal. For example,

```
460     INPUT BOOK$, O, R, S, L
```

will allow the book title and inventory information to be entered from the keyboard. However, in Example 3-2 the data is stored in the file INVEN.DAT that has been opened on communication channel #1 (line 320 of Figure 3-4). This channel number provides the means for letting the system know that the input will be coming from an external file (see Figure 3-6). We should note that INPUT (or PRINT) is followed by the channel number, and then the list, as with terminal input/output. Technically speaking, the terminal is considered channel #0 and the following pairs of INPUT and OUTPUT statements are equivalent.

```
200     INPUT A, B, C
210     INPUT #Ø, A, B, C

300     PRINT X, Y, Z
310     PRINT #Ø, X, Y, Z
```

Reading From an Existing File

Needless to say, whenever we must process data from an input file, we must know exactly what data is stored. For instance, the problem definition for Example 3-2 states exactly what fields are included in the file. Then the input list must correspond to the data read. This is identical to the concept of processing from the DATA statements in Figure 2-20. Each time the INPUT statement is executed, the next record is accessed. If the input process is repeated (with no end-of-file test), an error condition will occur when an attempt is made to read beyond the last record.

Printing to a New File

Following is the PRINT statement from the program of Figure 3-4.

Figure 3-6
Using the channel number for I/O operations

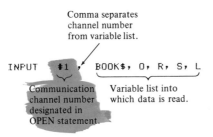

```
500    PRINT #2, C, BOOK$, O, N
```

In general form, the PRINT is identical to the INPUT in that the list is preceded by the channel number to which the output file has been associated. Each time the PRINT statement is executed, a new line will be written to the output file. It is imperative to recognize that the output would appear exactly as if it had been written directly to the terminal. Any output list that is allowable with the PRINT statement can be used with the PRINT # form of the statement. For instance,

```
800    PRINT "LENGTH:"; L; TAB(20); "WIDTH:"; W
```

will cause the output to be displayed on the terminal. The form

```
810    PRINT #7, "LENGTH:"; L; TAB(20); "WIDTH:"
```

will cause the exact same line of output to be written to the file associated with channel 7.

A word of caution is appropriate here. Special procedures must be followed in printing to a file if that file is to be used later as an input file with a program.

Exercise 3-5 Following is the skeleton of a program that a student prepared.

```
100 !    OPEN FILES
110          OPEN 'TEST.DAT' FOR INPUT AS FILE #2
120          OPEN 'TEST.OUT' FOR OUTPUT AS FILE #3
130 !    PROCESSING LOOP
140          INPUT #2, A, B
150          IF A = 0 THEN 200
160          C = 2*A + 2*B
170          D = A*B
180          PRINT #2, A, B, C, D
190          GOTO 130
200 !    CLOSE FILES AND TERMINATE
210          CLOSE #2, #3
32767    END
```

The results of running the program were very strange—the file TEST.OUT did not contain anything. What is wrong with the program?

OPENING DEVICES AS FILES

To this point, all file reference has related to files stored on the primary disk storage unit of the computer. Actually, the file reference in the OPEN statement can include more than the simple file-name described in this chapter. Although a complete description of the possibilities is beyond the scope of this book, the opening of a particular device is appropriate at this point. For instance, if the computer system includes a separate printer available to users, then in order for it to be used by the program it must be opened as a file. For this, the system includes certain predefined names. Two of these are:

LP: The line printer
KB: The user's keyboard

Note that each of these device names includes the colon character. A simple program to calculate and print the perimeter of rectangles for lengths and widths entered at the terminal is shown in Figure 3-7. The terminal and printer are opened in statements 200 and 210 respectively. Actually, there is really little difference between input through an assigned channel and without the use of a channel number. The thing that the user immediately observes is that the "?" prompt is not issued when the keyboard is opened on a channel other than 0.

AUTOMATIC END-OF-FILE DETECTION

(*Note*: This topic may be omitted until the study of Chapter 11.)

The end of each sequential file is marked by the system with a special end-of-file indicator. If a program accidentally attempts to read this indicator as a data value, an error occurs and the program is terminated. However, Basic-Plus has provisions to give control back to the program upon detection of any errors. This is achieved by an error switch called the **ON ERROR**; its use is illustrated in the program of Figure 3-8. We should note that the **ON ERROR** statement (line 440) appears at the beginning of the program. In essence, it says the following.

> If any type of error occurs in execution of
> any statement in this program, then **GOTO**
> statement 530.

Since reading beyond the end of a file is an error condition, execution will be transferred automatically from the **INPUT** statement (line 470) to statement 530. Line 540 checks to ensure that this is indeed an end-of-file error. If it is not, a normal error message will be printed. The full meaning of statements 440 and 540 is covered in Chapter 11.

Figure 3-7
Opening devices
as files

```
100 !    USING THE KEYBOARD AND
110 !    LINE PRINTER AS FILES
200      OPEN 'KB:' AS FILE #1%
210      OPEN 'LP:' AS FILE #2%
220 !  PROCESSING LOOP
230      INPUT #1%, 'ENTER LENGTH & WIDTH: '; L, W
240      P = 2*L + 2*W
250      PRINT #2%, L, W, P
260      GOTO 220
32767  END
```

Answers to   **3-1** The READ statement obtains data from the DATA statements that are included as part
Preceding   of the program. The INPUT statement displays a question mark prompt and awaits
Exercises   entry of the data from the keyboard.

Figure 3-8

Automatic end-of-file
detection

```
100 !              EXAMPLE 3-2
110 !      PROGRAM TO UPDATE AN INVENTORY
120 !      INPUT QUANTITIES AND NAMES ARE:
130 !         BOOK$ - BOOK TITLE
140 !         O - OLD BALANCE
150 !         R - COPIES RECEIVED
160 !         S - COPIES SOLD
170 !         L - COPIES LOST AND DESTROYED
180 !      CALCULATED QUANTITIES AND NAMES ARE:
190 !         C - LINE COUNT
200 !         N - NEW BALANCE
310 !   OPEN FILES
320       OPEN "INVEN.DAT" FOR INPUT AS FILE #1
330       OPEN "INVEN.OUT" FOR OUTPUT AS FILE #2
340       ON ERROR GOTO 530
400 !
410 !   PRINT THE HEADINGS
420       PRINT #2, "LINE", "BOOK", "OLD", "NEW"
430       PRINT #2, "NUMBER", "TITLE", "BALANCE", "BALANCE"
440       PRINT #2
450 !
460 !   BEGINNING OF PROCESSING LOOP
470       INPUT #1, BOOK$, O, R, S, L
480       LET N = O + R - S - L
490       LET C = C + 1
500       PRINT #2, C, BOOK$, O, N
510       GO TO 450
520 !
530 !   PRINT MESSAGE & TERMINATE
540       IF ERR<>11 THEN ON ERROR GOTO 0
550       PRINT #2
560       PRINT #2
570       PRINT #2, "PROCESSING COMPLETE"
580       CLOSE #1, #2
32767     END
```

3-2 An entry of YES results in an equal condition in line 450. An entry of anything else (including NO) results in an unequal condition and, therefore, termination of the program.

3-3 Invalid: W2.BASIC—extension cannot be more than three characters; DATABANK.A4—file-name cannot be more than six characters; SET.1.2—file-name and extension must be separated by one period.

3-4 If, for some reason, the file TEST.DAT does not exist, the open will still be executed, but for output. Thus a new (empty) file would be created erroneously.

3-5 The output file is opened on channel 3; the PRINT statement prints to channel 2.

Programming Problems

3-1 An automobile rental agency charges for its car rentals on the following basis.

$19.95 per day plus
$0.19 per mile plus
a variable insurance charge

Write a program that accepts the following from the keyboard and then computes and prints the total charge.

Number of days rented
Total mileage
Insurance charge

Set the program up to terminate if the value entered for the number of days is zero.

3-2 Expand Problem 3-1 to include keeping a total for all the rentals processed. When the terminal value of zero is entered, print this total and the number of rentals processed.

3-3 A teacher wishes to be able to enter examination scores into the computer and have a program calculate the mean (average). Write an interactive program that will accept scores from the keyboard and calculate and print the mean and count of number of scores. Use a value for the score of −1 to terminate input.

3-4 Repeat Problem 3-3 assuming that the data is stored in the file TEST.FLE.

3-5 A teacher maintains the data file EXAM.DAT with each record containing the following information.

Student name
Exam 1 score
Exam 2 score
Final exam score

Write a program to calculate the total points earned for each student using the formula:

Total score = Exam 1 + Exam 2 + 2 × Final exam

Output for each student must include the student's name and total score. Also, calculate the average scores for each of the three exams and print them at the end of the report. A trailer record will be included with EOF in place of the student name.

4

Conditional Operations

LINE-TO-LINE STATEMENT CONTINUATION

Each statement in example programs to this point has been written on a single line. However, Basic-Plus provides the capability to continue a statement on one or more additional lines. This obviously is convenient for very long statements that will not fit on a single line. It is of interest to us at this point because it allows us to format statements in such a way as to improve the readability of the program.

To indicate that a statement is to be continued on the next line when entering the statement using the NO EXTEND mode, the user depresses the LINE FEED key rather than the RETURN. This is illustrated in Figure 4-1(a) in which we see that the RETURN key is used only when the entire statement has been entered. Through positioning of respective fields by tabbing and spacing, the clarity of even this simple statement is improved significantly.

When programming in the EXTEND mode, the recommended method is to type an ampersand (&) at the end of the current line and then press the RETURN key. This is illustrated in Figure 4-1(b). Any number of tabs and/or spaces may be entered preceding or following the ampersand.

Where statement continuation is used, it must not split basic elements of the statement. For instance, Figure 4-2 shows two valid and correspondingly invalid forms. There is no limit to the number of continuation lines that may be used with a statement.

Exercise 4-1 For each of the following that represent invalid line continuation forms, state the error. (Assume EXTEND mode.)

```
200      PRINT "THIS IS";          &
                  "CORRECT"

300      PRINT "THIS IS NOT        &
                  "CORRECT"

400      IF B=9999                 &
               THEN GOTO 500

500      GO TO                     &
         500

600      GO                        &
         TO 500
```

BASIC FORM OF THE IF STATEMENT

We have already encountered the IF statement in its simplest form in Chapter 2. The general form of that version of the IF is:

IF <*relational expression*> THEN <*statement*>†

†The conventions used for describing the general form of Basic statements (together with a summary of all the statements) are included in Appendix III.

Figure 4-1

Calculating a new inventory balance (a) NO EXTEND mode (from Figure 1-3). (b) EXTEND mode (from Figure 1-5)

```
420     N = O + R - S - L
420     N = O (lf)
          +R (lf)
          -S (lf)
          -L (cr)
```

(a)

```
430     NEW.BAL = OLD.BAL + RECEIVED - SOLD - LOST
430     NEW.BAL = OLD.BAL          & (cr)
          +RECEIVED                & (cr)
          -SOLD                    & (cr)
          -LOST (cr)
```

(b)

Note: There is no way of knowing by looking at the terminal output whether the line feed or RETURN key was depressed.

For instance, the program of Figure 2-18 includes the following IF statement.

```
430     IF B=9999 THEN GO TO 490
```

Relational expression — Statement

Relational Operators and Expressions

The component of the IF statement that forms the test basis is commonly called the *relational expression*. In general, a relational expression involves two arithmetic

Figure 4-2

Valid and invalid line continuation

```
*VALID*
200     PRINT "SMALLEST INPUT VALUE IS"; A,   &
             "LARGEST INPUT VALUE IS"; B

300     NEW.BAL = OLD.BAL + RECEIVED         &
             - SOLD - LOST
```

```
*INVALID*                    Cannot split within a quote.
200     PRINT "SMALLEST INPUT⌐                &
             VALUE IS"; A,                    &
             "LARGEST INPUT VALUE IS"; B
```

```
                               Cannot break variable.
300     NEW.BAL = OLD.⌐                       &
             BAL + RECEIVED                   &
             - SOLD - LOST
```

quantities and a *relational operator*. (For example, *B* and 9999 are simple arithmetic quantities and "=" is a relational operator.) In evaluating a relational expression, the computer preforms any necessary calculations and then makes the designated comparisons. The expression is determined to be either true or false. Relational operators available to the Basic programmer are the following.

SYMBOL	MEANING	EXAMPLES	
>	Greater than	200	IF H > 0 THEN GO TO 450
=	Equal to	300	IF H = -1 THEN GO TO 340
<	Less than	400	IF H < 100 THEN GO TO 100
>=	Greater than or equal to	500	IF H >= 50 THEN GO TO 230
<=	Less than or equal to	600	IF H <= 25.3 THEN GO TO 900
<>	Not equal to	700	IF 2*H-10 <> 90 THEN GO TO 650
==	Approximately equal to†	800	IF H==Y THEN GO TO 100

†Within the computer quantities with decimal points are stored in a binary floating-point format. Because of the characteristics of number systems, the fractional parts of two numbers that we would consider equal can differ by a miniscule amount. The "approximately equal to" operator takes this into account and compares numbers only to the first 6 significant digits.

It is important to recognize that the relational symbols are valid only in the form shown. That is, $>=$, $<=$, and $<>$ are valid but $=>$, $=<$, and $><$ are *not* valid.

Execution of the IF Statement

Execution of the IF statement involves first evaluating the relational expression to determine whether it is true or false. If it is true, execution of the statement following THEN is carried out; if false, execution continues to the next sequential statement. For instance, in the above cases if the value of H were 50, then the following would occur.

STATEMENT	EVALUATION OF RELATIONAL EXPRESSION	VALUE	ACTION
200	50 > 0	True	GO TO statement 450
300	50 = -1	False	Continue to next statement
400	50 < 100	True	GO TO statement 100
500	50 >= 50	True	GO TO statement 230
600	50 <= 25.3	False	Continue to next statement
700	2*50-10 <> 90	False	Continue to next statement

Note that quantities to be compared are not limited to single variables or constants; an arithmetic expression is used in statement 700.

Exercise 4-2 Consider the following IF statement.

```
180     IF 3.2*T7 > =16 THEN GO TO 290
```

(a) Identify the relational expression.
(b) What will occur for each of the following values?

$$T7 = -10$$
$$T7 = 5$$
$$T7 = 20$$

Other Statement Forms in the IF Statement

All IF examples to this point have involved the GOTO statement following the THEN. Actually, any executable statement can be used. For instance, let us consider the following example.

Example 4-1 Each salesperson record in a file contains the following.

Salesperson name
Total sales

Sales commission for each salesperson is to be calculated as 8% of the total sales. If the total sales exceeds $20,000, then add a bonus of $300 to the commission. Write a program segment to perform this operation.

A program segment to perform these operations is shown in Figure 4-3. Here we see that the commission calculation will be executed each time through the loop. However, in statement 420 it is increased by 300 only if the sales exceed $20,000; then execution will continue to statement 430. On the other hand, if the

Figure 4-3
Using the IF state-
ment—Example 4-1

```
100  !     EXAMPLE 4-1
  .
  .
  .
400        INPUT N$, SALES
410        COMMISSION = 0.08*SALES
420        IF SALES > 20000          &
             THEN COMMISSION = COMMISSION + 300
430        . . .
  .
  .
  .
```

condition is false, the LET statement following the word THEN is ignored and execution continues to statement 430 with no additional action.

Exercise 4-3 For each of the values of T given below, show what will be printed by the following PRINT statements.

```
200    PRINT "A";
210    IF T > = 50            &
          THEN PRINT "B";
220    PRINT "C"
```

(a) T = 0;   (b) T = 50;   (c) T = 100

MORE ON THE IF

The IF-THEN-ELSE Form

Example 4-1 illustrates a case of either taking a given action or not taking it. Let us consider a common variation of this in which either of two actions will be taken.

Example 4-2 The sales commission problem of Example 4-1 is to be modified as follows: If the sales are less than $20,000, then the salesperson commission is calculated as 8% of the total sales. If the sales reach $20,000, the commission is 10% of the total sales. Write a program segment to perform this operation.

The difference in logic between Examples 4-1 and 4-2 is illustrated in Figure 4-4. In Figure 4-4(a) (which corresponds to Example 4-1) an action either is or is not taken, depending upon the result of the test. In Figure 4-4(b) (which corresponds to Example 4-2) either of two actions is taken, depending upon the result of the test.

The general form of the IF-THEN-ELSE is:

IF *<relational expression>* THEN *<statement>* ELSE *<statement>*

Figure 4-5 is a program segment to perform the required operation. In statement 410 one of the two commission calculations will always be performed. Whichever occurs, execution will then continue to statement 420.

Alternate Forms of the IF Statement

The preceding examples have all shown a complete statement following THEN (and ELSE) in the IF statement. However, if the statement to be executed is a

Figure 4-4

Two forms of the
IF statement

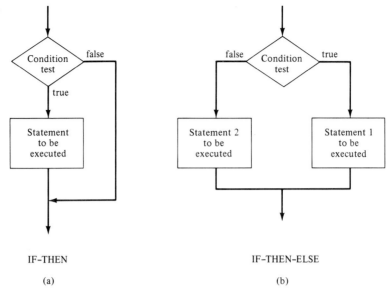

IF–THEN

(a)

IF–THEN–ELSE

(b)

GOTO, either of two abbreviated forms may be used. The general forms are as follows.

IF <*relational expression*> $\left[\begin{array}{l} \textbf{THEN} \ <statement> \\ \textbf{THEN} \ <line \ number> \\ \textbf{GOTO} \ <line \ number> \end{array} \right]$

IF <*relational expression*> $\left[\begin{array}{l} \textbf{THEN} \ <statement> \\ \textbf{THEN} \ <line \ number> \\ \textbf{GOTO} \ <line \ number> \end{array} \right] \left[\begin{array}{l} \textbf{ELSE} \ <statement> \\ \textbf{ELSE} \ <line \ number> \end{array} \right]$

Thus the following are equivalent as shown.

Equivalent $\left\{ \begin{array}{l} 200 \\ 220 \\ 220 \end{array} \right.$
```
IF A > 256 THEN GOTO 100
IF A > 256 THEN 100
IF A > 256 GOTO 100
```

Equivalent $\left\{ \begin{array}{l} 230 \\ 230 \end{array} \right.$
```
IF A > 256 THEN GO TO 100 ELSE GO TO 370
IF A > 256 THEN 100 ELSE 370
```

Exercise 4-4 Example 4-2 is to be modified to count each salesperson being paid 8% and each being paid 10%. (The counters CE and CT are to be used for 8% and 10% respectively.) Can incrementing of these counters, in addition to calculating the commission, be done by statement 410 in Figure 4-5? Explain.

Figure 4-5

Using the IF-THEN-
ELSE—Example 4-2

```
100     EXAMPLE 4-2
  .
  .
  .
400     INPUT N$, SALES
410     IF SALES < 20000                              &
          THEN COMMISSION = 0.08*SALES                &
          ELSE COMMISSION = 0.1*SALES
420     PRINT N$, SALES, COMMISSION
  .
  .
  .
```

BLOCKS OF STATEMENTS

The IF-THEN Block Form

The ability to execute a statement on a conditional basis as provided by the IF statement is a powerful tool. However, more often than not the programmer is faced with the problem of executing several consecutive statements on a conditional basis. Some versions of Basic include the capability conditionally to execute an entire block of statements as illustrated in Figure 4-6. This is an extremely convenient feature that eliminates a lot of programming headaches before they start. Although this precise feature is not available in Basic-Plus, it is easily simulated using the IF-THEN-ELSE form described in the preceding section. In addition, Basic-Plus includes a multiple-statement-per-line capability (described in a later section of this chapter), which can be used in many instances.

Example 4-3   The sales commission problem of Example 4-1 is to be modified as follows: For each salesperson who exceeds the $20,000 quota, add an additional $500 to the commission. A count of the total number of salespeople who exceed the quota is needed, so also increment the counter CNT by 1.

A program segment to perform this operation is shown in Figure 4-7. Although the particular form used here, including the comments, is not necessary, it clearly illustrates the logic of the sequence. The following commentary explicitly spells out the technique.

Figure 4-6

A block IF-THEN
statement type

```
500     IF A = B
510     THEN          ⎫  If test condition is true, all
520       .           ⎪  statements between the THEN
530       .           ⎬  and IFEND are executed, then
          .           ⎪  execution continues to line 580.
          .           ⎪
570     IFEND         ⎭  If false, execution falls through to line 580.
580       .
          .
          .
```

Figure 4-7

The block IF-THEN
concept in Basic-
Plus—Example 4-3

```
100  !    EXAMPLE 4-3
  .                                        Branch to        Branch to
  .                                        the THEN         the IFEND
  .                                        remark if true.  remark if
400       INPUT N$, SALES                                   false.
410       COMMISSION = 0.08*SALES
420       IF SALES >= 20000   THEN   430    ELSE    460
430  !    THEN
440          COMMISSION = COMMISSION + 500
450          CNT = CNT + 1
460  !    IFEND
470       PRINT N$, SALES, COMMISSION
  .
  .
  .
```

Indent all statements
within the IF for
clarity.

1. The IF statement itself marks the beginning of the block IF and the IFEND remark marks the end.

2. Corresponding to the IF-THEN form, the remark THEN marks the beginning of action to be taken.

3. Since the program is to perform particular operations if SALES are equal to or greater than 20,000, the IF statement is set up in this way; hence the use of the IF-THEN-ELSE in statement 420.

4. Each statement that makes up the conditional block is indented to indicate clearly the beginning and end.

Exercise 4-5 Rewrite statement 420 of Figure 4-7 using the IF-THEN form instead of IF-THEN-ELSE.

An IF Within an IF

The generality of this form of the block IF simulation is clearly illustrated by the following expansion of Example 4-3.

Example 4-4 The salespeople of Example 4-3 are identified by a special code field (CODE$) following their names. The code for management people is "M". For any manager-level salesperson, the salesperson name and commission must be written to the file open on channel 4. Also, the commissions for managers are to accumulated in the variable MCOMM.

This problem is similar to Example 4-3 in that a particular set of actions is to be taken if a given condition is met (SALES) equal to or greater than 20,000). In other words, for our first consideration we can think of this as the IF-THEN logic illustrated by Figure 4-4(a). Now in our stepwise refinement of the problem we see that the conditional action to be taken *also* includes a further action to be taken on a conditional basis. This **IF** within an **IF** action is illustrated by the flowchart of Figure 4-8(a). The segment of code to perform the desired operation is shown in Figure 4-8(b). Note the use of indentation, which serves as documentation to the programmer regarding the relationships between various segments of the program.

The IF-THEN-ELSE Block Form

Virtually the same format as that of Figure 4-7 (block **IF-THEN**) is used for the **IF-THEN-ELSE** form. Let us consider an example to illustrate this concept.

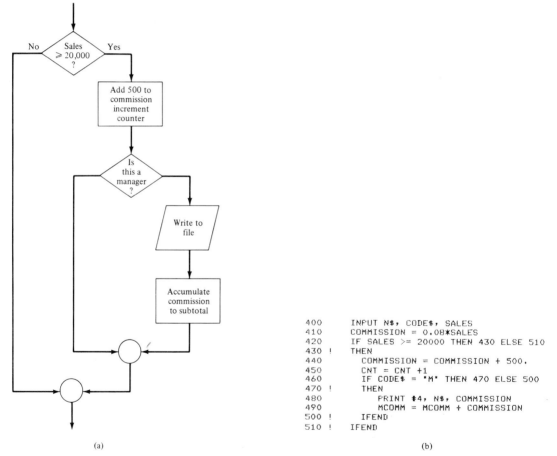

```
400        INPUT N$, CODE$, SALES
410        COMMISSION = 0.08*SALES
420        IF SALES >= 20000 THEN 430 ELSE 510
430 !      THEN
440           COMMISSION = COMMISSION + 500.
450           CNT = CNT +1
460           IF CODE$ = "M" THEN 470 ELSE 500
470 !         THEN
480              PRINT #4, N$, COMMISSION
490              MCOMM = MCOMM + COMMISSION
500 !         IFEND
510 !      IFEND
```

(a)   (b)

Figure 4-8 A condition test within a condition test—Example 4-4. (a) Flowchart (b) Basic program segment

Example 4-5 Each record in an employee payroll file includes the following.

> Shift code
> Employee number
> Employee name
> Pay rate
> Regular hours worked
> Overtime hours worked

Gross pay for each employee is to be calculated as:

> If shift code is equal to 2,
>
> > Regular pay = Regular hours × Pay rate
> >
> > Overtime pay = Overtime hours × Pay rate × 1.5
>
> If shift code is not equal to 2,
>
> > Regular pay = Regular hours × Pay rate × 1.1
> >
> > Overtime pay = Overtime hours × Pay rate × 2.0

For each employee calculate and print:

> Employee number
> Employee name
> Regular pay
> Overtime pay
> Total pay

The logic of this problem is clearly illustrated by the flowchart of Figure 4-9. Its significant features are as follows:

1. The input record is immediately checked to determine if it is the trailer (9999). If so, processing is terminated.

2. Pay is calculated using either of the two pay methods depending upon the value of Shift code. This is commonly called the *selection* procedure for obvious reasons.

3. Upon calculating regular and overtime pay (by whichever method was selected), the total pay is calculated.

4. Upon printing the output, execution is returned to the beginning of the loop to repeat the process.

Figure 4-9
The selection pro-
cess—Example 4-5.

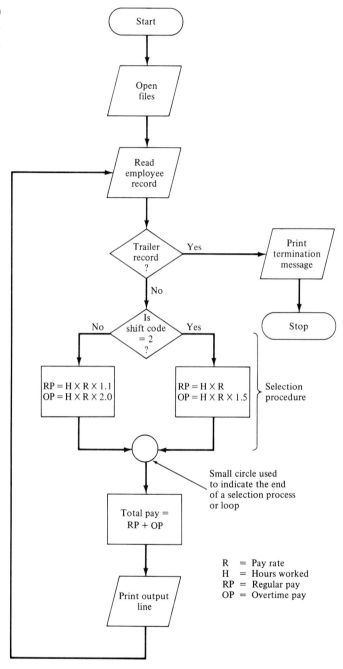

R = Pay rate
H = Hours worked
RP = Regular pay
OP = Overtime pay

Figure 4-10

The block IF-THEN-
ELSE concept in
Basic-Plus—
Example 4-5.

```
100  !   EXAMPLE 4-5
110  !   PAYROLL COMPUTATION
120  !   THIS PROGRAM CALCULATES GROSS PAY
130  !   INPUT QUANTITIES ARE:
140  !     SHIFT           SHIFT CODE
150  !     ENUM            EMPLOYEE NUMBER
160  !     ENAME$          EMPLOYEE NAME
170  !     RATE            PAY RATE
180  !     REGHOURS        REGULAR HOURS WORKED
190  !     OTHOURS         OVERTIME HOURS WORKED
200  !
210  !   THE INPUT FILE PAYROL.DAT IS TERMINATED BY A
220  !   TRAILER WITH 9999 FOR THE EMPLOYEE NUMBER.
230  !   CALCULATED RESULTS ARE:
240  !     REGPAY          REGULAR PAY
250  !     OTPAY           OVERTIME PAY
260  !     TOTPAY          TOTAL PAY
500  !
510  !   INITIAL SEQUENCE
520          OPEN "PAYROL.DAT" FOR INPUT AS FILE #1
530          OPEN "PAYROL.OUT" FOR OUTPUT AS FILE #2
540          PRINT #2, "EMPL NUM", "EMPLOYEE", "REG PAY", "OT PAY", "TOTAL PAY"
550          PRINT #2
560  !   INITIAL SEQUENCE END
570  !
600  !
610  !   MAIN PROCESSING LOOP
620          INPUT #1, SHIFT, ENUM, ENAME$, RATE, REGHOURS, OTHOURS
630          IF ENUM=9999          &
                 THEN GOTO 900    !      TERMINATE PROCESSING
640          IF SHIFT=2 THEN 650 ELSE 700
650  !       THEN
660  !           SHIFT 2 SEQUENCE
670             REGPAY = REGHOURS*RATE
680             OTPAY = OTHOURS*RATE*1.5
690             GOTO 740          !      EXIT THE IF STATEMENT
700  !       ELSE
710  !           SHIFT NOT 2 SEQUENCE
720             REGPAY = REGHOURS*RATE*1.1
730             OTPAY = OTHOURS*RATE*2.0
740  !       IFEND
750  !       NOW COMPUTE THE TOTAL PAY AND PRINT THE LINE
760             TOTPAY = REGPAY + OTPAY
770             PRINT #2, ENUM, ENAME$, REGPAY, OTPAY, TOTPAY
780  !   MAIN PROCESS LOOP END
790          GO TO 610
800  !
900  !   TERMINATION SEQUENCE
910          PRINT #2
920          PRINT #2, "PROCESSING COMPLETE"
930          CLOSE #1, #2
32767    END
```

Figure 4-10 is a complete program to perform this task. Note the extensive use of remarks to describe the actions that take place. We see that the IF statement causes a branch either to statement 650 (THEN) or to statement 700 (ELSE), depending upon the test for shift code. Execution of this statement will proceed as shown below.

```
         Condition True                                    Condition False

640      IF SHIFT=2 THEN 650 ELSE 700         640      IF SHIFT=2 THEN 650 ELSE 700
650  !   THEN                                 650  !   THEN
660  !       SHIFT 2 SEQUENCE                  660          SHIFT 2 SEQUENCE
670          REGPAY = REGHOURS*RATE            670          REGPAY = REGHOURS*RATE
680          OTPAY = OTHOURS*RATE*1.5          680          OTPAY = OTHOURS*RATE*1.5
690          GO TO 740 ! EXIT THE IF           690          GO TO 740 ! EXIT THE IF
700  !   ELSE                                  700  !   ELSE
710  !       SHIFT NOT 2 SEQUENCE              710  !       SHIFT NOT 2 SEQUENCE
720          REGPAY = REGHOURS*RATE*1.1        720          REGPAY = REGHOURS*RATE*1.1
730          OTPAY = OTHOURS*RATE*2.0          730          OTPAY = OTHOURS*RATE*2.0
740  !   IFEND                                 740  !   IFEND
```

Exercise 4-6 What would happen if statement 690 (the (GOTO) were accidentally left out of the program in Figure 4-10?

MULTIPLE STATEMENTS PER LINE

Basic Concepts

The first section of this chapter illustrates how to write a single statement over two or more terminal lines by using the ampersand character. Basic-Plus also allows the opposite; that is, it is possible to write two or more independent statements on a single line (using a single line number). For instance, let us assume that we must print two blank lines, then an error message. The obvious way to do this is shown in lines 200–220 of Figure 4-11. However, line 300, which includes all three of these statements, will do exactly the same thing. Note that statements are separated by the backslash (\) character. (Earlier versions of Basic-Plus used the colon, which is still supported by current versions.) A second example (line 400) is included to illustrate that the statements need not be all of the same type.

At this point it is well to distinguish among the *statement, line, and terminal line*. A *statement* is a single Basic language instruction. Thus in Figure 4-11 lines 200, 210, and 220 each include one statement. On the other hand, lines 300 and 400 each consist of *three* statements. In general, a *line* consists of a line number followed by one or more statements separated by backslashes. By contrast, a *terminal line* represents a physical line that may consist of one or more statements or a portion of a statement. For instance, the second example of line 430 in Figure 4-1 represents one line (and one statement) written on four terminal lines. Line 400 of Figure 4-11 is one line composed of three statements.

When multiple statements per line are used, it is wise also to use the line continuation feature so that the program is easier to read. This is illustrated in Figure 4-12. As a rule it is recommended that beginners avoid using this technique unless it is clearly of value. The one place where it is quite useful is in executing multiple statements within an IF statement. (Overall, this multiple-statement-per-line technique is useful for large programs in which storage must be used as efficiently as possible.)

Multiple Statements in the IF

The real value of multiple statements per line (at this point in our studies) lies in the IF statement. For instance, if we were to assume that lines 300 and 400 of Figure

Figure 4-11
Multiple statements per line

```
200     PRINT
210     PRINT
220     PRINT 'INPUT TOO LARGE'

300     PRINT \ PRINT \ PRINT 'INPUT TOO LARGE'
```
Backslash character separates one statement from the other.

```
400     C = C +1  \  PRINT C \ GOTO 100
```

Figure 4-12

Multiple statements
on continuation
terminal lines

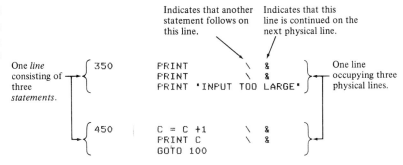

4-11 are to be executed on a conditional basis, they might appear as shown in Figure 4-13. In Figure 4-13(a) the entire **IF** statement is written on one terminal line. Note that in each case the action to be taken consists of three statements. The forms of Figure 4-13(b) are exactly equivalent to those of Figure 4-13(a), except that their documentation value is far greater.

A word of caution is appropriate at this point: Do not use this feature except for simple cases such as those shown in Figure 4-13 until you thoroughly understand how the multiple-statement-per-line feature is treated by the system! Although a detailed description of what occurs is beyond the scope of this chapter, Figure 4-14 includes some examples (without commentary) of both valid and invalid forms. The reader who wishes to pursue this topic may refer to the following exercise.

Figure 4-13

Multiple statements
in the IF

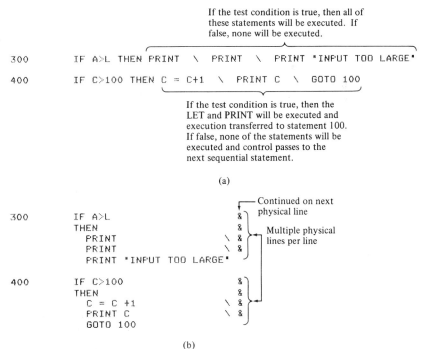

```
        Valid                                          Invalid

        415  !  REFER TO FIG. 4-7                       415  !  REFER TO FIG. 4-8
        420     IF SALES >= 20000          &            420     IF SALES >= 20000          &
                THEN                        &                    THEN                        &
                   COMM = COMM +500      \  &                       COMM = COMM +500      \  &
                   CNT = CNT +1                                     CNT = CNT +1          \  &
                                                                    IF CODE$ = "M"           &
                                                                    THEN                     &
                                                                       PRINT #4, N$, COMM \  &
                                                                    MCOMM = MCOMM + COMM

        200     IF A=B                      &            200     IF A=B                      &
                THEN                        &                    THEN                        &
                   PRINT "VALUES EQUAL"     &                       PRINT "VALUES EQUAL"  \  &
                ELSE                        &                    D = D +1                    &
                   PRINT "VALUES UNEQUAL" \ &                    ELSE                        &
                   C = C +1                                         PRINT "VALUES UNEQUAL"

        300     IF A=B                         &
                THEN                           &
                   X = Y+Z                  \  &
                   IF P$ = "Y" THEN PRINT X \  &
                   PRINT "OKAY"
```

Figure 4-14 Valid and invalid multiple statement IF forms

Exercise 4-7 What would occur in each of the two invalid forms of Figure 4-14?

ADVANCED PROGRAM LOGIC

Logical Operators

Frequently a problem will require that several tests be made on a data field to determine whether or not a particular action is to be taken. For instance, let us consider the following example.

Example 4-6 Each record in an employee file includes the following.

> Employee number
> Employee name
> Accumulated sick leave (days)
> Age
> Seniority (years)

Print the employee number and name of every employee who meets the following requirements:

> Accumulated sick leave equal to or greater than 120
> AND
> Age greater than 65 or seniority greater than 30

Great care must be used in dealing with problems of this type because it is very easy to become confused. There is a big difference between the foregoing statement and grouping the conditions as follows:

(Sick leave condition and Age condition) or Seniority condition

For instance, Sick leave = 100, Age = 50, and Seniority = 35 does not qualify by the example standard but it does by the alternate form above. Always be certain to double-check what is required and then program it carefully as is done in the program segment of Figure 4-15. As is often the case in programming, the action that will take place in statement 420 is rather apparent simply by reading the statement. Needless to say, care must be taken to write correct forms such as this.

Where $<$, $>$, $=$, and so on are called relational operators, AND and OR are called *logical operators*. Logical operators allow us to build complex test conditions for use in the IF statement. In general, we have

<relational expression> <logical operator> <relational expression>

For example, the following are all valid forms that can be used as the test condition in an IF statement.

WORK $<$ 20 OR HOURS $>$ 40

F1 $>$ 3 AND F2 $>$ 5 AND P=0

AGE $>$ 18 AND AGE $<$ 65

SALES $>$ 20000 OR (CODE=1 AND SALES $>$ 15000)

Overall, the AND and OR can be interpreted much the same as in ordinary English. That is, the overall expression

test condition 1 AND test condition 2

is true only if both test conditions 1 and 2 are true. Otherwise it is false. Similarly,

test condition 1 OR test condition 2

is true if either or both of the two individual conditions is true.

Figure 4-15
Multiple test conditions—Example 4-6

```
100 !    USING THE LOGICAL AND & OR
    .
    .
    .
400      INPUT #1, ENUM, ENAME$, LEAVE, AGE, SEN
410      IF ENUM=9999 THEN GO TO ...
420      IF LEAVE >= 120  AND  (AGE>65 OR SEN>30)         &
         THEN PRINT ENUM, ENAME$
430      GO TO 400
    .
    .
    .
```

Whenever a complex test form consisting of ANDs and ORs is evaluated, the ANDs are done first and then the ORs. (This is analogous to evaluating an arithmetic expression where multiplications are done before additions.) However, much confusion can be avoided by using parentheses because operations within parentheses are performed first. As this serves as good documentation and avoids confusion, all such examples in this book use parentheses for grouping. Thus statement 420 of Figure 4-15 will be evaluated as indicated by the numbered descriptions in Figure 4-16.

Exercises **4-8** Would the test condition of statement 420 (Fig. 4-15) be evaluated correctly if the parentheses around the OR grouping were removed? Explain.

4-9 An earlier example tests to determine if AGE is between 18 and 65 by using the following.

AGE > 18 AND AGE < 65

Since AGE is being tested in both cases, could this be written as follows? Explain.

AGE > 18 AND < 65

Validity Checking

As a final modification to Example 4-5, let us consider the following example.

Example 4-7 Processing is to be done as in Example 4-5, except that the only records to be processed are those containing a Shift code of 1, 2, or 3. Ignore all input records with other Shift codes.

In this example, if the Shift code is 1, 2, or 3, then the record is to be processed as before. If it is not 1, 2, or 3, then no processing is required and execution should continue to the next record. The logic of the problem is illustrated by the flowchart of Figure 4-17. We should note that the valid Shift code test

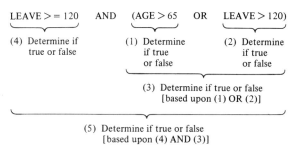

Figure 4-16
Evaluating multiple
test conditions

LEAVE > = 120   AND   (AGE > 65   OR   LEAVE > 120)

(4) Determine if
true or false

(1) Determine
if true
or false

(2) Determine
if true
or false

(3) Determine if true or false
[based upon (1) OR (2)]

(5) Determine if true or false
[based upon (4) AND (3)]

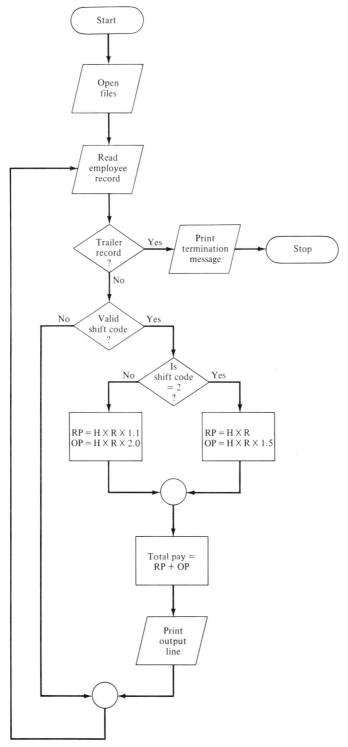

Figure 4-17
Flowchart for
Example 4-7

is illustrated as a selection process in which one of the two alternatives involves no

The main processing loop portion of this program is shown in Figure 4-18. We can see that it differs from the program of Figure 4-10 only by the addition of lines 635, 636 and 775. If the Shift code is 1, 2, or 3, then processing proceeds to line 640 and the pay is calculated as required. Otherwise execution jumps to the end of this sequence (line 775), which, in turn, proceeds to the repetition of the loop.

Exercise 4-10 Would it be possible to replace line 635 in Figure 4-18 with the following and achieve the same overall result?

(a) `635    IF SHIFT=1 OR SHIFT=2 OR SHIFT=3 THEN 640 ELSE 610`

(b) `635    IF SHIFT<>1 AND SHIFT<>2 AND SHIFT<>3 THEN 775`

Programming Techniques

For many years programming methods evolved rather loosely, more as an unorganized art than a science. As a result programming techniques vary widely from one programmer to another. And this is compounded by the fact that many programmers are inclined to begin writing the program *before* completely figuring how to solve the problem. The result has been chaos in the programming field. Excessive use of the GOTO statement to patch up errors and/or omissions due to poor planning is, unfortunately, quite common. The result is programs that are almost

Figure 4-18
Program for
Example 4-7

```
100  !  EXAMPLE 4-7
  .
  .
  .
610  !  MAIN PROCESSING LOOP
620        INPUT #1, SHIFT, ENUM, ENAME$, RATE, REGHOURS, OTHOURS
630        IF ENUM=9999          &
              THEN GOTO 900     !      TERMINATE PROCESSING
635        IF SHIFT=1 OR SHIFT=2 OR SHIFT=3 THEN 640 ELSE 775
636  !     THEN     !   SHIFT CODE VALID SO PROCESS THE RECORD
640            IF SHIFT=2 THEN 650 ELSE 700
650  !         THEN
660  !             SHIFT 2 SEQUENCE
670                REGPAY = REGHOURS*RATE
680                OTPAY = OTHOURS*RATE*1.5
690                GOTO 740     !     EXIT THE IF STATEMENT
700  !         ELSE
710  !             SHIFT NOT 2 SEQUENCE
720                REGPAY = REGHOURS*RATE*1.1
730                OTPAY = OTHOURS*RATE*2.0
740  !         IFEND
750  !     NOW COMPUTE THE TOTAL PAY AND PRINT THE LINE
760            TOTPAY = REGPAY + OTPAY
770            PRINT #2, ENUM, ENAME$, REGPAY, OTPAY, TOTPAY
775  !     IFEND
780  !  MAIN PROCESS LOOP END
790        GO TO 610
```

Figure 4-19

Structured program-
ming logical
components

The *process* structure, which consists of
one or more unconditional operations.

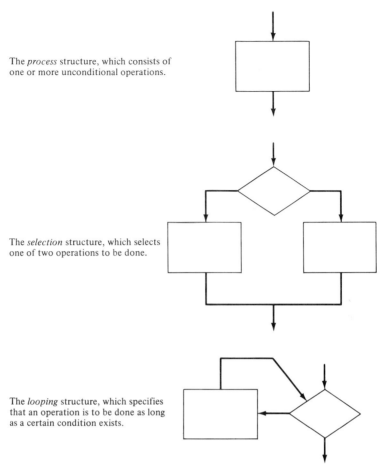

The *selection* structure, which selects
one of two operations to be done.

The *looping* structure, which specifies
that an operation is to be done as long
as a certain condition exists.

impossible to understand and modify because of all the jumping around. As a
general rule it has been observed that the quality of a program tends to decrease
with the increased use of GOTO statements.

Within recent years standardized techniques have evolved for coding programs; one is *structured programming*. Experience has shown that careful program planning and application of these techniques significantly improves programmer efficiency. The three basic structures shown in Figure 4-19 form the
basis for structured programming. Preceding example programs have involved the
process and selection structures, and each program has consisted of a main
processing loop. Both the selection and looping structures in these Basic examples
are implemented by use of the GOTO statement. A truly structured language
includes automatic loop control features that virtually eliminate the need for the
GOTO. Unfortunately, Basic is not one of these languages. However, structured
methods can be used very effectively in Basic.

General rules that are used in this book are as follows:

1. Work out a complete solution to the problem before beginning the coding. Use the basic flowchart structures of Figure 4-19.

2. On IF-THEN-ELSE forms, always exit from the selection process on an IFEND remark line (for example, see line 740, Figure 4-18). Thus the form illustrated in Exercise 4-10, which jumps to the beginning of a loop from a selection structure, should not be used.

3. Clearly mark the beginning of a loop with a remark, and when repeating the loop GOTO that line.

Careful use of these methods will usually result in a greatly reduced level of frustration for the beginning programmer.

Answers to Preceding Exercises

4-1 Statement 300; must not break a quoted quantity. Statement 600; the GOTO is considered a single element in Basic-Plus. Thus to break GOTO would be equivalent to, for instance, breaking PRINT following the R.

4-2 (a) The relational expression is $3.2*T7 >= 16$
  (b) $T7 = -10$; condition false; continue to next statement.
    $T7 = 5$; condition true; GOTO statement 290.
    $T7 = 20$; condition true; GOTO statement 290.

4-3 (a) AC;   (b) ABC;   (c) ABC

4-4 No. Following each the THEN and the ELSE there must be only one statement. To increment the counters in addition to calculating the commissions involves two statements each.

4-5
```
420          IF SALES <  20000 THEN GOTO 460
430     !      ELSE
440              COMMISSION=COMMISSION+500
450              CNT=CNT+1
460     !      IFEND
```

If SALES are less than 20,000, the condition is true and the sequence is skipped (as required). Otherwise execution "falls through" to statement 440 and the computations are performed. As we shall see, the form of Figure 4-7 is more consistent with the block IF-THEN-ELSE technique of the next section.

4-6 If statement 690 were omitted then, after computing the pay for a Shift 2 code, the pay would be recomputed as if it were not Shift 2. Thus all employees would be paid according to the not 2 formula.

4-7 In the first example (line 420), the statement

```
MCOMM = MCOMM + COMM
```

would *not* be associated with the second IF statement as required. The first IF would be interpreted to include four statements in the "action." In other words, it would be interpreted as if it had been written:

```
420    IF SALES > = 20000                              &
       THEN                                            &
         COMM = COMM + 500                          \  &
         CNT = CNT + 1                              \  &
         IF CODE$ = "M" THEN PRINT 4, N$, COMM      \  &
       MCOMM = MCOMM + COMM
```

In line 200 the ELSE and PRINT would be considered part of the preceding statement. Thus the system would "see" the statement as

```
D = D + 1 ELSE PRINT "VALUES UNEQUAL"
```

which violates the syntax rules.

4-8 No. Since ANDs are handled before ORs, removal of the parentheses would cause the condition to be evaluated as if it were

```
(LEAVE > =120 AND AGE > 65)   OR   SEN > 30
```

4-9 The form

```
AGE > 18 AND < 65
```

is not valid since <65 (to the right of AND) is not a relational expression. Remember, the form is

<relational expression> <logical operator> <relational expression>

4-10 (a) Yes, the loop would be repeated as in Figure 4-13. However, the form of Figure 4-13 is considered better practice, as described in the section that follows.

(b) Yes. If, for example, SHIFT were 4, then all three of the individual conditions would be false, the overall condition would be false, and execution would skip to line 775 as required.

Programming Problems

4-1 Each record in an input file contains three fields A, B, and C. Write a program to find the largest value for each set of A, B, and C and place it in the variable L. Print the input quantities and L. The file will be terminated with a trailer value of 9999 for A; no data value will be 9999.

4-2 Write a program for the data set of Problem 4-1 that will rearrange the values for each set of A, B, and C so that A contains the smallest value, B the next, and C the largest. In this problem it will be necessary to interchange values between variables that will require a temporary storage variable. For instance, A and B would be interchanged by the following.

```
100    T = A  !  SAVE A
110    A = B  !  PLACE VALUE OF B IN A
120    B = T  !  PLACE VALUE OF A SAVED IN T INTO B
```

4-3 This program is designed to perform a check of customer charge accounts to determine all customers who have exceeded their allowable charge limit. Each record in the data file includes the following information.

    Account number
    Customer name
    Balance at beginning of month
    Total charges during month
    Total credits during month
    Credit limit

A trailer record with 9999 for the account number is included in the file. Write a program to calculate the new balance (add charges to beginning balance and subtract credits) and compare the new balance with the credit limit. For only those accounts that exceed the credit limit, print the following.

    Account number
    Customer name
    New balance
    Credit limit

4-4 This problem is to compute gross pay of employees and company totals. Each record in the input file includes the following data.

    Employee number
    Hourly pay rate
    Hours worked: Monday
                Tuesday
                Wednesday
                Thursday
                Friday

The file will be followed by a trailer record with 9999 for the employee number. For each employee, calculate regular hours, overtime hours (anything over 40 hours per week), and gross pay. Pay at the rate of 1½ times the hourly rate for all overtime hours. Accumulate regular hours, overtime hours, and gross pay for all the employees. Output for each employee must include appropriate headings and the following.

    Employee number
    Regular hours
    Overtime hours
    Hourly rate
    Gross pay

After processing the last record print a summary line for accumulated values of regular hours, overtime hours, and gross pay.

4-5 Modify Problem 4-4 to calculate overtime hours as all hours worked in excess of 9 hours in any given day or 40 in the entire week; use the criterion that yields the maximum overtime. For instance, if an employee worked 12, 8, 8, 8, and 8 hours, the regular hours would be 40 and overtime hours 4 (based on 44 hours for the week). However, one who worked 12, 8, 8, 8, and 6 hours would be credited with 39 regular hours and 3 overtime hours (based on 12 hours for Monday).

4-6 Each record of a college class file includes the following.

> Actual enrollment
> Course name (maximum of 14 letters)
> Instructor name (maximum of 12 letters)
> Course number
> Section number
> Maximum permissible enrollment
> Minimum permissible enrollment

A trailer record will be included that has a value of 9999 for the course number. A report is to be printed with one line for each class that includes the course number, section number, course name, instructor name, actual enrollment, and the word

> OVER if Actual enrollment > Maximum permissible
> UNDER if Actual enrollment < Minimum permissible
> Blank otherwise

4-7 Each record in a salesperson file includes the following information (the trailer of EOF in the Salesperson name).

> Salesperson name
> Units sold
> Unit commission
> Base pay
> Bonus point
> Bonus

Write a program to calculate the commission (units sold × unit commission) and determine the gross pay for each salesperson as follows:

$$
\text{Gross pay} = \begin{cases} \text{base pay} & \text{if commission less than base pay} \\ \text{commission} & \text{if commission between base pay and} \\ & \quad \text{bonus point} \\ \text{commission+bonus} & \text{if commission greater than bonus point} \end{cases}
$$

As output, print the salesperson name, commission, and gross pay.

4-8 The "change-maker problem" is a classical one in programming. A person makes a purchase and pays with a one-dollar bill. The change can be anything from nothing to 99 cents. Write a program to determine the number of half dollars, quarters, dimes, nickels, and pennies that a person would receive for a given amount. Note that the number of half dollars, quarters, and nickels can only be one or zero. Print the input amount and number of half dollars, quarters, dimes, nickels, and pennies in change. Write this program to accept input from the keyboard; output, which is to consist of each input value and results, is to be written to an output file. Terminate execution upon entering a value of –1.

4-9 A credit card company assesses a monthly service charge of 1½% on the first $500 of the balance due and 1% on the balance due above $500. The input record for each customer includes the balance due as follows:

Customer number
Customer name
Balance due (dollars and cents)

Write a program to calculate the service charge; print all input quantities, service charge, and total amount (balance due plus service charge). Use appropriate headings.

4-10 Using a file of registered voters as a source, write a program that will produce a listing of the names of Democrats who are married and have an annual income of at least $15,000. The registered-voter records contain the following data.

Name
Street address
City, state, ZIP code
Annual income (dollars)
Party of registration:　R = Republican
　　　　　　　　　　　D = Democratic
　　　　　　　　　　　I = Independent
Marital status:　1 = Married
　　　　　　　　2 = Not married

5

Arithmetic Operations & Predefined Functions

THE NATURE OF NUMERIC VARIABLES

Numeric Quantities

Thus far we have studied two types of variables: numeric and string. Actually, numeric quantities fall in two different categories: *floating point* and *integer*. In a nutshell, floating-point numbers are numbers that include a decimal point. By contrast, integer numbers are, as the name implies, whole numbers. They have no decimal point. For instance:

FLOATING POINT	INTEGER
123.456	478
0.009703	−32
0.0	0
2501.	32767 (largest allowable integer)
−386.2	−32768 (smallest allowable integer)

Normally, all numeric values (variables and constants) specified in a Basic program are stored internally in binary floating-point format. For each floating-point variable or constant used in a program, the computer reserves 32 binary digits (64 if the system has been defined with double precision). The 32-bit format provides the capability for accurately storing up to 6 significant digits. The decimal positioning is determined by use of an exponent that allows the number to range from 10^{-38} to 10^{38}. As a rule we need not be concerned with such details since the system automatically converts numbers to our familiar form with the decimal point.

In many cases the power of floating point is simply not required. For instance, several example programs in preceding chapters have involved counters that begin at 0 and are incremented by 1 for each execution. In cases such as this, the use of integers is quite appropriate. For one thing, arithmetic operations involving integer quantities are much faster and more efficient than that with floating point or a combination of the two. For another, an integer occupies but 16 bits in storage (this is the reason for its relatively limited range of −32768 to 32767). This saving in storage could be critical in a large program, especially if large arrays are being used (the subject of Chapter 9).

Specifying Integer Quantities

As we already know, we indicate to the system that a variable is to store string data by adding the $ to the name. Similarly, the % is used to indicate that a quantity is to be treated as integer: this applies to *both* variables and constants. Following are some examples.

FLOATING POINT	INTEGER
A	A%
WORK	WORK%
CREDIT.LIMIT	CREDIT.LIMIT%
25	25%
−231.	−231%

Integer quantities may be used within the program in much the same way as floating point. For instance, the counter used in an earlier example would appear as

```
420    CNTR% = CNTR% + 1%
```

rather than as

```
420    CNTR = CNTR + 1
```

Input and output with integer quantities are handled in exactly the same way as with floating point and string. For instance, let us assume that a student ID number (4 digits), name, grade-point average, and total units must be read from a file open on channel 4. The following statement could be used.

```
500    INPUT #4%, ID%, STUDENT$, GPA, UNITS
```

Arithmetic Operations

Arithmetic operations with integer quantities are performed in the same way as those with floating-point quantities, with one exception. That is, integer division always gives an integer result that is truncated, not rounded off, as illustrated in Figure 5-1. The results produced by lines 150–170 are a bit subtle and demonstrate the importance of hierarchy of operations.

In some cases it is desirable to perform an arithmetic operation on two or more floating quantities and store the result as an integer. For instance, if $A = 26.0$ then the LET statement

```
200    X% = 2.1*A
```

Figure 5-1
Integer arithmetic
```
100    A% = 5%
110    B% = 13%
120    C% = 8%
130    X1%= B%/A%        !    RESULT IS 2   (REMAINDER OF 3 IS LOST)
140    X2%= A%/B%        !    RESULT IS 0
150    X3%= A%/B%*C%     !    RESULT IS 0   (A%/B% GIVES 0, TIMES C%)
160    X4%= A%*C%/B%     !    RESULT IS 3
170    X5%= A%/B% + C%/B%   ! RESULT IS 0   (0 + 0)
```

will produce a result for the expression of 54.6. However, it will be truncated to 54 before being stored in the integer variable X%.

The situation is somewhat more complex when integer and floating point are combined in an expression. This is called *mixed mode arithmetic* and is rather inefficient as it requires that the system convert integer quantities to floating point before proceeding. However, from time to time program needs dictate its use. For example, assume that we are dealing with grade-point averages of a group of students. The number of students is stored in CNTR% and the sum of their GPA's is stored in TGPA.

```
500    AVE.GPA = TGPA/CNTR%
```

Exercise 5-1 What will be stored in each of the variables P1%–P5% by the following statements?

```
100     X%  = 12%
110     Y%  = 18%
120     Z%  = 7%
130     P1% = Y%/Z%
140     P2% = (Z% + 11%)/Y%
150     P3% = X%/Y%*2%*Z%
160     P4% = Y%/X% + Y%/Z%
170     P5% = Y%/(X%+Z%)
```

INTEGERS AS LOGICAL VARIABLES

One very convenient feature of integers is that integer variables (or expressions) may be used within an IF statement in place of a logical expression. The integer value of 0% corresponds to the logical FALSE. Although any nonzero integer value will be interpreted as a logical true, the value –1% is normally used as it yields all binary ones in integer format. To illustrate this concept, let us consider the following example.

Example 5-1 A program loop involves reading, verifying, and processing certain input data. If a particular condition is detected during verification of the data, execution of the loop should not be repeated upon completion of the current pass.

Here we are dealing with an occurrence at one place in the program that will determine whether the loop is repeated at a later place in the program. Figure 5-2 illustrates three methods of performing this operation. The sequence on the left uses the string variable LOOP$ in a manner that is quite familiar to us by now. The first sequence on the right (which uses the integer variable LOOP%) functions in exactly the same way. In statement 400, if LOOP% contains –1%, the "condition" is true and the branch occurs. If LOOP% has been changed to 0% at line 210, the condition at line 400 is false and execution falls through.

Figure 5-2

Integers as logical
variables

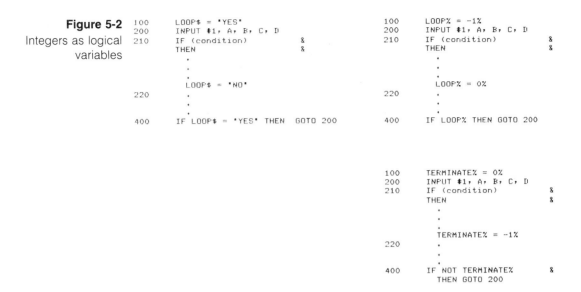

```
100    LOOP$ = "YES"                      100    LOOP% = -1%
200    INPUT #1, A, B, C, D               200    INPUT #1, A, B, C, D
210    IF (condition)        &            210    IF (condition)        &
       THEN                  &                   THEN                  &
         .                                         .
         .                                         .
         .                                         .
       LOOP$ = "NO"                              LOOP% = 0%
220      .                                220      .
         .                                         .
         .                                         .
400    IF LOOP$ = "YES" THEN  GOTO 200    400    IF LOOP% THEN GOTO 200


                                          100    TERMINATE% = 0%
                                          200    INPUT #1, A, B, C, D
                                          210    IF (condition)        &
                                                 THEN                  &
                                                   .
                                                   .
                                                   .
                                                 TERMINATE% = -1%
                                          220      .
                                                   .
                                                   .
                                          400    IF NOT TERMINATE%     &
                                                 THEN GOTO 200
```

The second example on the right is similar, except that the negation operator (NOT) is used. Prior to execution of line 210 TERMINATE% will contain 0% (FALSE), which means that NOT TERMINATE% (the opposite) is TRUE. Thus the GOTO at line 400 will be executed.

As we see in Chapter 7, this particular example will be easily adaptable to automatic loop control of Basic-Plus.

MATHEMATICAL FUNCTIONS

The Concept of the Function

In programming many operations exist that are general in nature and commonly performed. These include such basic operations as calculating a square root or taking the absolute value of a number. Since Basic includes no specific arithmetic operators beyond +, −, *, /, and ** (^) these quantities must be obtained by programming means. Fortunately for the user, many of the common operations are "preprogrammed" and available to the user as *functions*. For instance, the following statement 200 calculates the squate root of X and places the value in Y.

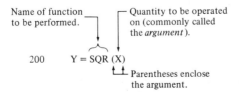

Name of function
to be performed. ┐ ┌ Quantity to be operated
               │ │ on (commonly called
               ↓ │ the *argument*).
    200   Y = SQR (X)
                   └┴ Parentheses enclose
                      the argument.

During execution of the program, the computer will

1. Obtain the value for the argument (X in this case).
2. Give this value to a special routine named SQR (included as part of the Basic system), which will calculate the square root of X.
3. Assign the result to Y by virtue of the LET statement.

Using Functions in Expressions

In general, functions such as this may be handled pretty much as variables in forming expressions. For instance, all of the following are valid forms and produce the results indicated.

Assume X = 25, LIM = 10

Y = 7.5*SQR(X) + LIM
    7.5*SQR(25) + 10
    7.5*5 + 10
    37.5 + 10
    47.5

IF   SQR(X) + 5 < LIM THEN 200
    SQR(25) +5 < 10
    5 + 5 < 10
    10 < 10
    Condition false

It is important to recognize that once the function is evaluated its result is included in the evaluation of the expression as if the function name were an ordinary variable.

Versatility of the function is further increased by the fact that the argument may be any acceptable expression. For instance, the following are valid and give the result indicated.

Assume X = 10

Y = SQR(X + 90)
    SQR(10 + 90)
    SQR(100)
    10

Z = 3*SQR(2*X + 16)
    3*SQR(2*10 + 16)
    3*SQR(36)
    3*6
    18

Basic-Plus Mathematical Functions

The various mathematical functions available in Basic-Plus are the following.

ABS(X)	Returns the absolute value of X. For instance, ABS(–10)=10 and ABS(10)=10.
SGN(X)	Returns a value of 1 with the sign of X. For instance, SGN(–27)=–1, SGN(23)=+1. However, note that SGN(0)=0.
INT(X)	Returns the greatest integer that is less than or equal to X. For instance, INT(23.7)=23, INT(23)=23, and INT(–26.8)= –27.
FIX(X)	Returns the truncated value of of X. For instance, FIX(23.7)=23, FIX(23)=23, and FIX(–26.8)=–26. Note the difference between FIX and INT when dealing with negative numbers.
COS(X)	Returns the cosine of X (X in radians).
SIN(X)	Returns the sine of X (X in radians).
TAN(X)	Returns the tangent of X (X in radians).
ATAN(X)	Returns the arctangent of X (X in radians).
SQR(X)	Returns the square root of X. If X is negative, an error condition will occur.
EXP(X)	Returns the value of the natural logarithm base *e* raised to the X power.
LOG(X)	Returns the natural logarithm of X.
LOG10(X)	Returns the common logarithm of X.
RND	Returns a random number between 0 and 1.

Since the argument of a mathematical function can be any arithmetic expression, it is possible to use another function as an argument. For instance,

```
200    X = SQR(ABS(Y))
```

is equivalent to

```
300    A = ABS(Y)
310    X = SQR(A)
```

It is necessary only to take care in matching up opening and closing parentheses.

Random Number Generation

Many actual phenomena that cannot be solved by ordinary mathematical methods can be solved by simulation techniques. The key to simulation is the use of numbers that are selected (over a given range) completely at random. Basic includes a random number function that will generate numbers between 0 and 1 completely at random. Unlike most of the other functions, RND does not involve an argument (if one is included, it is ignored). The generation of 20 random numbers is illustrated by the simple program of Figure 5-3. By inspecting the results, we see that the two different runs produced exactly the same sequence. Thus we might wonder just how random the numbers really are. The answer to this dilemma relates to the fact that, while debugging a program, we usually require that results be predictable so that we know whether or not our program is correct. However, once the program is ready for use, we would desire that each time it is run, a new sequence of random numbers will be generated. This can be accomplished with the RANDOMIZE statement shown in Figure 5-4. As a general rule, programs using random numbers are written and tested without the RANDOMIZE statement. When the program is ready for use, this statement is inserted, thus causing the system to generate a different sequence each time it is executed.

To illustrate the use of the RND function to generate integer random numbers within a given range, let us consider the following simple example.

Example 5-2 An elementary school teacher desires a simple multiplication table drill and practice program. The program is to display two one-digit numbers (0–9) selected at random and ask the pupil the product. The program is to indicate whether or not the answer is correct and to keep score.

Figure 5-3
Random number generation

```
LISTNH
10 !     RANDOM NUMBER DEMO
20       I% = 0%
30 !     PROCESSING LOOP
40       R = RND                    ! NOTE:  Statements 40 and 50 could
50       PRINT R,                   !        be replaced with PRINT RND
60       I% = I% +1%
70       IF I% < 20% THEN GOTO 30
32767    END

Ready

RUNNH
 .204935       .229581       .533074       .132211       .995602
 .783713       .741854       .397713       .709588       .67811
 .682372       .991239       .806084       .915352       .237358
 .185981       .979664       .204159       .40798        .610446

Ready

RUNNH
 .204935       .229581       .533074       .132211       .995602
 .783713       .741854       .397713       .709588       .67811
 .682372       .991239       .806084       .915352       .237358
 .185981       .979664       .204159       .40798        .610446

Ready
```

Figure 5-4

Random number
generation

```
LISTNH
10 !     RANDOM NUMBER DEMO
15         RANDOMIZE
20         I% = 0%
30 !     PROCESSING LOOP
40         R = RND                   !  NOTE:  Statements 40 and 50 could
50         PRINT R,                  !         be replaced with PRINT RND
60         I% = I% +1%
70         IF I% < 20%  THEN GOTO 30
32767  END

Ready

RUNNH
 .457144        .7428        .342504       .369828      .13643
 .490131        .712917      .866321       .78167       .893137
 .32379         .904507      .51293        .937015      .57157E-2
 .601162        .555531      .922726       .53658       .914946

Ready

RUNNH
 .842705        .559781E-1   .751522       .532917E-2   .268276
 .561695        .955686      .678855       .471959      .72206
 .847283E-1     .983073E-2   .296429       .6901        .472736
 .625513        .498457      .361124       .68063       .83367

Ready
```

A simple program to perform this operation is shown in Figure 5-5. Although the program illustrates several techniques covered in earlier chapters, the item of primary importance is the use of RND in statements 310 and 320. Although the function itself only produces random numbers in the range 0 to 1, appropriate manipulation can produce any desired range. The form from lines 310 and 320 is explained in Figure 5-6.

Exercises **5-2** Make the appropriate change to line 310 to generate an integer in the range 10 to 99.

5-3 Rewrite the IF test of statements 350–400 using multiple statements per line.

OTHER FUNCTIONS

In addition to the preceding mathematical functions, Basic-Plus includes a number of other functions for performing a variety of operations. For instance, Chapters 10 and 14 involve extensive manipulation of string data through the use of string functions. These and others are described at appropriate places in later chapters. However, let us consider two of the so-called system functions that will be useful to us immediately. One of them, DATE$, returns the current date and the other, TIME$, returns the clock time. Their use is illustrated in Figure 5-7. Note that the argument used to obtain the current date and time is 0 for both functions. Since the computer includes an internal clock, this information is always available. The dating of program output is a common and useful practice.

Figure 5-5

Multiplication drill
and practice—
Example 5-2

```
LISTNH
100 !    MULTIPLICATION DRILL AND PRACTICE
200 !    INITIAL ROUTINE
210        PRINT "WELCOME TO MULTIPLICATION DRILL & PRACTICE"
220        PRINT "I WILL GIVE YOU TWO NUMBERS AND YOU"
230        PRINT "MUST ENTER THEIR PRODUCT.   GOOD LUCK!"
240        RANDOMIZE
250        I%, CORRECT% = 0%
300 !    INNER PROCESSING LOOP
310        N1% = INT(10 * RND)
320        N2% = INT(10 * RND)
330        PRINT N1%; "TIMES"; N2%; "EQUALS";
340        INPUT P%
350        IF P% = N1%*N2%   THEN 360    ELSE 380
360 !      THEN
370          PRINT "CORRECT, THE ANSWER IS INDEED"; P%     \ &
             CORRECT% = CORRECT% +1%                       \ &
             GOTO 400
380 !      ELSE
390          PRINT "SORRY, THE ANSWER IS"; N1%*N2%
400 !      IFEND
410        I% = I% + 1%
420        IF I% < 10% THEN GOTO 300
500 !    END OF ONE SESSION (10 QUESTIONS)                   &
    !    PRINT THE SCORE THEN TERMINATE
510        PRINT "YOUR SCORE IS:" ;CORRECT%; "OUT OF 10."
520        IF CORRECT% = 10%                                 &
           THEN                                              &
             PRINT "VERY GOOD!'                              &
           ELSE                                              &
             IF CORRECT% >= 8%                               &
             THEN                                            &
               PRINT "PERFORMANCE OKAY."                     &
             ELSE                                            &
               PRINT "IMPROVEMENT NEEDED."
32767   END

Ready

RUNNH
WELCOME TO MULTIPLICATION DRILL & PRACTICE
I WILL GIVE YOU TWO NUMBERS AND YOU
MUST ENTER THEIR PRODUCT.   GOOD LUCK!
 1 TIMES 9 EQUALS? 9
CORRECT, THE ANSWER IS INDEED 9
 1 TIMES 5 EQUALS? 5
CORRECT, THE ANSWER IS INDEED 5
 1 TIMES 6 EQUALS? 6
CORRECT, THE ANSWER IS INDEED 6
 8 TIMES 2 EQUALS? 16
CORRECT, THE ANSWER IS INDEED 16
 1 TIMES 0 EQUALS? 0
CORRECT, THE ANSWER IS INDEED 0
 1 TIMES 7 EQUALS? 1
SORRY, THE ANSWER IS 7
 6 TIMES 0 EQUALS? 0
CORRECT, THE ANSWER IS INDEED 0
 4 TIMES 9 EQUALS? 40
SORRY, THE ANSWER IS 36
 7 TIMES 5 EQUALS? 35
CORRECT, THE ANSWER IS INDEED 35
 5 TIMES 0 EQUALS? 0
CORRECT, THE ANSWER IS INDEED 0
YOUR SCORE IS: 8 OUT OF 10.
PERFORMANCE OKAY.
```

Figure 5-6
Random generation
of digits

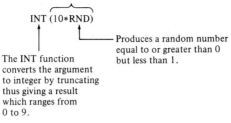

10 times the random number
produces a result equal to or
greater than 0 but less than 10.

INT (10*RND)

The INT function
converts the argument
to integer by truncating
thus giving a result
which ranges from
0 to 9.

Produces a random number
equal to or greater than 0
but less than 1.

Examples:	RND gives	.099713	.321766	.999999
	10* .397713 gives	0.99713	3.21766	9.99999
	INT (3.97713) gives	0	3	9

Figure 5-7
(a) Basic statements
using DATE$ and
TIME$. (b) Output
from statements

```
200     PRINT "SUMMARY REPORT DATED "; DATE$(0)
300     PRINT "UPDATE COMPLETED AT "; TIME$(0); DATE$(0)
```

(a)

```
SUMMARY REPORT DATED 21-FEB-84
UPDATE COMPLETED AT 13:29     21-FEB-84
```

(b)

Answers to Preceding Exercises

5-1 P1% = 2%; P2% = 1%; P3% = 0%; P4% = 3%; P5% = 0%

5-2 Approach this in two steps. If the requirement were 0 to 89, then we could use a simple multiplier of 90 (this is consistent with the technique of Figure 5-6). But adding 10 to the result gives what we desire, thus

```
310     N1% = INT (90*RND) + 10%
```

5-3
```
350     IF P% <> N1%*N2%                                    &
        THEN                                                &
            PRINT "SORRY, THE ANSWER IS"; P%                &
        ELSE                                                &
            PRINT "CORRECT, THE ANSWER IS INDEED"; P%    \ &
            CORRECT% = CORRECT% + 1%
```

Programming Problems

5-1 Write a program that will allow a number of seconds to be entered from the keyboard into an integer variable. Using integer arithmetic, calculate the number of hours, minutes, and seconds. For each entry print the input followed by the hours, minutes, and seconds. Allow for program termination by entering –1 for the seconds. Use an appropriate prompt at the terminal and appropriate headings for output.

5-2 Expand Problem 5-1 to keep a running total of hours, minutes, and seconds for each value entered. Note that it will *not* be possible to sum the input seconds because the integer capacity may be exceeded. The output from Problem 5-1 must be expanded to include a total line at the end.

5-3 Using integer arithmetic (and some ingenuity), it is possible to strip any desired digit from an integer quantity. Write a program that will accept an integer of up to 4 digits, then strip out and print each digit. For instance, the dialog might appear as follows:

INTEGER VALUE? *2593*

FIRST DIGIT	2
SECOND DIGIT	5
THIRD DIGIT	9
FOURTH DIGIT	3

5-4 In trigonometry the law of cosines relates the sides of a triangle and one of the angles. If A, B, and C represent the lengths of the three sides and a is the angle opposite the side A, then the law can be written as

$$A = \sqrt{B^2 + C^2 - 2BC \cos(a)}$$

Write a program that will accept B, C, and a from the keyboard (with suitable prompts) and calculate and print A. Allow for the value of a to be entered in degrees; check to ensure that it is greater than 0 and less than 90. Allow for termination of the program by entering a value of 0.

5-5 Although this problem is a bit far-fetched, it illustrates use of the random number generator for simulations. It seems that there once was a frog who enjoyed his evenings at a local tavern. He periodically found himself in the center of the nearby road with little control over his legs. His objective, of course, was to hop off the road into the ditch.

For this problem, you are to write a program to simulate the frog's activity. Make the following assumptions.

1. The road runs due east and west and is exactly 14 feet wide.

2. With each jump, the frog will travel exactly 1 foot either north, south, east, or west (at random).

Write a program to simulate the frog's activity each night for one week. For each night, print the night number, number of hops required, and whether the frog ended up in the north or south ditch. Also print two summary lines. The first should indicate the average number of hops for the seven nights. The second should be as follows:

FROG SIMULATION PROGRAMMED BY *yourname* ON *system-date*

5-6 If you wish more of a challenge, use the random number generator to generate a random length of each jump (between 9 inches and 23 inches).

5-7 As a further modification to Problem 5-6, use trignometric functions and allow the frog to jump in any direction of the compass.

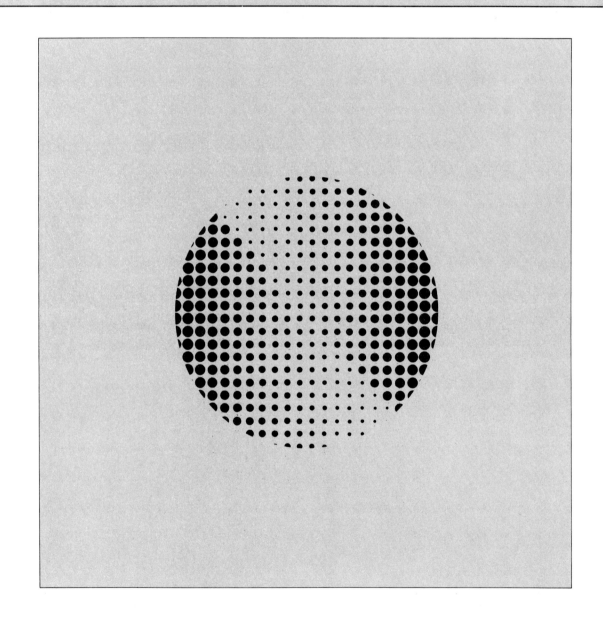

6

Report Generation

EDIT MASKS

The Concept of the Edit Mask

Up to this point not much attention has been given to details of formatting program output. Previous examples involved relatively simple headings and use of the TAB function to override the preset tab positions. Perhaps the most obvious shortcoming has been our inability to control decimal positioning and alignment in a column of numbers. For example, if a program is to print dollar and cent amounts, the following column of numbers on the right would be far better than that on the left.

```
257.33          257.33
16.87            16.87
482.6           482.60
31               31.00
1.732             1.73
```

Our output has been that shown on the left; let us now consider how to get that shown on the right. To begin with, whenever we are writing a program, we will know (or had better find out) the nature of the data. For instance, a program to calculate gross pay for employees will be dealing in the hundreds, or perhaps thousands, of dollars for each employee, certainly not millions. So usually we will have a good idea of the general size of results that we expect from a program. With this information we can plan the *format* of our output in order to obtain an appealing, easy-to-read end result. For instance, let us assume that we wish to print a dollar and cent quantity that will range from zero to 999.99 (refer to the preceding examples). What we really need is a means to describe the exact form in which the number is to be printed out. In programming, such a device is commonly referred to as an *edit mask* or a *format image*. For instance, the format image in which we are interested would appear as:

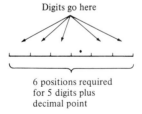

Digits go here

6 positions required
for 5 digits plus
decimal point

In Basic-Plus the pound sign (#) is used to indicate a digit position with a mask. Thus the edit mask for our dollar and cent amount would appear as shown in Figure 6-1.

Simple Form of the PRINT-USING

Special formatting of output via edit masks is done with the PRINT-USING statement. In essence, this statement says: "PRINT the indicated quantities USING a designated image." Let us assume that the variable A contains the dollar and cent amount in which we are interested. Then statement 600 of Figure 6-2 would print it in the way to which we have become accustomed in Basic.

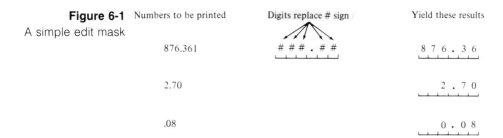

Figure 6-1
A simple edit mask

Numbers to be printed	Digits replace # sign	Yield these results
876.361	# # # . # #	8 7 6 . 3 6
2.70		2 . 7 0
.08		0 . 0 8

However, the **PRINT-USING** statements (700 and 800) direct the system to "use" the image following the keyword **USING** in determining output format. The output of these two statements would be exactly as shown in Figure 6-1. (In the case of statement 700, output will be to the terminal; in 800, it will be to the designated file.) The following commentary relates to the **PRINT-USING**.

1. Pound signs (#) to the left of the decimal for which there are no digits are replaced with blanks. For instance, the amount 23.78 would be edited into the image ####.## as bb23.78.

2. If the image includes a pound sign to the left of the decimal point, then a zero will be placed there whenever the output field is less than 1.0. For example, .23 would be edited into the image of item 1 as bbb0.23.

3. If the variable value to be printed contains more digits to the right of the decimal than space is provided for, the system automatically rounds off.

4. If the variable value to be printed is larger than the edit mask provides, then the mask is ignored and the quantity is printed preceded by a % sign. For instance, if **A** = 2578.13, the statement

```
400    PRINT USING "###.##", A
```

will cause the following to be printed.

%2578.13

The general form of the **PRINT-USING** statement is as follows:

PRINT #<channel number>, **USING** <mask string>, <variable list>

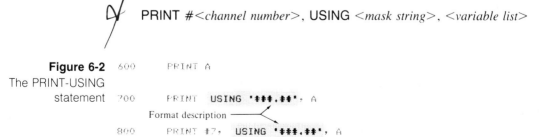

Figure 6-2
The PRINT-USING
statement

Edit Images for String Fields

Although string fields do not present the same type of problem as numeric fields, edit images are essential for overall line formatting. To illustrate editing string fields, let us assume that we have a description field **N$** that will never be more than nine positions. The edit image and its corresponding use are shown in Figure 6-3. It is important to note that only the first and last positions of the string edit image use the backslash characters. The string data (whatever characters are included) will be placed in the image area beginning in the position of the first backslash and not proceeding beyond the ending backslash.

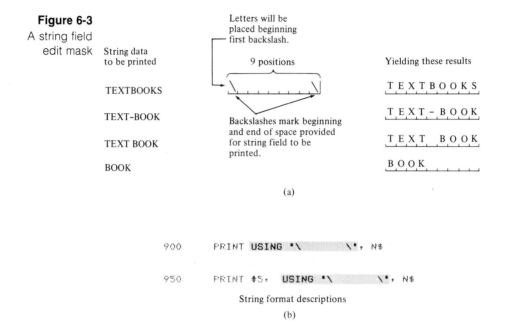

Figure 6-3
A string field edit mask

String data to be printed

TEXTBOOKS

TEXT–BOOK

TEXT BOOK

BOOK

Letters will be placed beginning first backslash.

9 positions

Backslashes mark beginning and end of space provided for string field to be printed.

Yielding these results

T E X T B O O K S

T E X T – B O O K

T E X T   B O O K

B O O K

(a)

```
900      PRINT USING "\        \", N$

950      PRINT #5,  USING "\        \", N$
```

String format descriptions
(b)

Exercise 6-1 What will be printed by the statement

```
500    PRINT USING "#####.#", C
```

for the following values of C (use ƀ to indicate a blank position)?

12345.6
12345.
683.11
12.9
0.68

EDITING A COMPLETE LINE

Format Planning

Obviously the capability of using a single string edit mask presents little advantage over simple printing of string fields as in earlier chapters. However, the power and flexibility come from the ability to designate the format of numerous fields in an entire line. To illustrate this concept, let us reconsider Example 4-5, which calculates gross pay and prints the following:

> Employee number (assume always 4 digits—treat as string)
> Employee name (maximum of 16 positions)
> Regular pay (maximum of 999.99)
> Overtime pay (maximum of 999.99)
> Total pay (maximum of 1999.98)

In an actual programming environment one of the important tasks is laying out how the results are to be printed. This is often referred to as *format planning* and is a painstaking job regardless of which programming language is being used. It involves such tasks as laying out column headings that are descriptive and are aligned above the columns, determining spacing between various fields, and defining edit images to be used for output quantities. To accomplish this with a minimum of effort requires that some type of a layout form be used, such as that shown in Figure 6-4. Here we see that the spacing has been coordinated between fields of both the heading lines and the detail line (actual data which is processed) to give a neat, balanced form.

A Program Segment

The format planning of Figure 6-4 is reflected directly in the program segment of Figure 6-5. In statements 210–240 we see the string variables being assigned

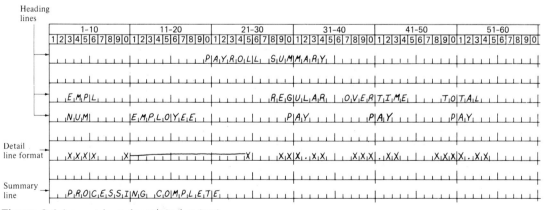

Figure 6-4 Layout form for printed output

values with the **LET** statement. Although this may be new to us, it is effectively no different than the same operation with numeric quantities. For instance, the following statement 500

```
500    A = 25.6
600    INPUT #4, B
```

assigns the value 25.6 to the numeric variable A and 600 reads a new value into the variable B. Similarly, statement 700

```
700    A$ = "EXAMPLE"
800    INPUT #4, B$
```

assigns the string value **EXAMPLE** to the string variable A$ and 800 reads a new value into the variable B$.

Referring again to Figure 6-5, the headings (H1$, H2$, and H3$) are printed by the corresponding statements of lines 260, 280, and 290. Needless to say, these **PRINT** statements (and the corresponding statements 210–230) could have been replaced by the following.

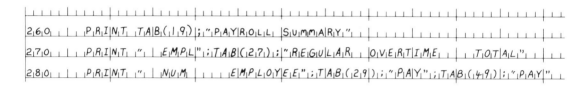

As a general rule, this form is somewhat more clumsy and errors in alignment are more easily made than when laying them all out as with statements 210–240 of Figure 6-5.

The **PRINT-USING** statement of line 530 uses this same approach; that is, the edit mask for the entire line is defined as a separate field (D$). Figure 6-6 illustrates how Basic-Plus handles this statement. When the **PRINT-USING** is executed, an image of the mask (D$ in this case) is used and fields in the output list are matched up with individual edit images within the designated string. It is important to realize that the string field containing the edit image (D$ in this case) is *not* destroyed by the **PRINT** statement. Thus it is not necessary to execute statement 240 each time the **PRINT-USING** is executed.

Alignment of Headings and Detail Lines

Now we can see the advantage of defining the heading lines and edit mask(s) all together in a separate portion of the program. Here we can readily see whether the information to be printed includes proper spacing. In fact, statements 210–240 of Figure 6-5 correspond almost exactly to the format planning chart of Figure 6-4. This process can often eliminate a lot of frustration and wasted time in attempting to align output quantities.

Figure 6-5

The PRINT-USING
statement in
a program

```
200  !   DEFINE OUTPUT FORMATS
210      H1$ = "                          PAYROLL SUMMARY"
220      H2$ = "   EMPL                   REGULAR  OVERTIME    TOTAL"
230      H3$ = "   NUM       EMPLOYEE        PAY      PAY       PAY"
240      D$ = " \    \       \           \  ###.##   ###.##   ####.##"
250  !   PRINT REPORT HEADINGS
260          PRINT H1$
270          PRINT
280          PRINT H2$
290          PRINT H3$
300          PRINT
     .
     .
     .
400  !   MAIN PROCESSING LOOP
     .
     .
     .
530          PRINT USING D$, ENUM$, ENAME$, REGPAY, OTPAY, TOTPAY
540          GOTO 400
     .
     .
800  !   TERMINATE PROCESSING
810          PRINT " PROCESSING COMPLETE "
     .
     .
     .
```

Exercise 6-2 The following statements appear in a program.

```
200    L$ = "#####ЬЬЬ###.###ЬЬЬ/ЬЬЬЬЬЬЬЬЬЬ/ЬЬЬ##"
400    PRINT USING L$, A, B, C$, D
```

Note: The character b̶ is included only to indicate spacing.
Assuming the following values for the list variables, sketch the output line as it would
be printed (use the b̶ to indicate a blank position).

A   37
B   256.8338
C$ EXAMPLE D
D   2

MORE ON THE PRINT-USING

Inserting Commas in Numeric Quantities

For numeric quantities that are 1000 or greater, it is convenient to insert commas to
improve readability. That is, 13865 and 5681372 are normally written as 13,865
and 5,681,372 respectively. Basic-Plus provides for the insertion of commas
every 3 digits to the left of the decimal point (if any). For this, the programmer
need insert but *one* comma *anywhere* to the left of the decimal point in the edit
image. Figure 6-7 illustrates this concept; remember, only one comma in each
individual mask is required to trigger the automatic insertion of commas as needed
by the number.

Including a Dollar Sign in Numeric Output

If the edit mask for a numeric field begins with $$, then a single dollar sign will be
printed immediately preceding the first digit of the number. This is commonly
called a *floating dollar* sign and can be used with or without commas. Figure 6-8
illustrates its use.

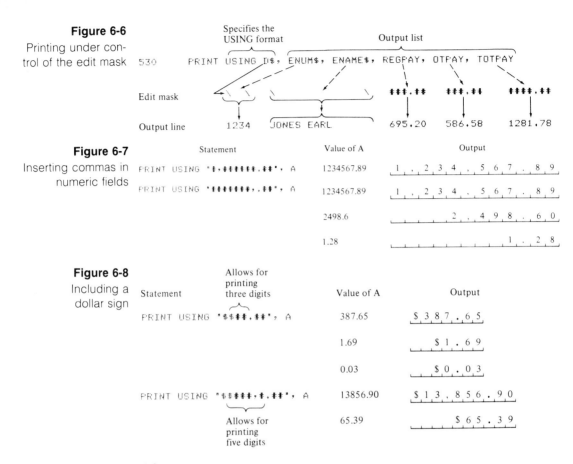

Figure 6-6
Printing under control of the edit mask

Specifies the USING format / Output list

530   PRINT USING I$, ENUM$, ENAME$, REGPAY, OTPAY, TOTPAY

Edit mask   ###.##   ###.##   ####.##

Output line   1234   JONES EARL   695.20   586.58   1281.78

Figure 6-7
Inserting commas in numeric fields

Statement	Value of A	Output
PRINT USING "#,#######.##", A	1234567.89	1,234,567.89
PRINT USING "#######,.##", A	1234567.89	1,234,567.89
	2498.6	2,498.60
	1.28	1.28

Figure 6-8
Including a dollar sign

Statement	Allows for printing three digits	Value of A	Output
PRINT USING "$$##.##", A		387.65	$387.65
		1.69	$1.69
		0.03	$0.03
PRINT USING "$$###,#.##", A	Allows for printing five digits	13856.90	$13,856.90
		65.39	$65.39

Exercises **6-3** Using the edit mask

####,##.##

how would each of the following be printed?

62534.21
1249.6
0.01698
7891507

6-4 Repeat Problem 6-3 for the following edit mask.

$$######,#.##

Answers to Preceding Exercises

6-1 12345.6, 12345.0, bb683.1, bbb12.9, bbbb0.7

6-2 bb37bbb256.834bbbEXAMPLEbDbbbbbbbb2

6-3 b62,534.21
bb1,249.60
bbbbbb0.02
%7891507—number too large for mask

6-4 bbb$62,534.21
bbbb$1,249.60
bbbbbbbb$0.02
$7,891,507.00

Programming **6-1** For Problem 4-3 assume that the input quantities have the following restrictions:
Problems

> Account number—always 4 digits (treat as a string)
> Customer name—maximum of 20 positions
> New balance—never exceed 9999.99
> Credit limit—never exceed 9999.99

Expand the requirements of Problem 4-3 as follows: Main headings and column headings should appear as:

OVER-LIMIT REPORT   31-FEB-84
CUSTOMER ACCOUNT SYSTEM

CUST		NEW	CREDIT
NUM	NAME	BALANCE	LIMIT

Numeric quantities in the detail line should be edited to include the comma and decimal point as appropriate.

6-2 For Problem 4-9 assume that the input quantities have the following restrictions:

> Account number—6 digits
> Customer name—maximum of 20 positions
> Balance due—less than $8,000

Expand Problem 4-9 to include two lines of appropriate main headings (include the system date) and one or more lines of column headings. (See the example of Problem 6-1.) Edit all numeric quantities as is appropriate considering their size.

6-3 For the purpose of issuing checks, a company maintains a file with the following information for each check to be written:

> Payee—maximum of 20 positions
> Amount—not to exceed $5,000

Because checks are printed on preprinted forms, only the variable information need be printed. Write a program that will print the following for each payee.

PRINT LINE	FIELD	BEGINNING PRINT POSITION
First	Check number	46
Second	Current date	41
Third	Payee	6
	Amount	40

7

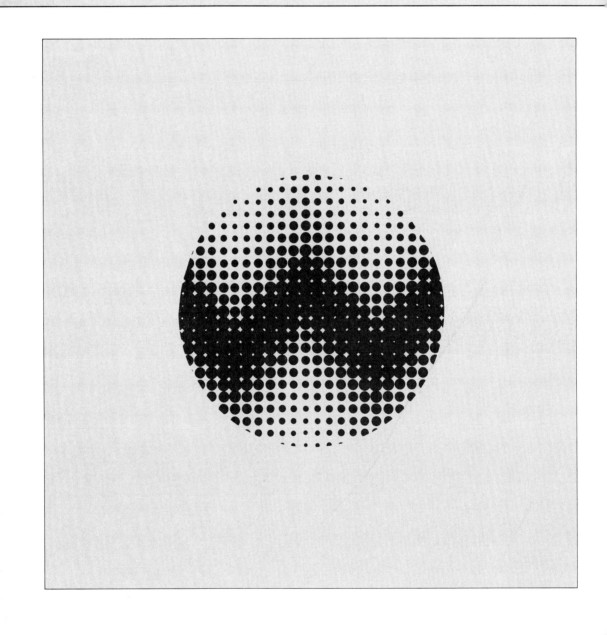

Program Loops

USE OF IMMEDIATE MODE

Statements in Immediate Mode

The subject of this chapter is program loops—the real heart of programming. Overall, if a program is carefully planned and modularized, problems associated with getting it running can be minimized. However, loops do tend to cause problems, especially for the careless beginner. One device that sometimes is helpful in debugging a program is the immediate mode facility of Basic-Plus. As we have learned, one distinction between commands and statements is that commands are executed immediately and statements later on during execution of the program. But this is not exactly true since many of the statements can be entered at the terminal *without* a line number, thus causing them to be executed immediately (as if they were commands): hence the term *immediate mode*. For instance, the following is a direct dialog with the computer.

```
LET A% = 3%
Ready
LET B% = 12%
Ready
LET C% = A% * B%
Ready
PRINT A%, B%, C%
 3              12              36
Ready
```

At first thought this may appear to be of little value to us. However, it is important to recognize that whenever program execution is terminated, all variables contain their values at termination. Thus if a program terminates at the wrong point or is giving incorrect results, we can inspect any variables in the program. For instance, assume that our program is calculating the mean of a data set and the program input statement is

```
510    INPUT 2%, N$, Q%, AMNT
```

Furthermore, the program has terminated on an error condition and we are suspicious of the input quantities and the internal loop variable I%. We can then use the following immediate mode PRINT to get the desired values printed at the terminal:

```
PRINT I%, N$, Q%, AMNT
```

This is a powerful and useful feature of the language.

Interrupting Execution

Sometimes a program will become locked up in a loop and never break out (bad program logic). If the loop involves no input or output, we will not see anything happening at the terminal. With Basic-Plus it is possible to stop the program, make inquiries, change variable values if desired, and then continue. Following is an example of how such a sequence might be used. We will assume that the program is running and appears to be in a never-ending loop.

1. Hold down the CONTROL key then simultaneously depress the letter C. This is called a *control C* and immediately causes program execution to terminate and the system to return to the command mode.

2. Enter the immediate mode statement:

   PRINT LINE

   The predefined variable LINE contains the line number at which execution was interrupted.

3. We can then refer to a program listing to determine just where we are in the program. Furthermore, we can use the LIST command to list all or part of the program without disturbing the "state" of the program.

4. Let us assume that the variables J% and MAX% appear to be the culprits. We can find their values with the immediate mode statement:

   PRINT J%, MAX%

5. More often than not, it is "back to the drawing board" at this stage. However, if we wished to continue execution at the point of interruption, then we would enter the command:

   CONT

   which means continue. Execution would then continue as if it had never been interrupted.

With these capabilities the programmer can often spot errors very quickly that otherwise would be difficult to detect. However, these methods are no substitute for careful program design *prior* to coding and testing. All too often the beginner has a tendency to get on the terminal and start poking around. Remember, an ounce of thinking is worth a pound of poking.

BASIC CONCEPTS OF LOOPS

Counted Loops

All of the sample programs in this book have involved a program loop which causes the repeated execution of a sequence of statements. Exit from the loop has been achieved by detecting a trailer record that has indicated the end of the file. This chapter deals with loops in a much more general way. The concept of the *controlled loop* involves performing a sequence of operations until a particular condition arises. This can range from detection of a trailer record to execution a predetermined number of times. The latter commonly occurs in programming and is called a *counted loop*. As an illustration, the program segment of Figure 7-1(a) will cause repeated execution of the loop exactly five times. The following commentary relates to this example.

1. The variable I% is used as a counter (commonly called the *control variable*) to control the loop. Its value is initialized to 1 prior to entering the loop (statement 210).
2. The test for loop completion is made by statement 230 where I% is compared with 5. When the condition is satisfied, execution is transferred to the loop exit point.
3. The *body* of the loop consists of the two statements 240 and 250. These will be executed repeatedly.
4. Upon completion of each pass through the loop, the control variable I% is increased by 1.

Printed output for this example is shown in Figure 7-1(b) where we see that the loop is executed exactly five times before execution breaks out.

Figure 7-1
(a) A counted loop.
(b) Loop output

```
200 !    LOOP ENTRY POINT
210         I% = 1%              ! INITALIZE LOOP INDEX I% TO 1
220 !    BEGINNING OF LOOP
230         IF I%>5% THEN GO TO 280    ! TEST LOOP INDEX FOR EXIT CONDITION
240           PRINT "TEST LINE"; I%    !   BODY
250           PRINT                    !   OF LOOP
260           I% = I% + 1%             !   INCREMENT COUNTER
270         GOTO 220
280 !    LOOP EXIT POINT
290         PRINT "LOOP TERMINATED"
    .
    .
    .
```
(a)

```
TEST LINE 1

TEST LINE 2

TEST LINE 3

TEST LINE 4

TEST LINE 5

LOOP TERMINATED
```
(b)

Figure 7-2

Loop control with the FOR-NEXT

```
200 !   BEGINNING OF FOR-NEXT LOOP
210       FOR I% = 1% TO 5%
220         PRINT "TEST LINE"; I%
230         PRINT
240       NEXT I%
250 !   END OF FOR-NEXT LOOP
260       PRINT "LOOP TERMINATED"
      .
      .
      .
```

Figure 7-3

Details of the FOR-NEXT

Initial value which is given to the index upon entering the loop.

Test value—control variable value is compared to this. Execution of the loop continues as long as index does not exceed this value.

Control variable (index) which controls execution of the loop.

Increment is the amount by which the index is increased with each execution of the loop. If omitted, 1 is assumed.

```
210       FOR   I% = 1%   TO   5%   STEP   1%
      .
      .
      .
240       NEXT   I%
```

Indicates the end of the loop and causes incrementing of the index to occur.

Exercise 7-1 What would happen in the sequence of Figure 7-1 if each of the following conditions occurred?

(a) The index I% were initialized to 10 instead of 1.

(b) The test for I% (statement 230) were I% = 5% instead of I% > 5%.

(c) A value of 1 were subtracted from I% rather than added in statement 260.

(d) Line 270 said GOTO 200.

The FOR-NEXT Statements

Counted loops are so common in programming that Basic includes a special pair of statements that provide automatic control of the loop. The loop of Figure 7-1 is rewritten in Figure 7-2 using a FOR-NEXT loop. This loop will function in exactly the same way as that of Figure 7-1 and will produce the same output. Details of how the FOR-NEXT works are given in Figure 7-3. Upon entering the loop (the FOR statement at line 210), the control variable I% is set to the initial value. Upon encountering the NEXT statement, it is increased by the increment of the STEP value. If the increment is 1, then the STEP may be omitted as in statement 210 of Figure 7-2. The test value (5 in this case) is the maximum allowable value for which the loop will be executed. When this value is exceeded execution automatically continues to the statement following the NEXT.

General Form of the FOR Statement

The general form of the FOR statement is

FOR <*variable*> = <*expression*> TO <*expression*> STEP <*expression*>

The following examples further illustrate the characteristics of the FOR statement.

```
FOR J% = 5% TO X%+3%
```

Note that the initial value need not be 1. Furthermore, the initial value, the test value, and the increment can all be expressions. If X% contained 4, then this loop would be executed for values of 5, 6, and 7, or three times.

```
FOR I% = 0% TO 13% STEP 2%
```

In this case the loop would be executed for values of 0, 2, 4, 6, 8, 10, and 12. Note that the index need not end up equal to the test value. The rule is that the loop will be executed as long as the index does *not* exceed the test value.

```
FOR A = -1.5 TO 2.4 STEP 0.1
```

Fractional quantities are allowable in the FOR statement. This loop would execute 40 times.

```
FOR C% = 0% TO -5% STEP -1%
```

It is possible to use a negative increment. Here the loop would be executed for values of C% of 0, –1, –2, –3, –4, and –5 (six times).

Exercise 7-2 How many times would the loops controlled by each of the following FOR statements be executed?
- (a) `FOR J% = 3% TO 13%`
- (b) `FOR J% = 3% TO 13% STEP 3%`
- (c) `FOR J% = 5% TO -5% STEP -1%`
- (d) (Assume X% = 4%) `FOR J% = 0% TO 3%*X%-1%`

A Flowchart Representation of the FOR-NEXT Loop

The counted-loop example of Figure 7-1 includes user-prepared code to perform the initializing, incrementing, and testing functions. The flowchart of Figure 7-4 displays each of the operations of Figure 7-1. Since these operations are performed automatically by the FOR-NEXT, the detail of Figure 7-4(a) does not seem quite appropriate. The form illustrated in Figure 7-4(b) is commonly used to indicate a FOR-NEXT loop. The correspondence between these two forms and between the FOR-NEXT and its flowchart equivalent are readily apparent.

Figure 7-4
(a) Flowchart for
counted loop.
(b) Flowchart for
FOR-NEXT loop

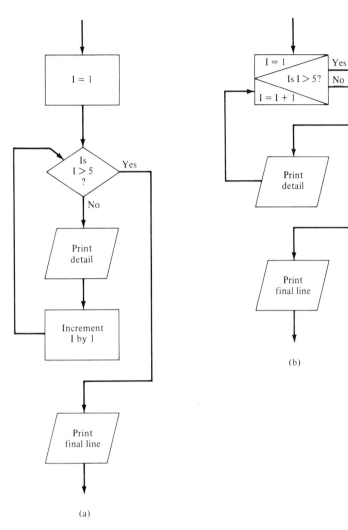

(a)

(b)

PROGRAMMING EXAMPLES WITH FOR-NEXT

Calculating a Table

Inflation, and the decreasing purchasing power of the dollar, is a prime problem today. We continually read how $10 of goods today will cost us $11 or $12 next year, $13 or $14 the year after, and so on. Predictions such as these are based on the expected annual rate of inflation. To illustrate, let us assume that economists predict a 12% annual inflation rate. Then the cost of purchasing $10 worth of goods in 1, 2, and 3 years would be calculated as follows:

The general form for the calculations is

Cost next year $\quad= $ Cost this year $\times (1 +$ Inflation rate$)$

Current year: $10 purchases $10 worth of goods

Cost after 1 year $\quad= 10 \times (1 + 0.12)$
$\qquad\qquad\qquad\quad= \$11.20$

Cost after 2 years $\quad=$ Cost after 1 year $\times (1 + 0.12)$
$\qquad\qquad\qquad\quad= 11.20 \times 1.12$
$\qquad\qquad\qquad\quad= \$12.54$

Cost after 3 years $\quad=$ Cost after 2 years $\times (1 + 0.12)$
$\qquad\qquad\qquad\quad= 12.54 \times 1.12$
$\qquad\qquad\qquad\quad= \$14.05$

Let us consider this as the basis for illustrating use of the **FOR-NEXT**.

Example 7-1 Prepare a program that will accept an annual inflation rate as input, then calculate a 10-year table of the cost of $10 worth of goods related to the base year. The program must print appropriate headings and a termination message.

Program Planning and Solution

The logic of this problem is relatively straightforward, as illustrated by the flowchart of Figure 7-5. Here we should note use of the special box to indicate the obvious need for a **FOR-NEXT** control structure. Prior to beginning the coding itself, it is essential to plan the output format. A print layout form and a sample output (from the program) are included in Figure 7-6.

Figure 7-7 is the complete program for this example. We can see the **FOR-NEXT** loop in statements 620–650; it is reasonably straightforward. Attention should also be paid to the preparation of headings, the **PRINT-USING**, and use of the **DATE$** function.

Exercise 7-3 In statement 630 of Figure 7-7 the new value of COST is calculated as

```
COST * (1. + INF/100.)
```

The quantity within the expression is calculated on each pass through the loop. This is not very efficient. Explain this and show what change might be made.

Figure 7-5
Flowchart for
Example 7-1

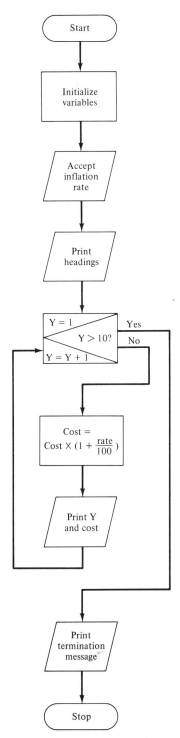

Start

Initialize
variables

Accept
inflation
rate

Print
headings

Y = 1
Y > 10?   Yes
Y = Y + 1 No

Cost =
Cost × $(1 + \frac{\text{rate}}{100})$

Print Y
and cost

Print
termination
message

Stop

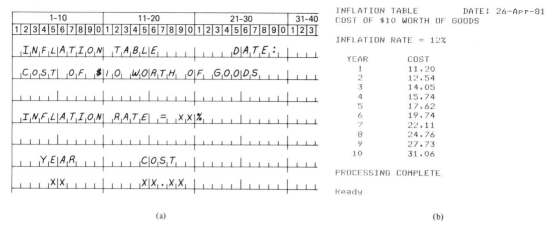

Figure 7-6 Example 7-1. (a) Print layout. (b) Sample output

Figure 7-7

Program for

Example 7-1

```
100 !    INFLATION RATE - EXAMPLE 7-1
110 !    THIS PROGRAM CALCULATES THE PURCHASING
120 !    POWER OF THE DOLLAR OVER A 10-YEAR
130 !    PERIOD.  INPUT IS THE INFLATION RATE.
140 !    OUTPUT IS A TABLE OF THE AMOUNT REQUIRED
150 !    TO PURCHASE $10 WORTH OF GOODS RELATIVE
160 !    TO THE BASE YEAR.
170 !      VARIABLES USED ARE:
180 !        Y%    -- YEAR
190 !        INF   -- INFLATION RATE IN PERCENT
200 !        COST  -- AMOUNT NEEDED TO MAKE "$10
210 !                 PURCHASE" FOR A GIVEN YEAR
300 !
310 !    DEFINE EDIT MASKS
320         H1$ = "INFLATION TABLE        DATE: "
330         H2$ = "COST OF $10 WORTH OF GOODS"
340         H3$ = "INFLATION RATE = ##%"
350         H4$ = "   YEAR        COST"
360         D$  = "   ##         ##.##"
370 !    INITIAL OPERATIONS
380         INPUT "WHAT INFLATION RATE DO YOU WISH"; INF
390         COST = 10.     !INITIAL YEAR COST
500 !    PRINT HEADINGS
510         PRINT H1$; DATE$(0)
520         PRINT H2$
530         PRINT
540         PRINT USING H3$, INF
550         PRINT
560         PRINT H4$
600 !
610 !    TABLE PROCESSING LOOP
620         FOR Y% = 1% TO 10%
630            COST = COST * (1. + INF/100.)
640            PRINT USING D$, Y%, COST
650         NEXT Y%
660 !    END OF TABLE PROCESSING LOOP
800 !
810 !    TERMINATION OPERATIONS
820         PRINT
830         PRINT "PROCESSING COMPLETE"
32767    END
```

Nested Loops

Frequently programming needs involve a loop completely within another loop. These are called *nested loops*, and are easily handled with the FOR-NEXT. Example 7-2, which is an expansion of Example 7-1, illustrates this concept.

Example 7-2 This example involves inflation tables as in Example 7-1. However, the user is to key in a range of inflation rates. For example, if the "beginning" rate is entered as 8% and the "ending" rate as 12%, then complete tables must be produced for each of the rates 8%, 9%, 10%, 11%, and 12%.

This program will involve an overall or *outer* loop, which will execute for values of inflation rate ranging from 8 to 12. For each of the inflation rate values an *inner* loop (identical to that of Example 7-1) will execute 10 times. The logic of this solution is shown in the flowchart of Figure 7-8. Here the problem has, in a sense, been *modularized*. The main flowchart in Figure 7-8(a) shows the entire sequence of calculating and printing the table as a single block. Details of this operation are expanded in Figure 7-8(b), which is almost identical to Figure 7-6.

The program of Figure 7-7 has been expanded in Figure 7-9 to include repetitious calculation of tables. From the use of indentation, the inner and outer loops are readily apparent. Each pass through the outer loop will cause entry into the inner loop (statement 620), which will produce a complete table, including headings, for the current value of R%.

Exercise 7-4 In your opinion, how many tables would be prepared (that is, how many passes through the outer loop) if the initial and final values entered were the same? What if the final value were smaller than the initial value?

EARLY EXIT FROM A FOR-NEXT LOOP

Searching a Table

Frequently the needs of a program will require that a loop be executed a certain number of times. However, if a particular condition occurs, then the exit is to be made immediately. The FOR-NEXT loop allows this to be done. To illustrate, let us consider a simple example.

Example 7-3 This example is a greatly simplified version of an online information system. The user will enter a student number through a terminal and the computer will search a DATA table containing the student number, name, and grade-point average. Upon finding the student number the name and GPA are to be displayed. If no such student is found, the message at the top of the following page will be printed.

STUDENT *nnnn* NOT IN TABLE

This problem involves searching a table for a particular entry, which is a common operation in programming. The table will be stored in a series of **DATA** statements with each statement containing the student number, name, and GPA such as illustrated in the sample on the next page.

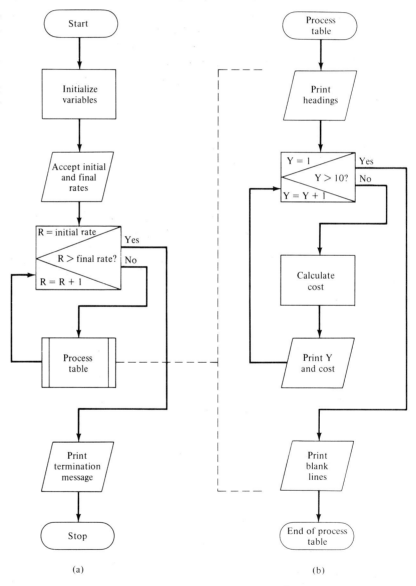

(a) (b)

```
1000 !    DATA TABLE FOR EXAMPLE 7-3
1005      DATA 37
1010      DATA 1572, "BAKER ALICE", 3.62
1020      DATA 9713, "COLUMBO ERNEST", 2.11
1030      DATA 4613, "DICKEY SCOTT", 3.91
  .
  .
  .
1370      DATA 2218, "ZENER DONALD", 2.88
```

Preceding the first student record is a separate **DATA** statement with the number of entries in this table. Thus the example table includes 37 entries in the table; this value will be used to control the **FOR-NEXT** loop.

The logic of this problem solution is illustrated in Figure 7-10. Some points of importance that will be reflected in the program are as follows:

1. To terminate processing the user can enter a value of zero for the student number.

2. Whether or not the student number is found during the search is indicated by use of a string variable whose value initially is set to "NO." If the student number is found, this variable is given a value of "YES." Outside the loop the variable is tested to determine what is to be printed.

3. After each search of the table, which will involve **READ**ing the **DATA** statements, the **DATA** pointer must be "restored" to the first student.

Figure 7-9
Program segments
for Example 7-2

```
380      INPUT "ENTER THE BEGINNING & ENDING INFLATION RATES"; &
               INIT%, FINAL%
400 !
410 !    OUTER LOOP - CONTROLS INFLATION RATE INCREMENTS
420          FOR R% = INIT% TO FINAL%
430              FACTOR = 1. + R%/100.
440              COST = 10
500 !            PRINT HEADINGS
510              PRINT H1$; DATE$(0)
520              PRINT H2$
530              PRINT
540              PRINT USING H3$, R%
550              PRINT
560              PRINT H4$
600 !
610 !            TABLE PROCESSING (INNER) LOOP
620              FOR Y% = 1% TO 10%
630                  COST = COST * FACTOR
640                  PRINT USING D$, Y%, COST
650              NEXT Y%
660 !            END OF TABLE PROCESSING LOOP
700 !
710              PRINT
720              PRINT
730              PRINT
740          NEXT R%
750 !    END OF OUTER LOOP
800 !
810 !    TERMINATION OPERATIONS
32767    END
```

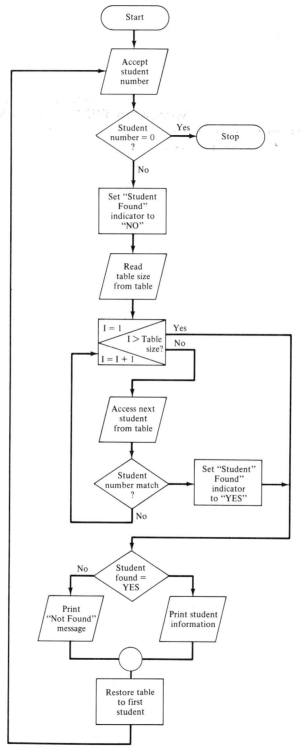

Figure 7-10
Flowchart for
Example 7-3

Start

Accept
student
number

Student
number = 0
?

Yes

Stop

No

Set "Student
Found"
indicator to
"NO"

Read
table size
from table

I = 1

I > Table
size?

Yes

No

I = I + 1

Access next
student
from table

Student
number match
?

No

Set "Student"
Found"
indicator
to "YES"

Student
found =
YES

No

Print
"Not Found"
message

Print student
information

Restore table
to first
student

The RESTORE Statement

As was learned in Chapter 1, the system forms a data pool from the entries in program DATA statements. As the program READs through the data pool, the system maintains a pointer within the pool in order to keep track of the next value that is available. Although this pointer is handled automatically by the system, the programmer can set it back to the beginning of the data pool by use of the RESTORE statement. Execution of the RESTORE moves the pointer back to the beginning regardless of where it happens to be, and allows the DATA table to be read again from the beginning. This capability is needed in Example 7-3.

An Example Program

The program of Figure 7-11 conforms to the logic of the flowchart in Figure 7-10. Points of note in this program are as follows:

Figure 7-11
Program for
Example 7-3

```
100 !    TABLE SEARCH -- EXAMPLE 7-3
110 !    THIS PROGRAM ACCEPTS A STUDENT NUMBER ENTRY FROM A
120 !    KEYBOARD AND SEARCHES A TABLE FOR THAT STUDENT.
130 !    IF FOUND, THE STUDENT NUMBER AND GPA ARE DISPLAYED.
140 !       VARIABLES USED ARE:
150 !         STUDENT%  - STUDENT NUMBER ENTERED FROM KEYBOARD
160 !         FOUND$    - SWITCH TO INDICATE WHETHER OR NOT
170 !                     STUDENT FOUND
180 !         LAST%     - NUMBER OF ENTRIES IN TABLE
190 !         SNUM      - STUDENT NUMBER FROM TABLE
195 !         SNAME$    - STUDENT NAME
200 !         GPA       - GRADE POINT AVERAGE
300 !    ACCEPT STUDENT NUMBER
310         INPUT "STUDENT NUMBER < ENTER 0 TO TERMINATE>"; STUDENT%
320         IF STUDENT% = 0%            &
                THEN GOTO 32767               ! TERMINATE PROCESSING
330         FOUND$ = "NO"
340         READ LAST%       ! GET NUMBER OF STUDENTS IN TABLE
350 !    TABLE SEARCH LOOP
360         FOR I% = 1% TO LAST%
370         READ SNUM%, SNAME$, GPA       ! READ NEXT TABLE ENTRIES
380         IF STUDENT% <> SNUM% THEN 420
390 !          STUDENT NUMBER FOUND
400            FOUND$ = "YES"
410            GOTO 430                   ! EXIT THE LOOP
420         NEXT I%
430 !    END OF TABLE SEARCH LOOP
440 !
500 !    PRINT APPROPRIATE MESSAGE
510         IF FOUND$ = "YES"           &
                THEN PRINT SNAME$; GPA  &
                ELSE PRINT "STUDENT"; STUDENT%; "NOT IN FILE"
520         PRINT
530         PRINT
540         RESTORE                      ! RESTORE THE DATA TABLE
550         GO TO 300
560 !    END OF MAIN PROGRAM
1000 !   DATA TABLE FOR EXAMPLE 7-3
1005     DATA 37
1010     DATA 1572, "BAKER ALICE",    3.62
1020     DATA 9713, "COLUMBO ERNEST", 2.11
1030     DATA 4613, "DICKEY SCOTT",   3.91
      .
      .
      .
1370     DATA 2218, "ZENER DONALD",   2.88
32767    END
```

1. The variable **FOUND$** is used as a *switch* to determine whether or not the student number is found. It is set to NO prior to searching in statement 330. If the number is found, it is set to YES in statement 400. Its value determines the message printed by statement 510.

2. The comparison between the search student number and the table number is made in statement 380. Note that to repeat the loop, the branch is to the **NEXT** statement (line 420), *not* the **FOR** statement that begins the loop. Execution of the **NEXT** causes the index to be incremented. Branching to the **FOR** statement would cause the index to be initialized again.

3. Upon printing the appropriate output message, the **DATA** table is RESTOREd at line 540.

Exercise 7-5 What would happen if statement 330 were accidentally left out of the program in Figure 7-11?

RULES REGARDING FOR-NEXT LOOPS

Previous examples illustrate many of the features of **FOR-NEXT** loops. Let us consider a summary of these and other characteristics of the **FOR-NEXT**.

1. The control variable is "just another variable" in the program. Within the loop its value can be used as that of any other variable. That is, it can be printed, used in a calculation, and so on. As a rule it should not be changed—leave it alone for automatic control by the **FOR-NEXT**. However, Basic-Plus *does* allow it to be modified by the program within the loop.

2. Upon exiting from a **FOR-NEXT** the value of the control variable remains at the last value used. For instance, upon completing the loop controlled by

```
FOR I% = 1% TO 10% STEP 2%
```

the value of I% will remain at 9 (*not* 11). If the loop is exited by a branching statement such as in the table search of Figure 7-11, the control variable remains at its value when the exit occurred.

3. For positive **STEP** values the loop is executed until incrementing the control variable would cause it to be greater than the final value. For negative step values the loop is executed until incrementing the control variable would cause it to be less than the final value.

4. Entry to a **FOR-NEXT** loop is only through the **FOR** statement. *Do not branch into the body of the loop from outside the loop.*

5. Example 7-3 involves a nested loop (one loop within the other). There is no limit to the number of loops that may be nested one within the other. However, care should be taken not to use the same variable as the control variable for two or more nested loops. Also, be certain not to overlap the ranges of two loops. Figure 7-12 illustrates correct and incorrect nesting of loops.

Figure 7-12
(a) Three-level nesting—VALID.
(b) Overlapped loops—INVALID

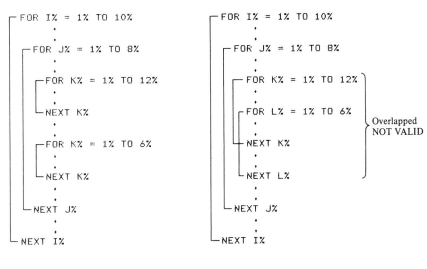

(a)

(b)

Exercise 7-6 What will be the value for the variable A% in each of the following sets of nested loops, assuming that all loops run to completion?

(a)
```
A% = 0%
FOR I% = 1% TO 10%
   .
   .
   .
FOR J% = 1% TO 10%
A% = A% + 1%
NEXT J%
   .
   .
   .
NEXT I%
```

(b)
```
A% = 0%
FOR I% = 1% TO 10% STEP 2%
    .
    .
    .
FOR J% = 7% TO 13%
A% = A% + 1%
NEXT J%
    .
    .
    .
NEXT I%
```

(c)
```
A% = 0%
FOR I% = 7% TO -2% STEP -1%
    .
    .
    .
FOR J% = 0% TO 5%
    .
    .
    .
NEXT J%
A% = A% + 1%
NEXT I%
```

(d)
```
A% = 0%
FOR I% = 1% TO A%
    .
    .
    .
FOR J% = 1% TO 9%
A% = A% + 1%
NEXT J%
    .
    .
    .
NEXT I%
```

THE WHILE AND UNTIL OPTIONS OF THE FOR-NEXT

Another form of the FOR statement that is sometimes convenient to use is

$$\text{FOR } <variable> = <expression> \{\text{STEP } <expression>\} \begin{bmatrix} \text{WHILE} \\ \text{UNTIL} \end{bmatrix} <condition>$$

The *condition* has the same structure as that used in the IF statement. Execution of the loop continues as long as the condition is true (WHILE) or is false (UNTIL).

This is a powerful tool that provides the capability for implementing structured programming techniques. However, as we shall see in the following examples, it does have its limitations and should be used within them. As a first illustration, let us reconsider Example 5-1 (Figure 5-2), in which a loop is executed until a particular condition occurs. The program segments of Figure 7-13 are equivalent to those of Figure 5-2. Following are some important points relating to this example.

1. The variable that forms the basis for the test (**LOOP$**, **LOOP%**, or **TERMINATE%**) must be given an initial value before entering the loop.

2. Both the conditional test and the branching operations of Figure 5-2 are automatically controlled by the **FOR-WHILE** and **FOR-UNTIL** forms in Figure 7-13.

3. Although the control variable I% is not used in this example, it will still be incremented by 1 on each pass and is available for use.

4. The condition test is made when the loop is first entered and then only *after* the completion of each pass. Execution does *not* exit from the loop the instant the value of, for instance, **LOOP$** changes to "NO" at line 220. In many cases this may result in an undesired pass through the loop, as illustrated by the next example.

Figure 7-13
The FOR-UNTIL and FOR-WHILE

```
100    LOOP$ = "YES"
200    FOR I% = 1%  WHILE LOOP$ = "YES"
210        INPUT #1, A, B, C, D
220        IF (condition)            &
           THEN                      &
           .
           .
           .
           LOOP$ = "NO"
230        .
           .
           .
400    NEXT I%    ! END OF LOOP
```

```
100    LOOP% = -1%
200    FOR I% = 1% WHILE LOOP%
210        INPUT #1, A, B, C, D
220        IF (condition)   &
           THEN                      &
           .
           .
           .
           LOOP% = 0%
230        .
           .
           .
400    NEXT I%    ! END OF LOOP
```

```
100    TERMINATE% = 0%
200    FOR I%=1% UNTIL TERMINATE%
210        INPUT #1, A, B, C, D
           IF  (condition)           &
           THEN                      &
           .
           .
           .
           TERMINATE% = -1%
230        .
           .
           .
400    NEXT I%    ! END OF LOOP
```

Example 7-4 Each record in an input file includes the following information (the trailer contains EOF in the name field):

> Student name
> Total points earned
> Number of exams taken

Write a program to calculate and print the average score for each student. Print a summary line at the end with the count of the number of students processed.

The logic of this program is relatively simple for us at this stage of the game. We could easily program it utilizing the techniques of earlier chapters, but what about using the **FOR-UNTIL**? If we expect the program of Figure 7-14 to do the job, we are in for a disappointment. Before proceeding further the reader should evaluate this program carefully and determine what will take place.

The loop for this program comprises lines 310–360. On each pass through the loop, **STUDENT$** is tested. If it is not "EOF," then execution of the loop proceeds. However, at line 320 the new value for **STUDENT$** is read. If it is EOF, the loop will still be completed. Thus the trailer record will be processed as if it were data. If the value for **EXAMS** is 0, then execution will be terminated by an error condition at line 330 (division by zero).

Different techniques can often be devised to allow use of the **FOR-UNTIL** or **FOR-WHILE** for situations of this type. However, they should be used only if they simplify overall program logic. They should never be used solely as a means to eliminate an **IF** statement and/or a **GOTO** statement.

Exercise 7-7 Modify the program of Figure 7-14 to work properly using the **FOR-UNTIL**. Do not include an **IF** statement. Give some thought as to what is required to place the **INPUT** statement at the end of the loop rather than at the beginning.

Figure 7-14
An invalid use of the FOR-UNTIL—
Example 7-4

```
100 !    EXAMPLE 7-4                      &
    !    AN INVALID USE OF THE            &
    !       FOR-UNTIL                     &
    !
200 !    INITIAL SEQUENCE
210      OPEN 'TEST.FLE' FOR INPUT AS FILE #1%
220      OPEN 'TEST.OUT' FOR OUTPUT AS FILE #2%
230      STUDENT$ = ''
240      CNT% = 0%
300 !    PROCESSING LOOP   ** BEWARE ** INVALID **
310      FOR I% = 1%  UNTIL STUDENT$ = 'EOF'
320        INPUT #1%, STUDENT$, PNTS, EXAMS
330        AVE = PNTS/EXAMS
340        PRINT #2%, STUDENT$; TAB(30%); AVE
350        CNT% = CNT% + 1%
360      NEXT I%
400 !    TERMINATION SEQUENCE
410      PRINT #2%  \ PRINT #2%, CNT%; 'STUDENTS PROCESSED'
420      CLOSE #1%, #2%
32767    END
```

THE FOR AS A STATEMENT MODIFIER

Occasionally the programmer encounters a situation in which a single statement must be executed repeatedly a predetermined number of times. For instance, an output report might require six blank lines. The sequence of statements

```
500    FOR I% = 1%  TO  6%
510       PRINT #4%
520    NEXT I%
```

can be replaced by the following single statement using a FOR modifier.

```
600    PRINT #4%    FOR I% = 1%  TO  6%
```

Causes the preceding
statement to be
repeatedly executed.

The FOR modifier can assume any form allowed with the conventional FOR statement. Following are two additional examples.

```
800    CLOSE I%    FOR I% = 1%  TO  12%

900    READ TEST%, N$    FOR I% = 1%  UNTIL TEST% = DESIRED%
```

Statement 800 causes all 12 I/O channels to be closed. In statement 900 values will be read from the DATA pool until a value is read that is equal to the value stored in DESIRED%.

Answers to Preceding Exercises

7-1 (a) The condition at line 230 would immediately be true and the body of the loop would never be executed.
   (b) The loop would be exited when I% reached 5 rather than 6, thereby printing only for values of 1–4.
   (c) The value of I% would never exceed 5 (it would progress from 1 to 0, –1, –2, . . .). The loop would never be terminated; this is called an *infinite loop*.
   (d) The value of I% would continually be set back to 1 and the loop would never be terminated as in part (c).

7-2 (a) 11;   (b) 4;   (c) 11;   (d) 12

7-3 INF remains unchanged throughout the program so the same thing is being recalculated each time. The following two statements inserted in Figure 7-7 would be more efficient.

```
385    FACTOR = 1. + INF/100.

530    COST = COST * FACTOR
```

7-4 The loop would be executed once if they are equal. Assume that the initial and final values were both 7. The control variable R% would be set to 7 and compared with the final value of 7 before proceeding. Since the control variable does not exceed the final value, the loop would be executed. However, upon incrementing, the control variable would exceed the final value, so the loop would not be executed again.

On the other hand, if the initial value exceeds the final value, the loop will not be executed at all. This results from the fact that the control variable R% upon first being assigned the initial value would already exceed the final value.

7-5 To illustrate, assume that five inquiries were made from the terminal as follows:

> First inquiry—student not in table
> Second inquiry—student in table
> Third inquiry—student not in table
> Fourth inquiry—student not in table
> Fifth inquiry—student in table

Now we must remember that initially **FOUND$** will be "empty" (will *not* be YES). Once a successful search is completed, line 510 will have placed YES into **FOUND$**, which will never change. The output for these five inquiries will be

> First inquiry—not found message
> Second inquiry—correct student information
> Third inquiry—student information for last student in table since this will be the last one read in the unsuccessful search
> Fourth inquiry—same as third
> Fifth inquiry—correct student information

7-6 (a)   100   (b)   35
(c)   10—the inner loop does not affect the value of **A%**;
(d)   0—the outer loop will never be executed.

7-7 The program of Figure 7-15 includes a technique commonly used in structured Cobol programming. Since the system has no way to "look at" the next record when repeating

Figure 7-15
Solution to
Exercise 7-7

```
100 !    EXAMPLE 7-4                          &
    !    A VALID USE OF THE                    &
    !       FOR-UNTIL                          &
    !
200 !    INITIAL SEQUENCE
210       OPEN 'TEST.FLE' FOR INPUT AS FILE #1%
220       OPEN 'TEST.OUT' FOR OUTPUT AS FILE #2%
230       STUDENT$ = ''
240       CNT% = 0%
250       INPUT #1%, STUDENT$, PNTS, EXAMS
300 !    PROCESSING LOOP
310       FOR I% = 1%  UNTIL STUDENT$ = 'EOF'
330          AVE = PNTS/EXAMS
340          PRINT #2%, STUDENT$; TAB(30%); AVE
350          CNT% = CNT% + 1%
355          INPUT #1%, STUDENT$, PNTS, EXAMS
360       NEXT I%
400 !    TERMINATION SEQUENCE
410       PRINT #2% \ PRINT #2%, CNT%; 'STUDENTS PROCESSED'
420       CLOSE #1%, #2%
32767    END
```

the loop, the next record is already available. This is accomplished by reading the first record outside the loop, and then reading the "next one" at the end of the loop. Although this technique does provide for better structured techniques, it is not very compatible with the automatic end-of-file detection features of Basic-Plus. This subject was broached in Chapter 2 and is covered in detail in Chapter 11.

Programming Problems

7-1 For counseling purposes a college uses a personality test that provides scores in each of four categories. The data for each student is included in a record of a data file as follows (the trailer contains 9999 for a student number):

> Student number
> Student name
> Intrinsic motivation (IM)
> Self-enhancement (SE)
> Person orientation (PO)
> Goal deficiency (GD)

A program is to be written to locate students requiring counseling for personality problems. The criteria are as follows:

> IM > 40
> PO < 20
> GD ⩾ 40

The results for each "problem" student should be printed in the form of a bar graph, as shown by the following example output.

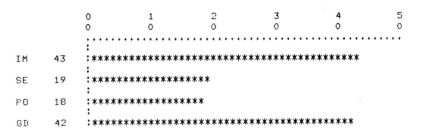

```
GERALD ERATA
15732

             0       1       2       3       4       5
             0       0       0       0       0       0
          :...........................................
          :
   IM    43 :*******************************************
          :
   SE    19 :******************
          :
   PO    18 :*****************
          :
   GD    42 :******************************************
```

7-2 For a manufacturing company one objective of inventory control is to minimize the overall cost resulting from carrying inventory and setting up for new production runs. The term *economic order quantity* refers to the most economical quantity of a given item to produce in a single run for specified cost conditions; more explicitly, the economic order quantity may be computed as

$$Q = \sqrt{\frac{2RS}{C}}$$

where Q = economic order quantity
R = annual number of units required
S = setup cost per order
C = inventory cost to carry 1 unit for 1 year

A manager would like a program that will calculate tables such as the following.

```
ECONOMIC ORDER QUANTITY
UNITS REQUIRED:   200,000
INVENTORY COST:   0.030


  SETUP COST          QUANTITY

    12.00               12649
    12.50               12910
    13.00               13166
    13.50               13416
    14.00               13663
```

Input to the program will be

	EXAMPLE VALUES
R	200000
C	0.030
Beginning value of S	12
Ending value of S	14
Increment of S	0.5

Upon completing the table, the program should ask the manager whether or not another table is desired.

Note: If you are scientifically inclined, then use the formula for the oscillating frequency of a spring-mass system:

$$f = 0.1592 \sqrt{\frac{k}{m}}$$

where f = frequency in cycles per second
k = spring constant
m = mass

Allow a single value to be entered for m and a range to be entered for k.

7-3 Modify Problem 7-2 to allow a range to be entered for both S and R and print a series of tables. Nested **FOR-NEXT** loops will be required for this.

7-4 Modify Problem 7-3 to print the results in a single table with the columns representing increasing values of S and the rows increasing values of C.

7-5 We are all familiar with the salesperson's approach of "for the low monthly payment of $20 you may have . . . ." This problem involves finding out what is behind "low monthly payments." The program to be written must:

1. Accept from the keyboard the amount to be borrowed, the annual interest rate in percent, and the number of months over which the loan is to be paid.

2. Calculate the monthly payment.

3. For each month, calculate and print how much was applied to interest and how much to the loan.

4. At the end of the report, print the total interest paid.

To calculate the monthly payment at the beginning of the program use the following formula:

$$\text{Monthly payment} = \frac{i \times (\text{Loan amount})}{1 - (1 + i)^{-n}}$$

where i = Monthly interest rate expressed as a decimal fraction. For instance, an annual rate of 18% would give: $i = (18/100)/12 = 0.18/12 = 0.015$
n = number of monthly payments

To calculate interest relating to each monthly payment use:

Monthly interest charge = Previous month balance $\times i$
New balance = Previous balance − (Payment − Monthly interest charge)

An example of how the output should appear follows.

LOAN SUMMARY
  AMOUNT OF THE PURCHASE: 100.00
  ANNUAL RATE OF INTEREST: 21
  NUMBER OF MONTHS: 12

  MONTHLY PAYMENT BASED ON ABOVE: $9.32

PAYMENT NUMBER	PREVIOUS PRINCIPAL	AMOUNT OF INTEREST	AMOUNT APPLIED TO PRINCIPAL	NEW PRINCIPAL
1	100.00	1.75	7.57	92.43
2	92.43	1.62	7.70	84.73
:	:	:	:	:
:	:	:	:	:

  TOTAL INTEREST PAID ON 100.00 LOAN = 11.73

Because of inherent "round-off" errors in floating-point calculations, the last payment will probably not be exactly correct. In an actual environment an adjustment would be made. Ignore this problem.

When processing is complete, the program should ask the user if another table is to be calculated.

7-6 A file contains examination score information for each student as follows:

> Examination group number (integer)
> Student number
> Examination score

The file has been sorted such that the records in the file are grouped by their examination group number. (For instance, all students in examination group 17 will be together in the file, followed by all students in group 18, and so on.) The file is ended with a trailer having 9999 for the examination group number.

Write a program that will calculate the average for each group and print the group number and average.

Also, keep a subtotal in order to calculate the overall average of all the scores. Upon completion, print the number of groups processed and the overall average. The technique of Figure 7-15 can be used to advantage in this problem.

7-7 Expand Problem 7-6 to print each examination group average as a bar graph in the manner illustrated by the statement of Problem 7-1.

7-8 This problem involves calculating the square root of a number using the Newton method of successive approximations. To illustrate, let us assume that we want the square root of 10 and we make a guess of 2. If our guess is correct, the quotient from dividing the guess (2) into the number (10) should be 2. Obviously 2 is not a good guess since the quotient is 5. However, we can now say that the square root must lie between 2 and 5 so let us take the average as follows:

$$\frac{2 + 10/2}{2} = 3.5$$

Thus 3.5 becomes our "refined" guess and we try it again:

$$\frac{3.5 + 10/3.5}{2} = 3.18$$

This process can be repeated indefinitely until the final result is as close as desired. This so-called *iterative* technique involves the basic relationship:

$$n = \frac{c + N/c}{2}$$

where N = a number whose square root is desired
c = the current estimate
n = the next estimate

Write a program that will accept a value from the keyboard and calculate the square root. Continue the iteration process until the new value differs from the previous one by less than 0.1%. Print the number, its square root, and the number of iterations required. Then ask the user if another number is to be processed; if yes, repeat the process, otherwise terminate. This program should be written without the use of a GOTO statement.

8

Manipulation of String Quantities

COMPARING OPERATIONS USING STRING FIELDS

String Quantities

Numeric and string quantities differ in one very important respect. That is, for each numeric quantity the Basic system reserves a set amount of storage (technically, one 16-bit word for an integer and normally two words for a floating-point quantity). Regardless of the number that we store in an integer variable, whether it be 0 or 32767, the allotted area is unchanged. String fields, on the other hand, are totally different. For instance, the string variable A$ might contain simply the letter C (one character). However, the next instant the program might store in it a string consisting of a thousand or more characters. There is no limit to the size of a string field other than a practical one determined by the amount of storage available. Thus in dealing with string fields we will often be interested not only in the data itself but also in its length.

As we know, numeric variables are given initial values of 0. Similarly, string variables are given initial values of *null* with a resulting length of zero. Occasionally it is necessary to initialize a string variable to null; this is easily done with the LET statement as follows:

```
A$ = " "
```

The Notion of Equality

Examples in earlier chapters involved comparing two string fields to determine if they were equal, for example:

```
IF SNAME$ = "EOF" THEN GO TO 900
```

The notion that string fields of the same length are equal is fairly straightforward. Obviously, EOF, ABC, and EFF are different and therefore not equal. However, what if two fields are identical except that one of them includes trailing spaces? The answer is that trailing spaces are ignored. This concept of equality and inequality is illustrated by the examples in Figure 8-1. Here each of the fields has

Figure 8-1
Comparison of string fields

	A$	B$	
(1)	JONES	JONES	Equal since they are identical.
(2)	JONES	JONAS	Unequal since they differ in fourth character.
(3)	JONES	JON	Unequal.
(4)	JONES	JONES	Equal since trailing blanks in B$ are ignored.
(5)	JONES	JONES	Unequal since leading blanks are not ignored.
(6)	EOF	E O F	Unequal since blanks are not ignored.

the length shown. For instance, the third example of B$ is five characters in length, the first three being JON and the last two being space characters. It is important to note that the space is a valid character just as are, for instance, the letter A, the digit 8, and the special character $. Although trailing spaces are ignored when comparing string fields, other spaces are not (refer to the examples).

If a program included the statement

```
IF A$ = B$ THEN GOTO 800
```

the test condition would be true (resulting in a branch to 800) in cases (1) and (4) of Figure 8-1. Similarly, in the statement

```
IF A$<>B$ THEN GOTO 900
```

the test condition would be true (resulting in a branch to 900) in cases (2), (3), (5), and (6).

If a comparison involves a string that contains null, the comparison will be equal if the other quantity is null or consists of all spaces.

Sometimes it is necessary to determine if two fields are identical, that is, are the same length and are composed of the same characters in the same order. This is done using the == relational operator. For instance, in the statement

```
IF A$ == B$ THEN GOTO 700
```

only case (1) of Figure 8-1 would result in a true condition and a subsequent branch to statement 700.

The Concept of Greater Than and Less Than

Briefly, the application of relational operators to string fields involves alphabetic sequencing. Thus SMITH is "larger than" JONES since it falls later in the alphabet. Technically, the comparison of two fields is carried out by comparing them character by character, beginning at the left of each field. Almost always, comparison of string fields involves fields consisting of letters and the space. However, string fields may contain digits and special characters. When this occurs the ordering of the character set is as listed in the summary of Appendix II. This ordering is commonly called the *collating sequence*. For the most commonly encountered characters in string comparisons, the order is space, digits, and letters. This concept is illustrated by the examples of Figure 8-2.

Exercise 8-1 In each of the following, determine whether A$ and B$ are equal, or if unequal, which is larger. (The symbol b̷ represents a space character.)

	A$	B$		A$	B$
(a)	ADAMS	ADAM	(d)	SMITH	ANDERSON
(b)	ADAM	ADAMb̷b̷b̷	(e)	TAGB	TAG7
(c)	Wb̷JONES	Bb̷JONES	(f)	SMITHb̷	b̷SMITH

Figure 8-2	A$	B$	Comments
Unequal string fields	S M I T H	J O N E S	A$ is larger since S falls after J.
	S M I T H	S M I T T	B$ is larger since T falls after H.
	S M I T H	S M I T	A$ is larger since H falls after space.
	W A 7 3 2	W A 7 3 P	B$ is larger since P falls after 2.
	J O N E S	J O N E S O N	B$ is larger since this comparison is made as if the fields were the same length and A$ were padded to the right with blanks. The O is larger than space.

A Summary of Relational Operators with Strings

The relational operators that may be used with string variables are summarized in Table 8-1.

The following example illustrates a commonly encountered procedure when dealing with string quantities.

Example 8-1 Each record in a data file includes an employee name (and other data). The last record is followed by a trailer with ZZZZ in place of the employee name. The file is to be scanned to ensure that the records are in alphabetic order (each name is larger than the preceding). Write a program segment to perform this operation.

Table 8-1
RELATIONAL OPERATORS USED WITH STRING FIELDS

OPERATOR	EXAMPLE	MEANING
=	A$=B$	The strings **A$** and **B$** are equivalent, except for possible trailing spaces.
<	A$<B$	The string **A$** occurs before **B$** in the collating sequence.
<=	A$<=B$	The string **A$** is equivalent to or occurs before **B$** in the collating sequence.
>	A$>B$	The string **A$** occurs after **B$** in the collating sequence.
>=	A$>=B$	The string **A$** is equivalent to or occurs after **B$** in the collating sequence.
<>	A$<>B$	The strings **A$** and **B$** are not equivalent.
==	A$==B$	The strings **A$** and **B$** are identical.

In this example it will be necessary to compare the name just read with the previous one. Thus a *save area* will be required. Use of this save area and the overall process are illustrated by the program segment of Figure 8-3.

Exercise 8-2 Rewrite the program segment of Figure 8-3 to use the **FOR-UNTIL** to control the loop.

STRING FUNCTIONS

The Length Function

In many applications it is necessary to know the length of a string. For instance, in checking Social Security numbers being entered, the string should always have a length of 9. Also, processing commonly involves working with one or more portions of a string. Considerable manipulation of strings is possible through special *string* functions. The simplest of these is the length (**LEN**) function. The following statements illustrate its use.

```
600    A$ = "ABCDEFG"
610    L% = LEN(A$)
620    PRINT "LENGTH OF A$ IS"; L%
```

The output of the sequence would be

```
LENGTH OF A$ IS 7
```

Although this sequence would be of little value in a program, let us consider the example on the next page.

Figure 8-3
Performing a
sequence check

```
500 !    ASSUME INPUT FILE OPEN ON CHANNEL #1
    .
    .
    .
550      PREV.NAME$ = ""            !ENSURE THAT SAVE AREA CONTAINS NULL
    .
    .
    .
600 !    READ & TEST LOOP
610        INPUT #1%, ENAME$
620        IF ENAME$="ZZZZ"       &
              THEN GO TO 670        ! END OF FILE TERMINATION
630        IF ENAME$ <= PREV.NAME$  &
              THEN GO TO 900        !  TO ERROR HANDLING
640        PREV.NAME$ = ENAME$      !  SAVE CURRENT NAME FOR NEXT LOOP
650        GOTO 600
660 !    END OF READ & TEST LOOP
670 !    CONTINUE PROCESSING AS REQUIRED
    .
    .
    .
```

Example 8-2 A program to accept and edit employee information from a keyboard is required. The Social Security number must be checked for the proper length of 9.

In statement 520 of the program segment in Figure 8-4 we see the length function used in forming the test condition.

Figure 8-4
A string field
length check

```
500 !   SOCIAL SECURITY LENGTH CHECK
510        INPUT "SOCIAL SECURITY NUMBER"; SSN$
520        IF LEN(SSN$) <> 9 THEN 530 ELSE 580
530 !      THEN
540           PRINT "SSN MUST BE 9 DIGITS."
550           PRINT "PLEASE REENTER IT."
560           PRINT
570           GOTO 500
580 !      IFEND
     .
     .
     .
```

Breaking a String Into Parts

The Social Security number in Example 8-2 is entered as 9 digits into the string variable **SSN$**. A number such as 532242005 is adequate for internal operations in the computer but leaves something to be desired for printed reports. As we know, Social Security numbers are grouped by the first 3, the next 2, and last 4 digits. In other words, the preceding number would be 532-24-2005. Basic-Plus provides three functions to break strings into "substrings"; **LEFT, MID,** and **RIGHT**. These are illustrated in Figure 8-5. It is important to note the difference between the **LEFT** and **RIGHT** functions. The **LEFT** says "how many" characters; the **RIGHT** says from "a given point on."

By use of these functions, the previous value of **SSN$** (532242005) will be printed as shown by both of the statements that follow. Note that the function may be used directly in the **PRINT** statement itself yielding exactly the same output as the **SSN1$, SSN2$, SSN3$** form.

```
532-24-2005

PRINT SSN1$; "-"; SSN2$; "-"; SSN3$

PRINT LEFT(SSN$,3%); "-"; MID(SSN$,4%,2%); "-"; RIGHT(SSN$,6%)
```

Exercise 8-3 If the value stored in A$ is ABC123456, what will be in B$ after each of the following statements?

(a) B$ = LEFT(A$,2%)
(b) B$ = MID(A$,1%,2%)
(c) B$ = MID(A$,3%,5%)

(d) B$ = RIGHT(A$,7%)
(e) B$ = RIGHT(A$,9%)
(f) B$ = MID(A$,9%,1%)
(g) B$ = RIGHT(A$,12%)

Figure 8-5

Substring functions

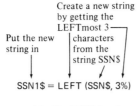

(a) The LEFT function

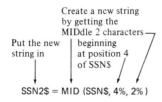

(b) The MID function

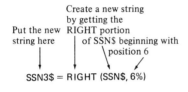

(c) The RIGHT function

Scanning the Elements of a String

Let us consider an expansion of Example 8-1 in which it is necessary to check each character of the Social Security number to make certain that it is numeric. In other words, each character must be between "0" and "9". A brute force approach would be to use the following.

```
IF MID(SSN$,1%,1%) < "0"  OR MID(SSN$,1%,1%) > "9" THEN ...
IF MID(SSN$,2%,1%) < "0"  OR MID(SSN$,2%,1%) > "9" THEN ...
IF MID(SSN$,3%,1%) < "0"  OR MID(SSN$,3%,1%) > "9" THEN ...
    .
    .
    .
```

Obviously this approach leaves much to be desired. However, if we inspect it closely, each of these statements is identical to the preceding except that the second argument in the MID function is one greater. This is a natural candidate for a **FOR-NEXT** loop as illustrated in the program segment of Figure 8-6. The combination of statements 550 and 560 executed within the **FOR-NEXT** loop checks each of the 9 digits. If a nondigit character is detected, a request for reentry is displayed at line 560.

CONCATENATION OF STRINGS

Editing a Social Security Number

A very common operation when working with string fields is to combine two or more to form another. This is called *concatenation* and is done with a **LET** statement and the operator +. For instance, in a preceding section the Social Security number was broken down into three parts, **SSN1$**, **SSN2$**, and **SSN3$**, and then printed with inserted hyphens. Let us assume that we have a program in which the Social Security number is printed in a number of different places. In such a case it would be convenient to build a copy of it that includes the hyphens. This is easily done by either of the following statements.

```
SSNH$ = SSN1$ + "-" + SSN2$ + "-" + SSN3$
SSNH$ = LEFT(SSN$,3%) + "-" + MID(SSN$,4%,2%) + "-" + RIGHT(SSN$,6%)
```

Of course, the first example assumes that **SSN1$**, **SSN2$**, and **SSN3$** have been previously extracted from **SSN$**. Thus if **SSN$** contained 532242005 (length of 9), the statement

```
PRINT SSNH$
```

would print the following.

```
532-24-2005
```

Figure 8-6
Check for nondigit
characters in a
string

```
500 !    SOCIAL SECURITY LENGTH CHECK
505 !    FIRST CHECK THE LENGTH
510        INPUT "SOCIAL SECURITY NUMBER"; SSN$
520        IF LEN(SSN$) <> 9                                    &
             THEN                                               &
               PRINT "SSN MUST BE 9 DIGITS."               \ &
               PRINT "PLEASE REENTER IT."                  \ &
               PRINT                                       \ &
               GOTO 500
530 !    NEXT CHECK FOR DIGITS
540        FOR I% = 1% TO 9%
550          SS$ = MID(SSN$,I%,1%)
560          IF SS$<"0" OR SS$>"9"                              &
               THEN                                             &
                 PRINT "THIS SSN CONTAINS NON-DIGITS"     \ &
                 PRINT "PLEASE REENTER IT."               \ &
                 PRINT                                     \ &
                 GO TO 500
570        NEXT I%
           .
           .
           .
```

Note that the string components have been "tacked on" to one another in the order indicated by the LET. Of course, the length of the result (SSNH$ in this case) is the sum of the lengths of the components (11).

The SPACE$ and STRING$ Functions

The programmer often encounters situations in which a long string composed of a given character is required. For instance, an image mask for a PRINT-USING might require a numeric field, a larger number of spaces, and another numeric field. Following is a typical image with two field definitions separated by 40 spaces that is defined by two different methods.

```
M$ = '###                                        ###.##'
M$ = '###' + SPACE$(40%) + '###.##'
```

Note the use of the SPACE$ function. It includes one argument that specifies how many spaces are to be generated. The concatenation operations build exactly the same result as that achieved by the first form.

Sometimes a string of other characters is desired. For instance, let us assume that we would like an entire line of hyphens (60 of them) printed across the page to separate the headings from the detail output. For this we can use the following form of the STRING$ function.

```
H$ = STRING$(60%,ASCII('-'))
```

We should note the exact form used here (see Figure 8-7 for an explanation). Use of the ASCII function is described in a later chapter—just use it here "because it works."

Exercise 8-4 What will be stored in L$ for each of the following? Assume that A$, B$, and C$ have been assigned as

```
A$ = "ABC"
B$ = "1234"
C$ = "X"
```

(a) `L$ = B$ + C$ + A$`
(b) `L$ = A$ + "99 99"`
(c) `L$ = A$ + RIGHT(B$,2%)`
(d) `L$ = SPACE$(7%) + C$`
(e) `X$ = STRING$(20%,ASCII("*"))`
     `L$ = X$ + SPACE$(30%) + X$`

Figure 8-7
The STRING$
function

Name of   Count of the number
the function   of this character
                   required
        ↓   ↓   ↓
STRING$ (60%, ASCII ("–"))
                ↑
         Required to make
         it work

8-1 In (b) A$ and B$ are equal; in all others A$ is larger.

8-2
```
605    FOR I% = 1% UNTIL ENAME$ = "ZZZZ"
610      INPUT #1%, ENAME$
630      IF ENAME$ <= PREV.NAME$    &
           THEN GO TO 900
640      PREV.NAME$ = ENAME$
650    NEXT I%
```

Note that this technique will work properly only if the trailer value is larger than the last name in the file.

8-3 (a) AB;   (b) AB—note: produces same result as (a);   (c) C1234;
(d) 456;   (e) 6;   (f) 6—note: produces same result as (e);
(g) null—A$ consists of only 9 characters.

8-4 (a) 1234XABC;   (b) ABC99 99;   (c) ABC234;   (d) 7 spaces preceding X (length of 8);   (e) a string of 20 "*" characters, followed by 30 spaces followed by 20 more "*" characters (total length is 70).

Programming Problems

8-1 This problem involves printing mailing labels. Each record in the input file contains the following.

> Number of labels to be printed for this person
> Name (last name, a space, first name)
> Social Security number
> City and state
> ZIP (treat it as a string quantity)

For each input record you are to print one or more labels as defined by the first field. For instance, a sample input record and the first label are illustrated below.

```
3,WRIGHT JAMES,123456789,987 OKAY STREET,OAKLAND CA,91234        (input)
```

```
123-45-6789                  ◀——— Note: hyphens
                        }    ◀———       two blank lines
JAMES WRIGHT                 ◀———       first name first
987 OKAY STREET
OAKLAND CA   91234
```

Note that the number of labels printed for each person will depend upon the value of the first field in that record. Also skip three lines between each label. Terminate processing upon detecting a value of zero for the number of labels.

8-2 One of the functions of a word processor is to format text information according to predefined formatting rules. Perhaps the most basic operation is to fill lines. For instance, text may be keyed into a computer with no regard to margins. The word processor takes the text, word by word, and fills the line until the specified margin is reached. This problem involves line filling. To simplify matters, the input file consists of one word per record. The first record contains a numeric quantity indicating the maximum line width (number of positions); the last record is a trailer with two consecutive periods. Write a program that will read the input file, word by word, and build an output line that is as long as possible without exceeding the line width. Each word should be separated by one space. Upon filling a line, write it to an output file and begin the next line.

8-3 Modify Problem 8-2 to search for words that end with a period (indicating end of a sentence). Following the period, include two spaces. If a word is preceded by a period, this means that a new paragraph is required. Write the present line to the output file, write a blank line, delete the period, and indent the new line five positions (insert five spaces) before beginning the new line.

8-4 True–false examinations consisting of 50 questions each are to be processed by the computer. Each record in an input file contains the student number, name, and a 50-position string field comprising the answers that will be T or F. For instance, an input record might appear as follows:

```
2573,JONES EARL,TTFTFTFFFTFTFFTFFFFTTTFTFTTFTFTTTFTFTTTFFFTFTFFTT
```

The first record in the file will consist of only the 50-position string field that is the answer key to the examination. (A trailer will include 9999 for the student number.) Write a program that will score each exam, and then print the student number, name, and score. After processing the last exam, print the average score for all exams graded.

8-5 Each record of a file contains one long string of characters (no punctuation). A program is required that will read each string, form a new string, and write it to an output file. Operations to be performed on the input string are as follows:

1. Eliminate all leading spaces (spaces at the front of the string).
2. Eliminate all trailing spaces (spaces at the end).
3. Reduce each group of spaces within the string to one space. For example, if two words are separated by five spaces in the input file, they will be separated by only one in the output file.

Terminate processing if the first character in an input string is a period. Note that this problem is more difficult than it first sounds. It is a natural candidate for using the **FOR-UNTIL** and **FOR-WHILE**. That is, positions in a string can be scanned (for instance, see lines 540–570 of Figure 8-6) **UNTIL** a space is encountered using the **FOR** statement modifier. Do *not* use the **CVT$$** function, which is covered in a later chapter.

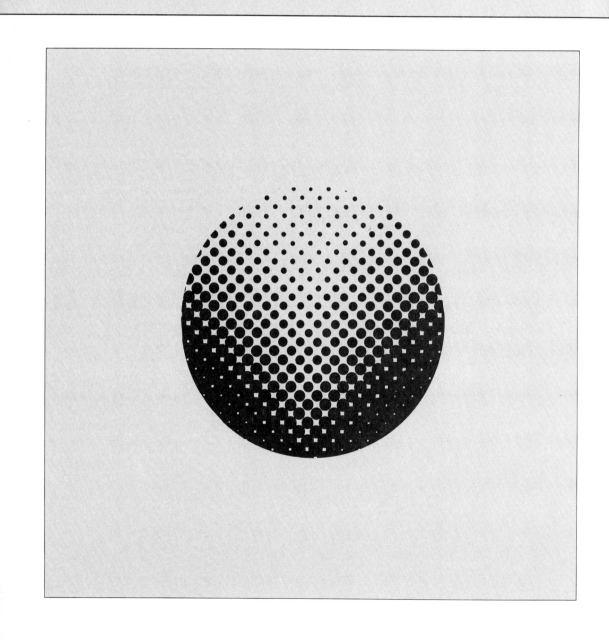

Subscripted Variables & Arrays

BASIC PRINCIPLES OF ARRAYS

Calculation of the Mean

Examples and techniques up until now have all involved the notion of reading a set of data values, operating on them, printing results, and then reading the next set of data values and so on. In other words each data record is read, processed, and then discarded in favor of the next one. However, some applications require that the data values be read *and saved* for later processing. To illustrate this concept let us consider the following example.

Example 9-1 An interactive program is required that will allow a user to enter a set of examination scores from the keyboard. The program is to calculate the mean (average) of the data set and determine how many test scores exceed the average. Assume that no more than 100 scores will ever be entered. The end of the data is to be signaled by entering a score of −1.

In this problem it will be possible to perform the accumulating function (required for calculation of the mean) as the data is being entered. Then it will be necessary to "see" the data set a second time in order to compare each score with the mean. Obviously the principles that we have used up to this point are not well suited to such an operation. This brings us to the principle of *subscripted variables*.

The Notion of Subscripting

In mathematics it is common practice to name a set of variables by the use of subscripts. For instance, assume that we have 16 different items that are similar in nature, such as examination grades for 16 students. Rather than name them a, b, c, . . . , p, which could be cumbersome, we might call them $a_1, a_2, a_3, . . . , a_{16}$. Thus in referring to the seventh data point we can speak of a_7 (which is called "a subseven" or simply "a seven") rather than g, which takes a moment to figure out. Furthermore, we can speak of the data set a consisting of 16 elements. More specifically, the mathematician will refer to the data set a_i where i ranges from 1 through 16. In speaking of the mean or average of the data set it becomes much simpler to be explicit (an important requirement in using Basic), since we can write a simple formula for the mean:

$$\text{Mean} = \frac{\text{Sum of elements } a_i \text{ where } i \text{ ranges from 1 to 16}}{16}$$

Of course, this could be written:

$$\text{Mean} = \frac{a_1 + a_2 + a_3 + \cdots + a_{16}}{16}$$

Let us refine this to a form that is basic to mathematics and indicative of the Basic forms we study in this chapter and the next. It is standard mathematical practice to use the Greek letter sigma (Σ) to represent "the sum of," and so the preceding form can be simplified to

$$\text{Mean} = \frac{\Sigma \, a_i}{16} \quad (i = 1, \, 16)$$

Now this may be generalized to any number of data points, the number of which we might refer to as n, yielding

$$\text{Mean} = \frac{\Sigma \, a_i}{n} \quad (i = 1, \, n)$$

Subscripted Variables in Basic

To this point in our studies, each variable named in a program reserves space for the storage of one value. Thus, for example, the variables X, Y, and Z would provide us with three "storage areas." Through use of the mathematical-type subscripting techniques, a single variable name can reserve space for many variables. Referring to Example 9-1, we will require space for up to 100 quanti-

Figure 9-1
(a) The DIM statement. (b) A subscripted variable

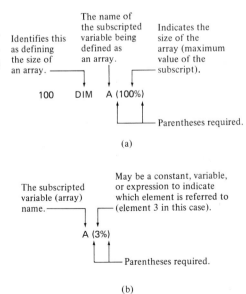

(a)

(b)

ties. This is done by *dimensioning* the array in a so-called **DIM** statement as shown in Figure 9-1(a). This statement will cause the system to reserve storage for the 100 values that we may enter in Example 9-1. As we shall see, we will be able to refer to them as elements 1 through 100.†

As a general rule all arrays in example programs in this book will be dimensioned in a **DIM** statement regardless of their size. However, if an array dimension is not to exceed 10 (for instance, **A(10)**), then it need not be dimensioned in a **DIM** statement. The system automatically assumes a dimension of 10 for any array not dimensioned. The same applies to two-dimensional arrays (described in a later section); the assumed size is 10×10.

In algebra the subscripted variable takes a form such as a_i. In Basic its form is identical to that in the **DIM** statement, as illustrated in Figure 9-1(b). Thus to read values into the first five elements of **A** (beginning with element 1), we could use the following sequence.

```
500      INPUT A(1%)
510      INPUT A(2%)
520      INPUT A(3%)
530      INPUT A(4%)
540      INPUT A(5%)
```

Obviously this "brute force" approach would leave something to be desired if we were to read 95 values instead of 5. One of the beauties of subscripted variables is that the subscript, as used in a program, can be a variable, or even an expression. Combine this with the **FOR-NEXT** and we have a powerful tool. Either of the following forms can be used to read 5 (or 95) values.

```
600      FOR I% = 1% TO 5%        700      INPUT A(I%) FOR I% = 1% TO 5%
610         INPUT A(I%)
620      NEXT I%
```

We can see that with the first execution of the **INPUT**, I% will have a value of 1 so statement 610 will be executed as if it were statement 500 in the previous sequence. With the second execution, I% will be 2, which will give the same result as statement 510, and so on.

Selecting Array Names

Since subscripted variables are, in fact, variables, the rules for selecting variable names apply equally to naming arrays. Furthermore, arrays can be floating point, integer (%), or string ($). Also, the same name can be used for a simple variable and a subscripted variable. That is, within a given program, **A** and **A(K%)** could both be used and would be every bit as different as **A** and **B(K%)**.

---

†Actually, space for 101 elements is reserved since Basic sets aside space for elements numbered 0 through 100. However, as a rule the element numbered 0 is generally not used since a counting sequencing beginning at 1 is less confusing than one beginning at 0.

PROCESSING AN ARRAY

Reading and Storing Data Values—Example 9-1

Let us consider the solution to the preceding Example 9-1 in two distinct parts. The first will read and save the input test scores, and calculate the mean. The second will scan the array to perform the required count. The logic of the mean calculation and a corresponding program are shown in Figure 9-2. The following commentary relates to this example.

1. Since we anticipate scores in the range 0 to 100 and no more than 100 values, then integer variables may be used. Thus the score, total, and subscripted variables are defined as integer; that is, S%, TOTAL%, and A%. Arrays may be defined as integer (as in this case), floating point, or string.

Figure 9-2

Calculation of the mean—Example 9-1. (a) A flowchart. (b) A program segment

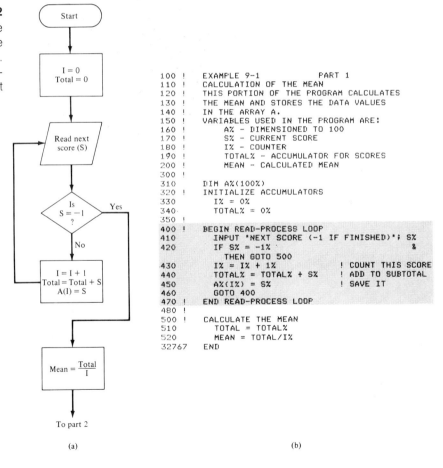

```
100 !    EXAMPLE 9-1              PART 1
110 !    CALCULATION OF THE MEAN
120 !    THIS PORTION OF THE PROGRAM CALCULATES
130 !    THE MEAN AND STORES THE DATA VALUES
140 !    IN THE ARRAY A.
150 !    VARIABLES USED IN THE PROGRAM ARE:
160 !        A% - DIMENSIONED TO 100
170 !        S% - CURRENT SCORE
180 !        I% - COUNTER
190 !        TOTAL% - ACCUMULATOR FOR SCORES
200 !        MEAN - CALCULATED MEAN
300 !
310      DIM A%(100%)
320 !    INITIALIZE ACCUMULATORS
330          I% = 0%
340          TOTAL% = 0%
350 !
400 !    BEGIN READ-PROCESS LOOP
410          INPUT "NEXT SCORE (-1 IF FINISHED)"; S%
420          IF S% = -1%                          &
                 THEN GOTO 500
430          I% = I% + 1%              ! COUNT THIS SCORE
440          TOTAL% = TOTAL% + S%      ! ADD TO SUBTOTAL
450          A%(I%) = S%               ! SAVE IT
460          GOTO 400
470 !    END READ-PROCESS LOOP
480 !
500 !    CALCULATE THE MEAN
510          TOTAL = TOTAL%
520          MEAN = TOTAL/I%
32767    END
```

(a)   (b)

2. In the processing loop, which is shaded, reading of a valid exam score will cause the counter I% to be incremented by 1 and S% to be added to the accumulator. In statement 450 the counter I% is used as the subscript for saving the current score into the array A%.

3. In statement 510 the integer variable TOTAL% is converted to floating point in TOTAL in order to yield a floating-point value for MEAN (statement 520).

4. The array will not necessarily be "full." That is, if only 37 scores were entered, then only A%(1) through A%(37) would contain data values. Subscripted variables, like simple variables, initially contain values of 0. Thus A%(38) through A%(100) (and A%(0)) will contain the value 0. The value stored in I% "points at" the last element of A%, which was loaded with a score.

Exercises 9-1 What would happen in the program of Figure 9-2 if the user entered more than 100 data values?

9-2 A programmer decides that each input value in the program of Figure 9-2 should be counted as soon as it is entered. What would happen if the programmer changed statement 430 to number 415?

Searching the Array

The "second half" of this example involves comparing the calculated mean with each of the values stored in the array A%. However, we must remember that I% contains the subscript number of the last value load. (For instance, if 37 exams were processed, the value in I% would be 37.) Thus this portion of the program would look at A%(1) through A%(I%). At this point it is important to note the role of the subscript: It is only a "dummy" variable that defines *which* A% element is desired. Thus if K% = 7 and J% = 8, then all of the following refer to the same element of A%—that is, the eighth one.

```
A%(8%)              A%(J%)              A%(K% + 1%)
```

Therefore, the following sequence on the left would print all scores that were entered and the sequence on the right would print them in reverse order.

```
800     FOR C% = 1% TO I%          900     FOR C% = I% TO 1% STEP -1%
810         PRINT A%(C%)           910         PRINT A%(C%)
820     NEXT C%                    920     NEXT C%
```

Note that the variable I% used as the subscript in Figure 9-2 is used as a control variable in the FOR-NEXT loop here.

The flowchart of Figure 9-3(a) illustrates such a FOR-NEXT loop for the solution to the second part of Example 9-1. The program itself shown in Figure 9-3(b) is fairly straightforward.

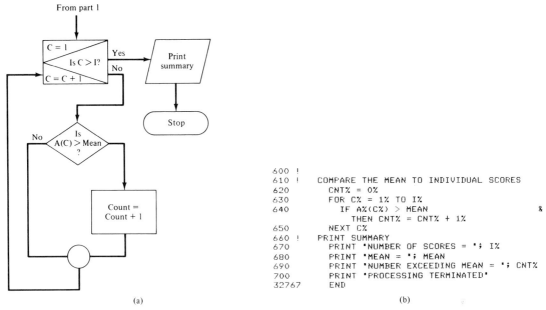

Figure 9-3 Searching the array—Example 9-1. (a) A flowchart. (b) A program segment

The program segment in the figure reads as follows:

```
600 !
610 !   COMPARE THE MEAN TO INDIVIDUAL SCORES
620       CNT% = 0%
630       FOR C% = 1% TO I%
640         IF A%(C%) > MEAN                              &
                THEN CNT% = CNT% + 1%
650       NEXT C%
660 !   PRINT SUMMARY
670       PRINT "NUMBER OF SCORES = "; I%
680       PRINT "MEAN = "; MEAN
690       PRINT "NUMBER EXCEEDING MEAN = "; CNT%
700       PRINT "PROCESSING TERMINATED"
32767   END
```

Exercises **9-3** Would the end result of processing in Figure 9-3(b) be any different if the array had been searched backward by changing statement 630 to the following?

630   FOR C% = I% TO 1% STEP -1%

9-4 Considering the complete program of Figures 9-2(b) and 9-3(b), what changes would be required to allow the user the option of repeating the loop for another data set?

TABLE SEARCHING

A Table Search Example

One of the important uses of subscripted variables is for the storage of tables that must be searched for a particular value. To illustrate this usage, let us consider the following example.

Example 9-2 This example involves two input data files: one containing employee data and the other table information. Each record of the employee file (EMP.DAT) includes

> Employee Social Security number
> Employee name
> Hours worked (floating point)
> Job code (integer <9999)

The last data record is followed by a trailer with a Social Security number field of 999999999. Each record of the table file (PAY.TBL) includes a job code and the corresponding pay rate; the last table entry is followed by a trailer with the pay code field of 9999. Calculate the gross pay for each employee.

We should note that the employee record contains the hours worked, but *not* the pay rate. It does, however, contain a job code. Furthermore, the table file consists of job codes and corresponding pay rates. Thus for each employee it will be necessary to search the table from the table file in order to obtain the pay rate for that employee.

The Concept of Arguments and Functions

Most of us are quite accustomed to using tables. For instance, a store clerk will total a sale, and then consult a tax table for the amount of tax corresponding to the purchase. Similarly, to find a person's telephone number we scan the directory of names and, upon coming to the one of interest, we read the corresponding telephone number. Of importance in these examples is that both of them involve two types of data: something that is known and something that is unknown. In using the telephone directory we know the name of the individual but we do not know the telephone number.

These table concepts are formalized in the job-code/pay-rate table shown in Figure 9-4. We can see that each entry in the table consists of two values: the *argument,* which we think of as the known quantity, and the *function,* which we think of as the unknown quantity. For example, if we wished to know the pay rate

Figure 9-4
The principle of a table

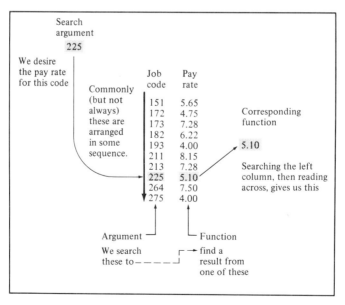

for the job code 225 (225 would be referred to as the *search argument*), we would scan the list of arguments to find that entry, then read across to obtain the corresponding function value of 5.10.

This type of operation is well suited to subscripted variables; let us see how it is implemented in Basic.

Loading a Table

Each table entry consists of two quantities (argument and corresponding function), and so this example will require two arrays. The process of loading the table is virtually identical to the task of reading and storing test score values in Example 9-1 [see Figure 9-2(b)]. This portion of the program is shown in Figure 9-5. Here it has been assumed that if the table file includes more than 100 entries, then only the first 100 will be used.

Exercises **9-5** At line 440 of Figure 9-5 the value of I% (table entry count) is set as I%–1%. Why is it necessary to decrease I% by 1?

9-6 The statements in line 450 seem unnecessary. Why not delete them and change 430 to the following?

```
430    INPUT #2%, CODE%(I%), RATE (I%)
```

Using the Table

In searching the table we must anticipate the possibility of not finding a job code. To indicate this possibility, the program will use the switch FOUND$. It will be set to N (for Not found) upon reading a new employee record. Upon finding the correct table entry during the search, its value will be changed to F (for Found).

Figure 9-5
Loading a table—
Example 9-2

```
100 !   TABLE LOOK-UP        EXAMPLE 9-2
110 !   THIS PROGRAM FIRST LOADS A PAY RATE
120 !   TABLE THEN PROCESSES AN EMPLOYEE FILE TO
130 !   COMPUTE GROSS PAY
200     DIM CODE%(100%), RATE(100%)
300 !
310 !   INITIAL HOUSEKEEPING
320        OPEN 'PAY.TBL' FOR INPUT AS FILE #2%
330        OPEN 'EMP.DAT' FOR INPUT AS FILE #1%
340        OPEN 'EMP.RPT' FOR OUTPUT AS FILE #3%
400 !
410 !   LOAD PAY RATE TABLE
420        FOR I% = 1% TO 100%
430           INPUT #2%, C%, R
440           IF C% = 9999%                    &
              THEN                             &
                 I% = I% - 1%              \ &
                 GOTO 470
450           CODE%(I%) = C%               \ &
              RATE(I%) = R
460        NEXT I%
470 !   END OF PAY RATE LOAD
480        TSIZE% = I%       !  SAVE THE TABLE SIZE
32767   END
```

Thus the search loop will exit under two conditions: one if the end of the table is encountered, and the other if the required argument is found. In the first case, exit from the loop should leave FOUND$ at N; in the second FOUND$ should contain F. Then the appropriate message can be printed, depending upon the value of FOUND$.

The logic of this solution is illustrated in the flowchart of Figure 9-6(a). Note that when a match is found the only action that occurs is that FOUND$ is set to F. Since the loop control involves an end-of-table test *and* a test for FOUND$, an exit from the search loop will occur with the next attempted pass. We find this loop control in the FOR-UNTIL statement of line 660 in Figure 9-6(b) (p. 172).

Overall, the key element of this program relates to lines 670 and 840. When an equal compare results at line 670, the subscript I% "points at" the matching argument. This means that it also points at the corresponding function when used with RATE. Since prior to the test at line 660, the varaible I% is incremented by 1, RATE(I%−1%) is the desired pay rate. (This concept is illustrated by Figure 9-4.) Thus RATE(I%) is used in the gross pay computation of line 840.

Exercise 9-7 What would happen in the program of Figure 9-6(b) if the OR in line 660 were accidentally entered as AND?

TWO-DIMENSIONAL ARRAYS

Rows and Columns of Data

Many applications, both business and scientific, deal with tables that have rows and columns—in other words, *two-dimensional* arrays. To illustrate this concept let us assume that we work for a company that manufactures four different models of "widgets." The shop in which the widgets are made includes five different machines, each of which is needed to make each type of widget. For production planning purposes, the management has summarized the time required by each model widget on each machine in Table 9-1.

Table 9-1
Product/ Machine Summary (Minutes)

WIDGET MODEL	MACHINE				
	1	2	3	4	5
1	23	6	18	6	2
2	17	4	21	5	3
3	6	5	30	6	0
4	17	4	22	6	4

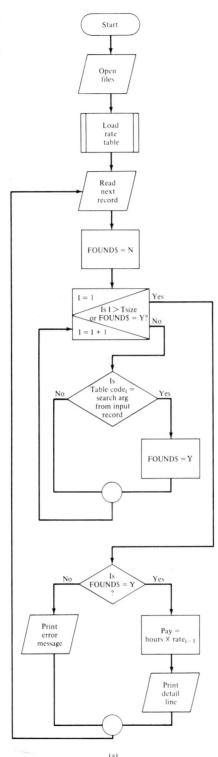

Figure 9-6a

Searching a table—
Example 9-2 —a
flowchart.

(a)

Figure 9-6b

Searching a table—
Example 9-2—a
program.

```
600 !
610 !    MAIN PROCESSING LOOP
620        INPUT #1%, SSN$, ENAME$, HOURS, JCODE%
630        IF SSN$ = "999999999"                              &
             THEN GOTO 930
640        FOUND$ = "N"
650 !      SEARCH FOR PAY RATE  -  WHEN THE CORRECT    &
   !       ENTRY IS FOUND (LINE 670) THEN FOR STATEMENT &
   !       (LINE 660) WILL BE EXECUTED ONCE MORE TO     &
   !       RECOGNIZE THAT THE CONDITION HAS BEEN        &
   !       SATISFIED.  AT THAT POINT, I% WILL BE 1 TOO  &
   !       LARGE.  AN ADJUSTMENT MUST BE MADE IN        &
   !       ACCESSING THE RATE TABLE (SEE LINE 840)
660          FOR I% = 1% UNTIL I% > TSIZE% OR FOUND$ = "Y"
670            IF JCODE% = CODE%(I%)                    &
                 THEN FOUND$ = "Y"
680          NEXT I%
690 !      END OF SEARCH
800 !
810 !      PRINT OUTPUT RECORD
820          IF FOUND$ = "Y" THEN 830 ELSE 870
830 !        THEN
840            PAY = RATE(I%-1%) * HOURS
850            PRINT #3%, USING "\            \  \          \  ##.#   $$##.##", &
                 SSN$, ENAME$, HOURS, PAY
860            GOTO 910
870 !        ELSE
880            PRINT #3%
890            PRINT #3%, "JOB CODE"; JCODE%; "NOT FOUND FOR EMPLOYEE "; SSN$
900            PRINT #3%
910 !        IFEND
920          GOTO 610
930 !    END OF MAIN PROCESSING LOOP
940 !
950 !    CLOSE FILES AND TERMINATE
960          PRINT #3%
970          PRINT #3%
980          PRINT #3%, "PROCESSING COMPLETE"
990          CLOSE #1%, #2%, #3%
32767    END
```

Here we see that the table consists of four rows (model) and five columns
(machine) arranged in a convenient, easy-to-use form. For instance, we can
immediately see that model 3 requires 6 minutes on machine 4. In other words, we
locate any item by its row and column. Using subscripting notation, we can refer to
the time t for this particular model as $t_{3,4}$. Furthermore, operations might be
performed on entire rows or columns. For instance, the production manager would
likely be interested in a bit more information: For example, how much total
machine time is required by each widget? This is easily obtained by summing the
figures in each row, thus producing the following one-dimensional array.

55
50
47
53

These and many other operations are commonly performed on two-dimensional
arrays. Let us examine how they are done in Basic.

Two-Dimensional Arrays in Basic

Exactly the same forms are used in Basic for two-dimensional arrays as for
one-dimensional arrays. For instance, Table 9-1 would require the following DIM
statement:

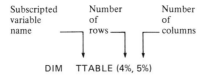

```
                                       DIM    TTABLE (4%, 5%)
```

A two-dimensional array such as this is commonly used as consisting of rows 1 through 4 and columns 1 through 5. However, like one-dimensional arrays it includes elements 0; that is, it consists of five rows—0 through 4, and six columns—0 through 5.

In referring to a particular element, for instance, time required by model 3 on machine 4, we refer to:

```
TTABLE%(3%,4%)
```

Similarly, if we are processing within a loop, we can use

```
TTABLE%(I%,J%)
```

In other words, the same rules apply to variables with one or two subscripts. Example 9-3 illustrates these principles.

Example 9-3 The production manager of Widget Corporation requires an interactive program to assist in production planning. It is to accept from the keyboard the desired number of a particular model widget, and then print the total number of hours required by each machine. Table 9-1 (p. 170) is to be included within the program in DATA statements.

As with Example 9-2, this program will consist of two basic components: loading the table into the array and processing the array. The complete program is included in Figure 9-7. The table is first loaded by the nested FOR-NEXT loops of lines 320–360. It is obviously important to vary the subscripts to correspond with the table in the DATA statements of lines 910–940. Since J% controls the inner loop, it will range from 1 to 5, while I% is held constant. Then I% will be incremented and the inner loop will be repeated. In other words, the subscript sequence will be

(1,1), (1,2), (1,3), (1,4), (1,5), (2,1), (2,2), . . . , (4,4), (4,5)

The required time calculations are performed in the loop of lines 460–490. In particular, details of the computation (line 470) are given by the description at the top of the next page.

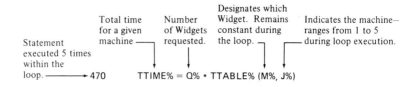

Statement executed 5 times within the loop. ────▸ 470   TTIME% = Q% * TTABLE% (M%, J%)

Exercises 9-8 Assume that the table has been entered in the DATA statements by columns rather than by rows, that is,

DATA 23,17,6,17,6,4,5,4,18,21,30,22,6,5,6,6,2,3,0,4

Modify the nested FOR-NEXT loops in lines 320–360 to reflect this change. Do not change the DIM statement.

9-9 Assume that the needs of the program required that the calculated times (line 470, Figure 9-7) be stored in an array. Define TTIME% as an appropriate array and make the required modification to the program.
Note: Exercise 9-10 is at the top of the next page.

Figure 9-7
Two-dimensional
array processing—
Example 9-3

```
100  !    TABLE PROCESSING -- EXAMPLE 9-3
110  !    WIDGET CORPORATION PRODUCTION TIME SUMMARY PROGRAM
120  !    ACCEPTS WIDGET MODEL NUMBER AND NUMBER OF UNITS
130  !    REQUIRED AND PRINTS TOTAL HOURS FOR EACH MACHINE.
140  !
200  !    DIMENSION ARRAY
210       DIM TTABLE%(4%,5%)
300  !
310  !      READ TABLE
320          FOR I% = 1% TO 4%
330            FOR J% = 1% TO 5%
340              READ TTABLE%(I%,J%)
350            NEXT J%
360          NEXT I%
370  !      END OF TABLE READ
400  !
410  !    MAIN PROCESSING LOOP
420          INPUT "MACHINE MODEL NUMBER "; M%
430          INPUT "QUANTITY "; Q%
440          PRINT
450          PRINT "WIDGET      TIME"
460          FOR J% = 1% TO 5%
470            TTIME% = Q% * TTABLE%(M%,J%)
480            PRINT USING "     #          ###", J%, TTIME%
490          NEXT J%
500          PRINT
510          PRINT
520          INPUT "DO YOU WISH TO CONTINUE "; Q$
530          IF Q$ = "YES" THEN GOTO 410
540  !    END OF MAIN PROCESSING LOOP
550          PRINT "PROCESSING COMPLETE"
900  !      TABLE ENTRIES
910        DATA 23,6,18,6,2
920        DATA 17,4,21,5,3
930        DATA  6,5,30,6,0
940        DATA 17,4,22,6,4
32767  END
```

9-10 One important feature of interactive programs is the checking of data values that are entered. In Figure 9-7 there is nothing to prevent the user from entering a nonexistent value for a widget number such as 12. This would cause an error termination since the array dimension in statement 470 would be exceeded. Write the necessary statements for preventing this occurrence.

Answers to Preceding Exercises

9-1 The system would attempt to store a value in A%(101) at line 450. Since the **DIM** statement only defines 100 elements, an error would occur.

9-2 The trailer value of –1 would be counted and the final count for computation of the mean (line 520) would be one too large.

9-3 No.

9-4 Since all accumulators and counters (I%, **TOTAL**%, and **CNT**%) are initialized to zero in the program it would only be necessary to add the following.

```
695      INPUT "DO YOU WISH TO PROCESS ANOTHER DATA SET";Q$
696      IF Q$ = "YES" THEN GOTO 320
```

Note that nothing need be done with regard to elements of A% since new values will be read into the array.

9-5 The trailer record is read and counted within the loop. Thus I% will reflect the table count plus one for the trailer.

9-6 If there are fewer than 100 table values, the trailer record will be read into the table. In this particular instance it would cause no problem since subsequent searching of the table is controlled by the table size variable **TSIZE**%. However, if there were 100 table values, then the trailer record would be 101. Upon reading it, the subscript at line 430 would exceed the **DIM** value.

9-7 If the search argument were not in the table, the error message would be printed as it should be. If the search argument were in the table, it would be found and **FOUND$** changed to F. However, searching would continue until *both* conditions were true. At that point I% would remain at the last used value of I%, which is **TSIZE**%, *not* **TSIZE**% + 1%. Thus everyone would be paid at the last pay rate in the table.

9-8 Lines 320–360 would be as follows:

```
320    FOR J% = 1% TO 5%
330       FOR I% = 1% TO 4%
340          READ TTABLE%(I%,J%)
350       NEXT I%
360    NEXT J%
```

9-9 The following statements would require the changes shown.

```
210    DIM TTABLE%(4%,5%), TTIME%(5%)

470    TTIME%(J%) = Q%*TTABLE%(M%,J%)
480    PRINT USING "    #          ###",J%,TTIME%(J%)
```

9-10

```
425    IF M% > =1% AND M% < =4% THEN 430
426        PRINT "MODEL MUST BE BETWEEN 1 AND 4"
427        GO TO 420

435    IF Q% > 0% THEN 440
436        PRINT "QUANTITY MUST BE GREATER THAN ZERO"
437        GO TO 430
```

Programming **9-1** The following file is used as input for several programming problems. A data file
Problems consists of statistical information (integer) stored one data value per record (line).
The last data value is followed by a trailer record with a value of 9999. There will
never be more than 100 data values in the file.

The data file is to be read into an array and printed as it is read. Then reverse the
contents of the array elements. For instance, if 37 data values were read, then the
array contents would be switched such that

X(1) is replaced by X(37)
X(2) is replaced by X(36)

.
.
.

X(37) is replaced by X(1)

Print the array contents after the switch and check the results.

9-2 The file of Problem 9-1 is to be processed as follows:
(1) Read the file into an array and search for the largest value.
(2) Duplicate the array into a second array.
(3) Divide each element of the new array by the largest value.
(4) Print both arrays side by side.
Upon completion of this operation the new array will have a largest value of 1; this is
called *normalizing* an array.

9-3 In statistics the mean, which is simply an arithmetic average, is used to study data.
However, it does not give the complete picture of a data set. For example, the
following two sets of

10, 50, 90
50, 50, 50

both have means of 50, but there is a significant difference in the two.
Another entity in statistics that gives an indication of the data spread is *standard
deviation,* calculated using the formula:

$$SD = \sqrt{\frac{\Sigma(x_i - \bar{x})^2}{n - 1}} \qquad i = 1, n \qquad \bar{x} = \text{mean}$$

Thus for the data points 10, 50, and 90 the standard deviation is

$$SD = \sqrt{\frac{(10 - 50)^2 + (50 - 50)^2 + (90 - 50)^2}{3 - 1}}$$

$$= \sqrt{\frac{1600 + 0 + 1600}{2}}$$

$$= 40$$

Using the data file of Problem 9-1, calculate and print the number of data values, the mean, and the standard deviation. Note that other forms are available for calculating the standard deviation that are more compatible with conventional computational methods. However, use the equation given here.

9-4 The problem of sorting a set of data into an ascending sequence (smallest first through the largest, which is last) is an important programming function. Many very efficient techniques exist but, as a rule, they are beyond the scope of this chapter. However, one simple (yet effective) technique involves searching the list to be sorted for the largest value and placing that value at the end of the list. For example, assume that we have the array X consisting of elements 1 through 100. Upon searching the array, element by element, we find that the 63rd element, that is, X(63), is the largest. If we interchange the values of the last element, X(100), and the largest element, X(63), the last element will now contain the largest value. Next we repeat the process for elements 1 through 99, moving the "next largest" value into X(99). At this point X(99) and X(100) are in their "proper" sequence. Continued application will rearrange the elements in the array to produce the desired ascending sequence. Sort the file of Problem 9-1 using this method.

9-5 The input file for this problem consists of a data set followed by a 9999 trailer (call this the A set), followed by another data set followed by its 9999 trailer (call this the B set). Assume that A and B will each consist of no more than 50 data values and that each is arranged in ascending sequence. Write a program to read these values into storage and merge the two sets into the single array C (which may therefore consist of up to 100 elements). The merging should be accomplished such that the elements in C are in ascending sequence.

9-6 Assume that the data values in the file of Problem 9-1 fall in the range 0–99. Write a program to determine how many values fall in each of the following categories.

0–9	50–59
10–19	60–69
20–29	70–79
30–39	80–89
40–49	90–99

Define an array T% consisting of 10 elements corresponding to the above 10 categories. Do not use a series of IF statements. In planning your solution, take some example scores, divide by 10 (using integer arithmetic), and then compare this result with the category number.

9-7   Eight ships are at sea and the location of each is specified by a special rectangular coordinate system. For example, consider the two ships 1 and 2 whose locations are shown in Figure 9-8. The location of ship 1 is represented as (x_1,y_1) and that of ship 2 by (x_2,y_2). The distance between the two can be calculated using the Pythagorean theorem as

$$d = \sqrt{(x_2 - x_1)^2 + (y_2 - y_1)^2}$$

Each record of a file contains the x and y coordinates of a ship. The file is terminated by a trailer with 9999 for x. Write a program to read each of the ship's coordinates into an X array and a Y array. Determine which pair of ships is the closest (assume that no two are the same distance away).

9-8   Expand Example 9-3 to request how many of each widget model are to be processed. For example, an order may consist of three model 1's, five model 2's, and so on. Calculate the total time required on each machine for a complete order.

9-9   Problem 9-8 (and Example 9-3) are to be expanded further. Following the last DATA statement for the table is another DATA statement consisting of five entries. These are cost per minute values of operating each machine. The program should now calculate for an order of widgets the cost of operating each machine and the total cost.

9-10   A teacher has decided to computerize a system for recording examination grades. Each class will consist of fewer than 100 students and the maximum number of exams given will be six. For the purpose of this program, students are identified by the student roster numbers, which are consecutive beginning with 1 (that is, 1, 2, 3, . . .). Similarly, exams are numbered 1, 2, 3, ... After each exam has been graded, the score (0–100) of each student is stored as one record in a file with the following information:

Figure 9-8
Coordinates for
ships at sea

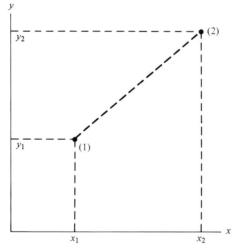

Student roster number
Examination number
Examination score

The file will be preceded by a header record with the number of students in the class followed by the number of exams given. The last record will be followed by a trailer with 9999 for a student roster number.

Write a program to do the following.

1. Read the data into the array SC(99, 6).
2. Calculate the class average for each exam.
3. Calculate the total points for each student; the score received in the first exam is to be doubled in computing total points since it is the final exam. For instance, if four exams were given, then the total points would be

$$\text{Total} = (2 \times \text{exam 1}) + \text{exam 2} + \text{exam 3} + \text{exam 4}$$

In planning your program take into account that some students will not have taken all the exams for the course and that there need not be one record for each student for each exam. However, every student will have taken the final exam.

Output is to include the averages for each of the six exams and the student roster number and total score for each of the students.

Matrix Operations

THE CONCEPT OF A MATRIX

An important field of mathematics deals with the concept of *matrices*. The word *matrix* is simply another name for an array. Whereas our operations in Chapter 11 deal with operations on individual elements of arrays (or matrices), mathematicians are commonly interested in operations dealing with entire arrays. This is so common that Basic includes capabilities of this type. These are the so-called MAT operations and operate on both one- and two-dimensional matrices. However, the zero elements of matrices [A(0), B(0,*m*), and B(*n*,0)] *are not included* in the operations performed by the MAT operations.

Some of the MAT operations involve advanced mathematical concepts, but others are relatively simple to use and provide the user capability that would be impossible without them.

MAT INPUT AND OUTPUT OPERATIONS

The MAT READ Statement

Table 9-1, which consists of machine times for widgets, was read into the array TTABLE% in Figure 9-7 by a nested FOR-NEXT loop, which is repeated here in Figure 10-1. Exactly the same operation will be performed by the following MAT READ statement.

```
210    DIM TTABLE%(4%,5%)

320    MAT READ TTABLE%
```

The system knows how many values to read from the DIM statement, and it automatically varies the second subscript most rapidly when reading them. This is a convenient form indeed.

The power of the MAT READ is further enhanced by its ability to redimension a matrix. For instance, let us assume that the Widget Corporation wishes to generalize the program so that it can handle up to 20 models (of whatever they manufacture) requiring up to 15 different machines. Then it would be necessary to dimension for 20 × 15. However, most of their products involve fewer than 20 models and 15 machines. Modifications necessary to handle this change are shown in Figure 10-2. In this case the size of the matrix is included in the first DATA statement. This is read by statement 320, thus storing the number of rows in R% and the number of columns in C%. Inclusion of dimensions in the MAT READ at

Figure 10-1
Reading a table—
from Figure 9-7

```
210        DIM TTABLE%(4%,5%)
300  !
310  !     READ TABLE
320          FOR I% = 1% TO 4%
330            FOR J% = 1% TO 5%
340              READ TTABLE%(I%,J%)
350            NEXT J%
360          NEXT I%
```

Figure 10-2
The MAT READ
statement

```
210      DIM TTABLE%(20%,15%)
300  !
310  !   READ THE NUMBER OF ROWS AND COLUMNS
320        READ R%, C%
330  !   READ THE TABLE & REDIMENSION
340        MAT READ TTABLE%(R%,C%)
  .
  .
  .
900  !   TABLE ENTRIES
905        DATA 4, 5
910        DATA 23, 6, 18, 6, 2
  .
  .
  .
```

line 340 causes the matrix to be redimensioned according to the values in R% and
C%. In this case the dimensions of **TTABLE%** will be changed from 20 × 15 to
4 × 5. Then the values are read accordingly. All subsequent processing will be as
if **TTABLE%** were originally dimensioned as 4 × 5.

Although both one- and two-dimensional matrices may be dimensioned to
smaller sizes than the **DIM**, no dimension may become larger than that specified in
the **DIM**.

The MAT INPUT **Statement**

If a matrix is to be read from the terminal keyboard, then the **MAT INPUT**
statement may be used. This statement works in exactly the same way as the **MAT
READ** (except for the source of the data). Like the **MAT READ**, the **MAT INPUT**
allows for input of integer, floating-point, or string matrices. For instance, let us
assume that the following statements are included in a program.

```
200    DIM A(10%,15%)
  .
  .
  .
300    MAT INPUT A(8%,12%)
```

Execution of statement 300 will immediately redimension the matrix A to 8 × 12.
Then the prompt ? will be displayed and the computer will await entry from the
keyboard. Data values will be stored into consecutive elements as follows:

(1, 1) (1, 2) . . . (1, 12) (2, 1) (2, 2) . . . (8, 11) (8, 12)

It is important to recognize that depression of the RETURN key terminates input of
data. (The LINE FEED key can be used if desired to display the entered data on
consecutive lines.) If the RETURN key is depressed prior to entering the full
number of values, then obviously the entire array will not be filled. Following the
input of a matrix, the predefined variable **NUM** contains the number of rows that
have been input (or for a one-dimensional array the number of elements). The
variable **NUM2** contains the number of elements in the last row that have received

values. For instance, if in response to the previous MAT INPUT of statement 300, 21 data values were entered, then NUM would contain 3 and NUM2 would contain 5 (three rows with five values in the last row).

Remember that the zero elements are not affected by the MAT READ or MAT INPUT statements.

The MAT PRINT Statement

The MAT PRINT statement can be used for printing all or a portion of an array. Figure 10-3 includes four examples of this statement. Note that the array name can be followed by nothing, a comma, or a semicolon with the indicated results. Furthermore, output can be limited to the number specified as illustrated by statement 500. Redimensioning of the matrix does *not* occur with MAT PRINT.

Two-dimensional arrays, if printed using the semicolon, are printed by rows, line per line.

Exercise 10-1 The statement DIM X(100%) is included in a program. Write a sequence of statements that will perform the following.

1. Ask the user how many values (up to 100) are to be entered.

2. Input into the matrix the required number of values and redimension the matrix as appropriate.

3. Give the user an error message if the proper number of elements has not been entered.

Enter your routine into the computer to make certain it works.

MANIPULATION OF MATRICES

The algebra of matrices is composed of many powerful problem-solving techniques for manipulating matrices virtually as if they were simple variables. Basic-Plus includes some of the common matrix manipulation operations.

Figure 10-3
The MAT PRINT statement

```
100       DIM A(15%)
  .
  .
  .
200       MAT PRINT A          Print all 15 elements in a single
                                  column (one per line).
300       MAT PRINT A,         Print across the page using the print zones;
                                  yields 5 elements per line.
400       MAT PRINT A;         Print on one or more lines in a packed fashion.
500       MAT PRINT A(12%)     Print only the first 12 elements of A in a
                                  single column. Does not redimension.
```

Figure 10-4
MAT initialization
statements

```
100        DIM A(25), B(15,10), C(20,20)
  .
  .
300        MAT A = ZER          Sets elements A(1) through A(25) to 0.

400        MAT A = ZER(15)      Sets elements A(1) through A(15) to 0 and redimensions A to 15.

500        MAT B = CON          Sets elements B(1, 1) through B(15, 10) to 1.

600        MAT B = CON(10,10)   Sets elements B(1, 1) through B(10, 10) to 1
                                  and redimensions B to (10, 10).
700        MAT C = IDN          Creates an identity matrix; that is, sets all elements to 0 except C(1, 1),
                                  C(2, 2), C(3, 3), . . . , C(20, 20) which are set to 1.
```

Initialization Statements

The matrix initialization statements provide for initializing all elements of an array (except the zero elements), and for redimensioning if desired. These statements, which are illustrated in Figure 10-4, provide for setting all elements of a matrix to 0, setting all elements to 1, and creating an identity matrix.

Matrix Arithmetic

The three arithmetic operations of addition (+), subtraction (−), and multiplication (*) can be performed on matrices. (The operation of division is not defined in matrix algebra.) In addition, it is possible to multiply each element in an array by a single quantity; this is called *scalar multiplication*.

For addition or subtraction the matrices must have the same dimension or dimensions (for two-dimensional matrices). Examples of both correct and incorrect addition of matrices are illustrated in Figure 10-5. Note that in statement 600 the matrix A will be redimensioned to be consistent with matrices D and E.

In order to multiply two matrices, they must be *conformable*; this means that the number of columns in the first matrix is equal to the number of rows in the second. For instance, in statement 500 of Figure 10-6 the number of columns in A and the number of rows in B are both 9. The resulting matrix will have dimensions equal to the number of rows in A and columns in B—12 × 6 in this case. The receiving array must be large enough to hold the resulting product. Note that statement 800 involves multiplying a two- and a one-dimensional matrix, producing a one-dimensional result.

Each element of a matrix can be multiplied by a constant, variable, or expression as illustrated in Figure 10-7.

Figure 10-5
Addition and sub-
traction of matrices

```
100        DIM A(20),B(20),C(15),D(15),E(15)
  .
  .
  .
500        MAT C = D + E        Valid operation.

600        MAT A = D + E        Valid operation; redimensions A to 15.

700        MAT C = A + B        Invalid since C is too small to hold the result.

800        MAT A = B + C        Invalid since B and C are different sizes.
```

Figure 10-6
Matrix multiplication

```
100     DIM A(12,9), B(9,6), C(9), D(15,20), X(15,15), Y(20)
  .
  .
  .
500     MAT X = A*B      Valid operation; X redimensioned to 12 rows and 6 columns.
600     MAT X = B*A      Invalid since B and A are not conformable in this order (number
                            of columns in B ≠ number of rows in A).
700     MAT A = X*D      Invalid since A is not large enough.
800     MAT Y = A*C      Valid operation; Y redimensioned to 12.
```

Figure 10-7
Scalar multiplication

```
100     DIM A(15,12), B(15,12)
  .
  .
  .
200     MAT A = (150)*B      Duplicates each element in B into A and multiplies
                                each element in A by 150.
300     MAT A = (X+5)*A      Multiplies each element in A by the value from X + 5.

400     MAT A = B            Copies each element of B into A.
```

Figure 10-8
Matrix transposition
and inversion

```
100     DIM A(12,9), B(15,15), C(15,15)
  .
  .
  .
300     MAT B = TRN(A)      Copies the rows of A into the columns of B and
                                redimensions B to (9, 12).
400     MAT A = TRN(B)      Not valid; A is not large enough.
500     MAT C = INV(B)      Inverts the matrix B into C and calculates the determinant
                                of B and stores it in DET.
600     MAT B = INV(A)      Not valid; A must be a square matrix.
700     MAT B = INV(B)      Not valid; Basic Plus does not allow the inverse to be
                                stored back into the original matrix.
```

Matrix Functions

Basic-Plus provides functions for the two matrix operations of transposition and inversion. These are illustrated in Figure 10-8. Note that inversion involves square matrices. Also, although none of the matrix operations operate on the zero elements, matrix inversion does destroy the previous contents of these elements.

Answer to 10-1
Preceding
Exercise

```
500     PRINT "HOW MANY VALUES DO YOU HAVE"
510     INPUT "TO ENTER (BETWEEN 1 AND 100)"; N%
520     IF N% < 1% OR N% > 100% THEN             &
            PRINT "MUST BE BETWEEN 1 & 100"       &
            PRINT "PLEASE TRY AGAIN"              &
            GO TO 500
530     MAT INPUT X(N%)
540     IF NUM < > N% THEN                        &
            PRINT "MATRIX NOT FILLED"             &
            STOP                                  &
```

Programming 10-1 This problem is similar to 8-4, except that it requires the use of arrays. True–false
Problems examinations consisting of up to 50 questions are to be graded by the computer. The
input file consists of the following information.

First record	Number of questions in exam
Second record	Answer key (up to 50 answers)
Following records	ID number
	Answers (up to 50 answers)

Answers are recorded as 1 (true) or 0 (false). For instance, the first three records of an examination consisting of 10 questions might be as follows:

10	Header record (number of questions)
1, 0, 1, 1, 0, 0, 1, 1, 0, 1	Answer key (10 answers)
2173, 1, 0, 1, 1, 0, 1, 0, 1, 0, 1	(ID number followed by answers)

Write a program to score each examination and print the results. Points of note relating to this program are as follows: (1) the **MAT INPUT** statement should be used to read the answer key into an answer key array. The value from the header (number of questions) can be used to redimension the array. (2) Each examination (records following the answer key) includes an ID number (integer) followed by the answers. A **MAT INPUT** should be used in reading each of these into an array. An appropriate adjustment will be required when comparing the answer key array with the data array. (3) The data file will be terminated with a trailer of 9999 for the ID number.

The program must print the score for each ID together with appropriate headings and descriptive information.

10-2 The subject of matrix algebra involves the algebra of array manipulation. For instance, consider the following linear system in the unknowns x, y, and z.

$$3x + 4y - 5z = -11$$
$$x - 5y + 2z = -8$$
$$-7x - y + 3z = 16$$

Using the laws of matrix algebra, this system could be represented as the following arrays.

$$\begin{pmatrix} 3 & 4 & -5 \\ 1 & -5 & 2 \\ -7 & -1 & 3 \end{pmatrix} \begin{pmatrix} x \\ y \\ z \end{pmatrix} = \begin{pmatrix} -11 \\ -8 \\ 16 \end{pmatrix}$$

This is commonly simplified as

$$AX = B$$

Here A represents the coefficient matrix, X the matrix of the unknowns, and B the constant matrix. In ordinary algebra we would solve this equation for X by dividing both sides of the equation by A. However, since these are really matrices and matrix algebra has no division operation, it is necessary to multiply both sides by the *inverse* of A. (The product of a quantity and its inverse produces a value equivalent to 1.) Thus we can solve for X as

$$X = A^{-1} B$$

where A^{-1} is the inverse of A.

Write a program that will read the coefficient and constant arrays of a linear system and solve for the unknowns using this method. Remember, the array X will contain the desired values for the unknowns (x, y, and z in the earlier example).

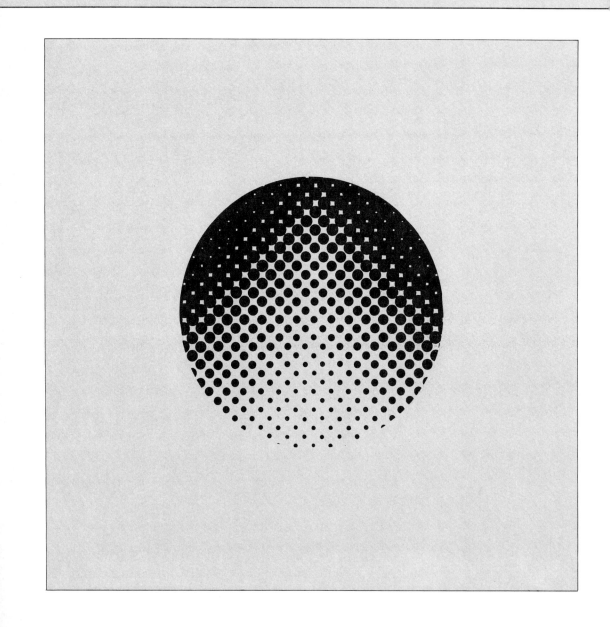

11

Error Trapping

BASIC ERROR-HANDLING CAPABILITIES

Basic-Plus Errors

Without a doubt the reader has encountered numerous error messages by this time. In Basic-Plus errors fall in two broad categories: recoverable and nonrecoverable. *Recoverable* errors are so-called because Basic allows the programmer to include code to detect and recover from those errors. These occur during execution of the program. The following are examples of recoverable errors.

```
?ILLEGAL NUMBER

?END OF FILE ON DEVICE
```

As the name implies, it is not possible for the program to recover from *nonrecoverable* errors. Many of these are detected by the compiler as the program is entered, for example,

```
?ILLEGAL EXPRESSION

?MODIFIER ERROR
```

Errors of this type must be corrected since the program will not execute beyond them.

Appendix VI is a summary for RSTS/E of the error messages and their meaning. Emphasis in this chapter is on recoverable errors—which, in general, can be grouped in two broad categories: computational errors and input/output errors. Although most of these errors cause termination of execution of the statement, some of them take a predetermined course of action and continue. The error message for the former is preceded by the ? character and for the latter by the % character (see Appendix VI). For instance, the message

```
%IMAGINARY SQUARE ROOTS
```

indicates that in a negative argument was used in the square root function (**SQR**). The system automatically uses the absolute value and continues—that is, unless error trapping has been specified.

The ON ERROR Statement

Many applications require that, when an error is detected, corrective program action be taken and then execution continued. This can be accomplished by use of the **ON ERROR** statement, an example of which follows.

```
100    ON ERROR GOTO 900
```

Execution of this statement says to the system, in essence:

If any recoverable error occurs at any point
in the program, then GOTO statement 900.

This amounts to a "delayed GOTO"—however, it is one that is executed *only* if an error occurs. Presumably statement 900 in the preceding example is the first statement of an error recovery routine.

Once corrective action has taken place, execution of the main program can continue. This is achieved with the RESUME statement.

The RESUME Statement

Let us assume that we have a program that asks the user the name of the data file to be used. Upon entering the desired file-name and extension, the program opens the file and proceeds with processing. However, what occurs if the file to be processed is PAYROL.DTA and the user keys in PAYROL.DAT (which does not exist)? The answer is that error number 5 occurs, the terminal displays

```
?CAN'T FIND FILE OR ACCOUNT
```

and execution terminates. The user must rerun the program and key in the correct name.

However, through use of the ON ERROR and corresponding RESUME the user is "given another chance" in the program segment of Figure 11-1. Here we see the error "switch" set at line 400. The file-name of a nonexistent file causes an error at line 420, which in turn results in the GOTO statement 900. Upon execution of that sequence the RESUME statement causes a return to the statement that caused the error. Every error-checking routine *must* contain a RESUME, since any detected error effectively disables the ON ERROR capabilities until the RESUME is executed. For example, if line 940 were replaced with GOTO 420 and a nonexistent file-name were entered the second time, execution would be terminated.

In many instances the user wishes to resume at some statement other than the one that caused the error. To illustrate, let us assume that we have an application in which the user may designate the name of the output file. However, we wish to ensure that an existing file is not accidentally destroyed. A relatively simple approach is to attempt opening for input. If an open failure occurs, then a file of the

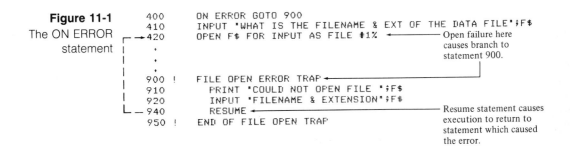

Figure 11-1
The ON ERROR
statement

```
400      ON ERROR GOTO 900
410      INPUT "WHAT IS THE FILENAME & EXT OF THE DATA FILE";F$
420      OPEN F$ FOR INPUT AS FILE #1%          Open failure here
  .                                             causes branch to
  .                                             statement 900.
  .
900 !    FILE OPEN ERROR TRAP
910          PRINT "COULD NOT OPEN FILE ";F$
920          INPUT "FILENAME & EXTENSION";F$
940      RESUME                                 Resume statement causes
950 !    END OF FILE OPEN TRAP                  execution to return to
                                                statement which caused
                                                the error.
```

name entered does not exist. However, if no open error occurs, such a file does exist. This technique is illustrated in Figure 11-2. Here we see that the RESUME statement includes a statement number. In other words, it is possible to resume at the statement that caused the error or at any other statement designated by the RESUME.

This example also illustrates disabling the error-trapping capability. Either of the following statements disables the error GOTO set by, for example, statement 500 in Figure 11-2.

```
610    ON ERROR GOTO 0

610    ON ERROR GOTO
```

This will prevent subsequent errors from trapping to statement 580 (in this example) and will return error handling to the system as if statement 500 never existed.

Exercise 11-1 Modify the program segment of Figure 11-1 to eliminate statement 920, which requests input of the file-name after the failure.

Resetting the Error Switch

In some instances the programmer may wish to trap only certain types of errors and let the system handle others. This is made possible by including ON ERROR GOTO 0 within the error routine itself. In fact, exactly this technique was used in the end-of-file termination of Figure 3-8, which is repeated here as Figure 11-3. We see that if ERR<>11, then the error switch is reset to zero. This effectively "retroactively" cancels the original error switch setting (line 440) and causes the system to handle the error as if line 440 never existed. However, if the error is an 11, then processing is handled by the error routine.

Figure 11-2
The ON ERROR and
RESUME

```
        '
        '
        '
500        ON ERROR GOTO 580
510        INPUT "FILENAME & EXTENSION FOR THE OUTPUT FILE";F$
520        OPEN F$ FOR INPUT AS FILE #3%
530  !      IF EXECUTION CONTINUES HERE THEN THE FILE F$ ALREADY EXISTS
540        CLOSE #3%
550        PRINT "FILE ";F$;" ALREADY EXISTS."
560        INPUT "DO YOU WISH TO DESTROY IT";Q$
570        IF Q$ = "YES"                          &
              THEN GOTO 600                        &
              ELSE GOTO 510
580  !   OPEN FAILURE -- NO SUCH EXISTING FILE SO OPEN FOR OUTPUT
590        RESUME 600      !        RESET ERROR SWITCH
600        OPEN F$ FOR OUTPUT AS FILE #3%
610        ON ERROR GOTO 0          !   DISABLE FURTHER ERROR TRAPPING
        '
        '
        '
```

Figure 11-3

Retroactively
disabling the
ON ERROR

```
530 !    PRINT MESSAGE & TERMINATE
540          IF ERR<>11 THEN ON ERROR GOTO 0
550          PRINT #2
560          PRINT #2
570          PRINT #2, "PROCESSING COMPLETE"
580          CLOSE #1, #2
32767    END
```

The ERR and ERL Variables

Often the recovery action to be taken in an error routine depends upon the type of error that occurred. For this purpose, the system places the error number of the occurring error (see Appendix VI) in the predefined variable ERR. For instance, if the "?END OF FILE ON DEVICE" occurred, the variable ERR would be loaded with a value of 11, the corresponding error number. Then the program can test ERR as it would any other variable. Let us consider an expansion of the file open check of Figure 11-1.

Example 11-1 A program segment is required that queries the user for a desired input file for opening. If the file exists and is available, then it should be opened. Provide for the following three possible error conditions.

2   ?ILLEGAL FILE NAME

5   ?CAN'T FIND FILE OR ACCOUNT

10   ?PROTECTION VIOLATION

In this example the variable ERR will be tested for a value of 2, 5, or 10, and the appropriate message will be printed. The program segment of Figure 11-4 performs these tests in lines 550, 560, and 570. Furthermore, if the error was not one of the three, then an error message is printed identifying the error number (ERR) and the line at which the error occurred (ERL). The variable ERL contains the line number at which the error occurred and, like ERR, is loaded by the system when the error occurs. Some sample dialogs are shown in Figure 11-5.

OTHER ERROR-TRAPPING TECHNIQUES

The WAIT Statement

Frequently, interactive programs are so designed that a user response is required within a certain amount of time. This can be programmed using the WAIT statement immediately prior to the INPUT statement. For instance, if the statement

100   WAIT 30

Figure 11-4

Using the ERR and
ERL variables—
Example 11-1

```
500        ON ERROR GOTO 540
510        INPUT "WHAT IS THE FILENAME & EXT OF THE INPUT FILE";F$
520        OPEN F$ FOR INPUT AS FILE #1%                          \ &
           GOTO 700        !  CONTINUE PROCESSING
530 !
540 !      FILE OPEN ERROR TRAP
550           IF ERR = 2                                            &
              THEN                                                  &
                 PRINT F$;" IS A BAD FILENAME"                    \ &
                 PRINT "PLEASE TRY AGAIN."                        \ &
                 GOTO 640
560           IF ERR = 5                                            &
              THEN                                                  &
                 PRINT "FILE ";F$;" DOES NOT EXIST."             \ &
                 GOTO 600
570           IF ERR = 10                                           &
              THEN                                                  &
                 PRINT "YOU ARE NOT AUTHORIZED TO USE ";F$ \ &
                 GOTO 600
580 !         ELSE
590              PRINT "UNEXPECTED ERROR"                         \ &
                 PRINT "ERROR = ";ERR                             \ &
                 PRINT "ERROR LINE = ";ERL                        \ &
                 PRINT "TERMINATING PROCESSING"                   \ &
                 GOTO 32767
600 !                                                               &
    !         RETURN POINT
610           INPUT "DO YOU WISH TO TRY AGAIN";Q$
620           IF Q$<>"YES"                                          &
                 THEN GOTO 32767
630           PRINT
640           RESUME 510
650 !      END OF FILE OPEN TRAP                                    &
    !
700 !   CONTINUE PROCESSING WITH FILE F$ OPEN
710        ON ERROR GOTO 0
```

Figure 11-5

A sample dialog for
Example 11-1

```
RUNNH
WHAT IS THE FILENAME & EXT OF THE INPUT FILE? PAY;DAT
PAY;DAT IS A BAD FILENAME
PLEASE TRY AGAIN.
WHAT IS THE FILENAME & EXT OF THE INPUT FILE? PAY.MAS
YOU ARE NOT AUTHORIZED TO USE PAY.MAS
DO YOU WISH TO TRY AGAIN? YES

WHAT IS THE FILENAME & EXT OF THE INPUT FILE? PAY.DAT
```

is executed within a program, then whenever an INPUT statement is executed, the user will be given 30 seconds to complete the input operation (and depress RETURN). If the indicated time expires, then error 15 (ERR=15, KEYBOARD WAIT EXHAUSTED) occurs. To illustrate use of the WAIT, let us consider the following example.

Example 11-2 A teacher requires a multiplication table drill and practice program. The student is to be given two numbers in the range 0 to 9 and must type in the product within 5 seconds. If the correct answer is not entered within 5 seconds, count it incorrect and continue. Maintain a count of the number of correct responses; a session must consist of 25 questions (pairs of numbers).

This program will consist of randomly generating pairs of numbers in the range 0 through 9, displaying them, and asking for their product. In handling the answer, four possibilities must be considered.

1. The correct answer is entered within the allotted time; a counter must be incremented for this case.

2. An incorrect answer is entered.

3. The WAIT time elapses (ERR=15). The student receives no credit but is given the correct answer. The student must be given time to look at the result before proceeding.

4. Invalid data is entered, for example, the student depresses a letter key by accident (an error but *not* ERR=15). The student is to be given another chance.

A complete program to perform this function is shown in Figure 11-6. Each use of the WAIT statement is shaded. The following commentary relates to this program.

1. Immediately prior to the INPUT requesting the student answer, the WAIT is executed. If the response is not received within 5 seconds, execution is transferred to statement 410 (because of the ON ERROR at line 230).

2. At line 400 the student is allowed to study the result (processing stops because of the INPUT). However, the WAIT applies to *any* INPUT statement that refers to the keyboard. In order to avoid the student timing out at line 400 (while studying the error), the WAIT 0 is included following the student response (line 370). This statement effectively cancels the WAIT and restores the keyboard to normal.

3. Within the error routine, the ERR variable is checked. If it is 15, a time-exceeded error has occurred and execution is resumed. If not 15 (an invalid integer entered at the terminal), the student is given another chance.

A sample dialog with the computer is shown in Figure 11-7. The reader should correlate this with the program of Figure 11-6.

Exercise 11-2 Why is it necessary to include WAIT 0 in the error routine at line 420 when it is already included in the program at line 370?

Figure 11-6

Using the WAIT
statement—
Example 11-2

```
100  !     MULTIPLICATION DRILL AND PRACTICE - EXAMPLE 11-2
110  !
200  !                                                        &
     !     INITIALIZE AND SET ON ERROR
210        CNT% = 0
220        RANDOMIZE
230        ON ERROR GOTO 410
300  !                                                        &
     !        BEGIN PROCESSING LOOP
310        FOR I% = 1% TO 25%
320           A% = INT(10*RND)
330           B% = INT(10*RND)
340           PRINT \ PRINT A%; " TIMES "; B%; " IS ";
350           WAIT 5
360           INPUT C%
370           WAIT 0
380           IF C% = A%*B%
                 THEN                                         &
                    PRINT "CORRECT!!"                    \  &
                    PRINT                                \  &
                    CNT% = CNT% + 1%                     \  &
                    GOTO 480
390  !           ELSE
400                 PRINT "SORRY -- CORRECT ANSWER IS "; A% * B%    \ &
                    INPUT "PRESS RETURN WHEN READY TO CONTINUE"; X$ \ &
                    GOTO 480
410  !                                                        &
     !     ERROR TRAP FOR WAIT
420        WAIT 0
430        IF ERR = 15                                        &
              THEN                                            &
                 PRINT "TIME EXPIRED -- CORRECT ANSWER IS "; A% * B% \ &
                 INPUT "PRESS RETURN WHEN READY TO CONTINUE"; X$     \ &
                 RESUME 480
440  !        ELSE
450              PRINT "ENTER NUMBERS ONLY -- TRY AGAIN"      \ &
                 RESUME 340
470  !     END OF ERROR TRAP                                  &
     !
480        NEXT I%
490  !  END OF MAIN PROCESSING LOOP                           &
     !
500  !  SUMMARY ROUTINE
510        PRINT "YOUR SCORE WAS "; CNT%; " OUT OF 25."
520        INPUT "WOULD YOU LIKE TO TRY ANOTHER SET"; Q$
530           IF Q$ = "YES"                                   &
                 THEN GOTO 200            ! REPEAT
540              PRINT "GOODBYE"
32767      END
```

Figure 11-7

A sample dialog for
Example 11-2

```
RUNNH

 2  TIMES  6  IS ? 12
CORRECT!!


 4  TIMES  8  IS ? 31
SORRY -- CORRECT ANSWER IS   32
PRESS RETURN WHEN READY TO CONTINUE?

 9  TIMES  0  IS ? 9
SORRY -- CORRECT ANSWER IS   0
PRESS RETURN WHEN READY TO CONTINUE?

 6  TIMES  6  IS ? 36
CORRECT!!


 4  TIMES  2  IS ? ^C
```

```
Figure 11-8      100        ON ERROR GOTO 19000        !   GENERAL ERROR TRAP
A generalized     .
error trap        .
                  .
                 520        INPUT "PLEASE ENTER THE MAXIMUM COUNT"; C%
                  .
                  .
                  .
                 690        INPUT "WHAT IS THE MINIMUM ACCEPTABLE VALUE"; M
                  .
                  .
                  .
                 820        INPUT #1%, A, B, C
                  .
                  .
                  .
                9000 !  FINISH UP ROUTINE
                9010        CLOSE #1%
                  .
                  .
                  .
               19000 !  GENERAL ERROR TRAP
                  .
                  .
                  .
               19100    IF ERL=520 OR ERL=690                     &
                        THEN                                      &
                            PRINT "BAD NUMBER - TRY AGAIN."   \   &
                            RESUME
               19200    IF ERR=11 AND ERL=820                     &
                        THEN                                      &
                            RESUME 9000
               19300    IF ERR<>11 AND ERL=820                    &
                        THEN                                      &
                            PRINT "THE INPUT FILE IS CORRUPT."   \   &
                            PRINT "THE FOLLOWING HAS BEEN FOUND:" \  &
                                .
                                .
                                .
                            CLOSE I% FOR I% = 1% TO 12%          \   &
                            GOTO 32767
                  .
                  .
                  .
               32767    END
```

On Error Routines in General

For many programming applications, especially those that are interactive in nature, the programming of error handling is a major task. On one hand, the programmer can simply ignore the error possibilities and allow the system to terminate execution with the appropriate error message. This is usually unacceptable. On the other hand, great care can be taken to provide recovery capabilities of all possible errors that might occur. In some applications this is essential. Since the **ON ERROR** statement provides a common branch point for all errors throughout the program, one major error-handling routine is commonly used and appropriate tests made to determine what occurred. This concept is illustrated by the skeleton program of Figure 11-8. Here various error conditions that can occur at lines 520, 690, and 820 are handled by statements within the error routine beginning at line 19000. At line 19100 execution resumes with whichever statement caused the problem. Line 19200 reflects detection of the end of file and so execution resumes with "FINISH UP ROUTINE" (line 9000). On the other hand, execution is simply terminated if execution proceeds to line 19300.

Exercise 11-3 Line 19300 in Figure 11-8 includes the condition ERR<>11. Is this condition test necessary? Explain.

In some instance it is clumsy, from a logical point of view, to have a program branch several pages forward to an error routine and then back. For situations of this type the ON ERROR address can be changed in a program as frequently as desired. To illustrate, consider the following example.

Example 11-3 A program includes a general error trap at line 19000. An INPUT statement within the program is to accept a single digit 1–9 as input. If the entry is out of this range or is nonnumeric, then a detailed description is to be printed and the user is requested to reenter the digit.

The program segment of Figure 11-9 demonstrates a technique of keeping the entire error-checking sequence together. Prior to executing the INPUT statement (line 620), the ON ERROR is reset to the local error trap. Two conditions will occur that cause the error message to be printed: detection of an out-of-range value at line 630; and an error condition representing bad data, which causes a branch to

Figure 11-9
Localizing an
error condition

```
100        ON ERROR GOTO 19000
  .
  .
  .
600  !     ACCEPT AND VERIFY INPUT
610        ON ERROR GOTO 640
620        INPUT "WHICH IS YOUR CHOICE (1-9)";N%
630        IF N%>=1% AND N%<=9%                           &
             THEN GOTO 700                                &
             ELSE GOTO 670
640  !       ERROR TRAP
650            RESUME 670
660  !       END OF ERROR TRAP
670  !                                                    &
     !       INVALID ENTRY RECOVERY ROUTINE
680            PRINT "THE VALUE ENTERED MUST BE A SINGLE DIGIT." \ &
               PRINT "REMEMBER, THE OPTIONS ARE ..."            \ &
                 .
                 .
                 .
               PRINT "PLEASE TRY AGAIN."                        \ &
               GOTO 620
690  !       END OF INVALID ENTRY RECOVERY
700  !                                                    &
     !     BRANCH-TO POINT FROM SUCCESSFUL INPUT
710        ON ERROR GOTO 19000
  .
  .
  .
```

the error trap at line 640. In both cases execution continues to the recovery routine at line 670. Upon entry of a valid value (line 620), execution of the main program continues at line 710 where the **ON ERROR** is immediately set to 19000.

Answers to Preceding Exercises

11-1 Eliminate statement 920 and change 940 to

```
940     RESUME 410
```

11-2 If the time elapsed or another error occurred with the **INPUT** statement (line 360), line 370 would not be executed. Then if the student took too long in responding at line 430, another time-exceeded error would occur.

11-3 No. Execution will never progress from line 19200 to line 19300 unless **ERR<>11**. The 11 code causes execution to continue from line 19200 to line 9000.

Programming Problems

11-1 The program of Figure 7-14 does not include any error-handling capabilities. This program involves writing the error-processing routine for the program. The program itself is to remain unchanged. However, the input data file will not include an EOF trailer for STUDENTS$; use the system end-of-file detection. (Assume that no student name will be EOF so that line 310 can remain unchanged.) In addition to the end-of-file error, your program must handle the following other possibilities.

1. The input file **TEST.FLE** does not exist; display an appropriate error message on the screen and terminate.

2. Invalid numeric data in the **TEST.FLE** file; display an error message, then ignore that data and continue processing.

3. The value of EXAMS might be zero, giving division by zero; display an appropriate error message, ignore that data, then continue processing.

4. Any other error: display an error message with the error code and line number, close the files, and terminate processing.

11-2 The table load and process program of Figures 9-5 and 9-6(b) does not include any error-handling capabilities. This problem involves writing the error-processing routines for the program. The program itself is to remain unchanged except that neither the **PAY.TBL** nor the **EMP.DAT** files will include trailer records. To this end, the statements of line 440 (Figure 9-5) and line 630 [Figure 9-6(b)] will be eliminated. End-of-file detection will be via the **ERR** 11. In addition, other errors that the routine must handle are:

1. The files **PAY.TBL** and **EMP.DAT** do not exist; display an appropriate error message at the terminal and terminate.

2. Invalid numeric data in the **PAY.TBL** file; print an error message to the screen, then ignore that data and continue loading the table.

3. Invalid numeric data in the **EMP.DAT** file; print an "invalid data" message to the file and the screen, then terminate processing.

4. Any other error: display an error message on the screen with the error code and line number, close the files, and terminate processing.

12

Principles of Subroutines

THE PROGRAMMED SWITCH

Basic Concepts

Earlier we learned that the conditional branch statement gives the computer the ability to modify the sequence of instruction execution according to conditions existing at a particular moment. We have seen how the IF can be used to determine whether or not a particular condition exists, and to specify what is to be done based on the result of the test. But sometimes the programmer faces a more complicated problem: that of not knowing whether a particular condition *has existed in the past* during execution of the program, as opposed to whether it currently exists. In such cases the program must modify its path on the basis of whether or not the particular condition has existed at *any time* during program execution. A technique has been developed whereby the program can "remember" whether or not a particular condition has occurred. This technique is often called the *programmed switch*.

The word "switch" brings to mind devices, such as the light switch, that are set in either of two ways that directly affect that which they control. The programmed switch does not immediately affect the path of the program, but it does have one thing in common with these other switches: It is set in one of two ways, and the ways are generally referred to as *on* and *off*. A programmed switch is nothing more than a storage area that can be assigned either of two values by the program, in order to indicate whether or not the desired condition has occurred. It is generally one character in length (although it may be more). The programmer commonly initializes the switch to one of its two values and then changes it to the other if the particular condition occurs. This is illustrated in Figure 12-1.

Using Integers as Logical Variables

We normally think of integer variables as containing numbers ranging from −32768 to 32767. However, they can be treated as *logical variables,* which are interpreted as being either true or false (refer to Chapter 5). An integer value of 0% corresponds to the logical value FALSE. Although any nonzero value is interpreted as true, the integer −1% (which is represented internally as all binary 1's) is normally used to represent the value TRUE. Referring to the example in Figure 12-1, the integer variable S% could be used as logical variable representing a switch as shown in Figure 12-2. In using the negation (for example, NOT S%), it is important to make certain that −1% is always used as the true value. Otherwise the negation will not work properly.

Figure 12-1
A programmed
switch

```
  .
  .
  .
220     S$ = "N"    !    SET SWITCH TO NO
  .
  .
  .
460     IF (condition) THEN S$ = "Y"  !  CHANGE SWITCH TO YES
  .
  .
  .
940     IF S$ = "Y" THEN (required action)
```

Figure 12-2

Using an integer as
a logical variable

```
  .                                                      .
  .                                                      .
220    S% = 0%   !   SET TO FALSE         220    S% = 0%   !   SET TO FALSE
  .                                                      .
  .                                                      .
  .                                                      .
460    IF  (condition)  THEN S% = -1%     460    IF  (condition)  THEN S% = -1%
  .                                                      .
  .                                                      .
  .                                                      .
940    IF S% THEN  (required action)      940    IF NOT S% THEN  (required action)
       ↑                                          ↑
```

S% will be treated
as a logical variable
having a value of either
TRUE (−1%) or
FALSE (0%) in this
context.

The NOT is called the
negation. If S% is
TRUE, then NOT S%
is FALSE. Here the
action takes place
only if S% is FALSE.

(a) Testing for the TRUE condition   (b) Testing for the FALSE condition

BASIC PRINCIPLES OF SUBROUTINES

The Concept of Modularizing

The programs we study in this book are relatively short in order to illustrate each new principle clearly. In business and industry applications programs usually consist of many somewhat individual components covering pages of code. If a large program is not well planned, the result can be a complete mess that is difficult to debug or understand, and is a disaster to attempt to modify or expand. With some creative thinking, most large jobs can be broken down into smaller components or *modules,* which are functionally independent of one another. For instance, consider Example 9-2 in which gross pay for employees is calculated. This program was broken down into two components. The first involves reading the pay rate table into an array (Figure 9-5), and the second involves actual processing of the employee file (Figure 9-6). Most large programming problems are well adapted to this approach. Furthermore, it makes good sense; the average human mind simply cannot grasp all the intracacies of a single large program. However, it can deal very well with a series of relatively small routines, each of which performs a specific function. To illustrate these principles, let us consider the following example.

Example 12-1 Each record in the payroll file PAYROL.FLE includes the following information.

> Code
> Employee Social Security number
> Pay rate
> Hours worked

For each employee with a Code value of 4, calculate the gross pay; for all hours over 40, use 1.5 times the regular rate. At the end of the report print a summary line of the total gross pay paid to all employees.

If we look at this problem from the point of view of logical functions to be performed, we can break it down into the following components.

> Initial operations:
>> Open files and perform initialization operations
>> Print headings
> Processing loop:
>> Read and locate next Code 4 record
>> Calculate pay
>> Accumulate subtotals and print
> Termination operations:
>> Print summary line
>> Close files

These can be represented schematically by the chart of Figure 12-3. Here the payroll program is shown to consist of the six indicated components. Note that this is *not* a flowchart. It does not indicate the program logic or the sequence in which components are executed. It merely shows the breakdown of the problem into components on the basis of the function they perform. These are often referred to as *top-down* charts and are very useful in representing the relationship of modules. To illustrate the further modularization of a component, consider the following exercise.

Exercise 12-1 In most applications payroll computations are quite complex. Assume that this module is to be further broken down into three others: gross pay calculation, withholding tax calculation, and Social Security withholding. Expand Figure 12-3 to represent these additions.

The GOSUB and RETURN Statements

In Chapter 5 we studied the concept of predefined functions for performing certain operations such as obtaining the square root of a quantity (SQR). Whenever the Basic system encounters the function name in a program, it brings in a special set of code from its library (a *subroutine*) and includes it within the program. Execution of the function involves branching to the subroutine where the computa-

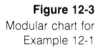

Figure 12-3
Modular chart for
Example 12-1

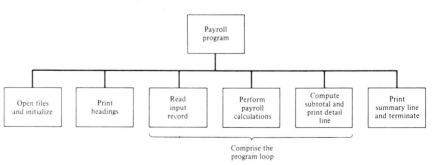

Figure 12-4

The concept of sub-
routine branching

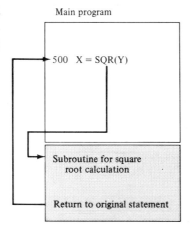

Main program

tions are performed, then branching back. This concept is illustrated in Figure 12-4. Here we see that control is transferred to the subroutine and then back to the statement that "called" the subroutine. With functions, these operations are automatic and we need not even be aware of them.

This broad "go to and return" capability is provided to the Basic programmer through use of the GOSUB and RETURN statements. For instance, let us assume that we have a special heading routine that we want executed at a certain point in the program. However, we wish to include the actual routine outside of the main program logic and place it beginning with line 2000. Use of the GOSUB and RETURN to accomplish this is shown in Figure 12-5. Here we see that

GOSUB 2000   and   GOTO 2000

operate the same in that they both cause a branch to statement 2000. However, the GOSUB causes the system to "remember" where it came from so that, upon encountering a RETURN, it returns to the statement following the GOSUB. In fact, since the system remembers, it is important always to terminate a subroutine such as this with a RETURN when continuing execution of a program.

Figure 12-5

The GOSUB and
RETURN statements

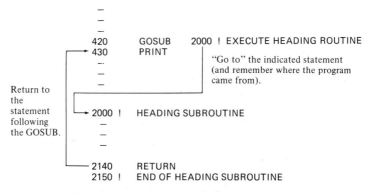

Figure 12-6

A modularized pro-
gram—Example
12-1

```
100 !      PAYROLL COMPUTATION - EXAMPLE 12-1                         &
    !
200 !      MAIN PROGRAM SEQUENCE
210 !                                                                  &
    !      INITIALIZATION OPERATIONS
220            GOSUB 1000                        ! OPEN FILES
230            GOSUB 2000                        ! PRINT HEADINGS
240 !                                                                  &
    !      PROCESSING LOOP
250            GOSUB 3000                        ! READ INPUT
260            IF FINISHED%                                            &
                 THEN GOTO 300                   ! EXIT LOOP
270            GOSUB 4000                        ! CALCULATE PAY
280            GOSUB 5000                        ! ACCUMULATE SUBTOTAL AND PRINT
290            GOTO 240                          ! REPEAT LOOP
300 !                                                                  &
    !      SUMMARY OPERATIONS
310            GOSUB 6000                        ! PRINT SUMMARY LINE & CLOSE FILES
320            GOTO 32767
330 !      END OF MAIN PROGRAM                                         &
    !      SUBROUTINES FOLLOW                                          &
    !
1000 !     *************************************************** &
     !     INITIALIZATION OPERATIONS                          &
     !     OUTPUT: FINISHED%, H$, D$, S$, FILES OPEN ON CHANNELS 1 AND 2
1010           OPEN "PAYROL.FLE" FOR INPUT AS FILE #1%
1020           OPEN "PAYROL.OUT" FOR OUTPUT AS FILE #2%
1030           ON ERROR GOTO 19000                               &
     !
1040           FINISHED% = 0%   ! FINISHED SWITCH - CHANGED TO   &
     !                                       "YES" ON EOF
1050 !                                                            &
     !     DEFINE IMAGE MASKS FOR PRINT USING
1060           H$ = "  SS NUMBER     HOURS       GROSS"    !HEADING
1070           D$ = "  \            \     ##.#     $$###,.##"  !DETAIL
1080           S$ = "             TOTAL GROSS:  $$#####,.##"   !SUMMARY
1090           RETURN
1100 !     END INITIALIZATION OPERATIONS                        * &
     !     *************************************************** &
     !
2000 !     *************************************************** &
     !     PRINT HEADING                                       &
     !     INPUT:   H$                                         &
     !     OUTPUT:  HEADING RECORD TO FILE
2010           PRINT #2%, USING H$
2020           PRINT #2%
2030           RETURN
2040 !     END PRINT HEADING
3000 !     *************************************************** &
     !     READ INPUT                                          * &
     !     INPUT:  FROM INPUT FILE                             * &
     !     OUTPUT:  C$, SSN$, RATE, HOURS
3010           INPUT #1%, C$, SSN$, RATE, HOURS
3020           IF C$<>"4"                                       &
                 THEN GOTO 3010          ! GET NEXT RECORD
3030           RETURN
3040 !     END OF READ INPUT                                    * &
     !     *************************************************** &
     !
```

Through use of the **GOSUB** capability, the program of Figure 12-6 is
completely modularized. The following commentary relates to this program.

1. The main program segment consists of a series of **GOSUB**s to various
routines illustrated in Figure 12-3. The overall program logic is relatively
straightforward.

Figure 12-6
(continued)

```
4000 ! ************************************************* &
     ! CALCULATE GROSS PAY                           * &
     ! INPUT: HOURS AND RATE                           &
     ! OUTPUT: GROSS
4010     RHOURS = HOURS      \ OTHOURS = 0.0
4020     IF HOURS > 40.0                               &
         THEN                                          &
             RHOURS = 40.0                         \ &
             OTHOURS = HOURS - 40.0
4030     GROSS = RHOURS * RATE + OTHOURS * RATE * 1.5
4040     RETURN
4050 ! END OF CALCULATE GROSS PAY                    * &
     ! ************************************************* &
     !
5000 ! ************************************************* &
     ! PRINT DETAIL LINE                               &
     ! INPUT: SSN$, HOURS, GROSS, D$                   &
     ! OUTPUT: TOTAL, RECORD TO FILE
5010     TOTAL = TOTAL + GROSS
5020     PRINT #2%, USING D$, SSN$, HOURS, GROSS
5030     RETURN
5040 ! END OF DETAIL LINE PRINT                      * &
     ! ************************************************* &
     !
6000 ! ************************************************* &
     ! PRINT SUMMARY AND CLOSE                        *
6010     PRINT #2%
6020     PRINT #2%, USING S$, TOTAL
6030     CLOSE #1%, #2%
6040     RETURN
6050 ! END OF PRINT SUMMARY                          * &
     ! ************************************************* &
     !
19000 ! ************************************************* &
      ! ERROR TRAP
19010     RESUME 19020
19020     IF ERR = 11                                  &
          THEN                                         &
              FINISHED% = -1%                      \ &
              GOTO 3030
19030 ! ELSE
19040         PRINT "UNEXPECTED ERROR:"
19050         PRINT "ERROR = "; ERR; "ERROR LINE = "; ERL
19060         PRINT "PROCESSING TERMINATED"
19070         CLOSE #1%, #2%
19080         GOTO 32767
19090 ! END OF ERROR TRAP ***************************** &
      ! ************************************************* &
      !
32767    END
```

2. The program is terminated by the switch **FINISHED%**, which is set to **TRUE** (−1%) in the error routine when an end of file is read in the read routine.

3. Each individual subroutine is documented regarding what it is, the input quantities required, and the output it produces. For instance, the pay calculation routine (beginning at line 4000) requires **HOURS** and **RATE** (input to the subroutine) and produces **GROSS** (output from the subroutine). This type of documentation is essential if modules of a particular program are divided among several programmers.

4. Each subroutine is terminated by a RETURN statement, which returns execution to the statement following the GOSUB.

One other important aspect of modularizing programs in this way is that later changes or additions are localized to individual modules. For instance, if the method of computing overtime pay is to be changed, the programmer knows exactly where to go in making the change. This is not the case with many large programs that were put together without much preplanning and subsequently have had patches added here and there over a period of time.

Exercise 12-2 A clever programmer decided to modify the processing loop of Figure 12-6 using the FOR-UNTIL as follows:

```
250    FOR I%=1% UNTIL FINISHED%
260        GOSUB 3000 !READ INPUT
270        GOSUB 4000 !CALCULATE PAY
280        GOSUB 5000 !PRINT DETAIL
290    NEXT I%
```

This involves a basic error. What is it?

More on the GOSUB

Another important feature of the GOSUB is that a given subroutine can be executed from two or more places in a program. To illustrate this, let us consider the following expansion of Example 12-1.

Example 12-2 The program of Example 12-1 is to be modified to provide for printing no more than 50 detail lines per page. After the 50th line skip to a new page; headings are to be printed at the top of each page.

This example involves a new concept: *page* control. The paper commonly used with computer printers is perforated so that, once printed, it can be separated into convenient sheets. Most computer printers include special features that allow the paper carriage mechanism to be coordinated with the page size. Upon performing a *form feed,* the printer will advance the paper to the top of the next page. For example, the Basic programmer who is preparing an output report and writing it to channel 2 would direct the printer to perform a form feed by using the following statement.

```
PRINT #2%, CHR$(12%);
```

For now we use this because it works; we will learn the significance of CHR$(12%) in Chapter 14.

Figure 12-7

Forms control—
Example 12-2

```
2000  !  PRINT HEADING
2005       PRINT #2%, CHR$(12%);
2006       L% = 0%   !  SET LINE COUNT TO 0
2010       PRINT #2%, USING H$
  .
  .
  .
5000  !  PRINT DETAIL
5010       TOTAL = TOTAL + GROSS
5015       IF L% = 50%              &
             THEN GOSUB 2000
5016       L% = L% + 1%   !   INCREMENT LINE COUNT
5020       PRINT #2%
  .
  .
  .
```

With this the modifications to our modularized program are relatively simple, as we can see by referring to the program segments of Figure 12-7. There are three items of importance to note in this example.

1. By modularizing the program the modifications required by this change consist simply of adding a few lines. They are: line 2005, to perform the form feed prior to printing headings; line 2006, to set the line counter to zero; line 5015, to execute the heading routine after 50 lines have been printed; and line 5016, to increment the line counter.
2. The heading subroutine is executed from two different points in the program: lines 230 and 5015. Execution will always return to the statement following the GOSUB from which the subroutine was executed.
3. A subroutine can be executed from within another subroutine. For instance, line 280 says GOSUB 5000. Within the subroutine at 5000 line 5015 says (on a conditional basis) GOSUB 2000. It is perfectly valid to execute a subroutine from within another subroutine. Upon encountering a RETURN, control is always returned following the last executed GOSUB.

Exercise 12-3 What would happen in the program modification of Figure 12-7 if statement 2006 were omitted?

MORE ON PROGRAM MODULARIZATION

The ON-GOSUB Statement

Occasions will sometimes arise in a program where one of several subroutines is to be executed depending upon a particular set of conditions at the time. For instance, let us assume that at a particular point in a program one of five different subroutines is to be executed depending upon the value of the variable I%; this is illustrated in Figure 12-8. The nested IF statements shown in Figure 12-9 will

Figure 12-8

Multiple selection

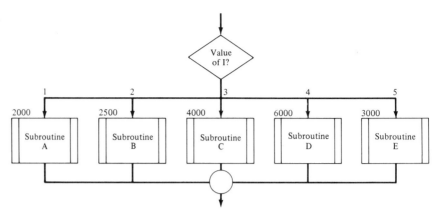

Figure 12-9

Multiple selection
using IF statements

```
      .
      .
      .
450   IF I% < 1% OR I% > 5%                            &
      THEN                                             &
        PRINT 'OUT OF RANGE IN GOSUB SELECTION' \ &
        STOP
460   IF I% = 1% THEN GOSUB 2000                       &
      ELSE                                             &
      IF I% = 2% THEN GOSUB 2500                       &
      ELSE                                             &
      IF I% = 3% THEN GOSUB 4000                       &
      ELSE                                             &
      IF I% = 4% THEN GOSUB 6000                       &
      ELSE GOSUB 3000
470   ...
      .
      .
      .
```

perform the required operation. Here if I% is 1, then the first condition test is true and the subroutine at 2000 is executed. Upon return from the subroutine execution continues to the next statement (at line 470). If I% has a value of 2, the first test condition is false so execution goes to the **ELSE** option. There the test condition is true so the subroutine at line 2500 is executed and, upon returning, execution continues to line 470, and so on.

For special cases such as this in which the test condition depends upon consecutive whole number values, a special multiselection statement may be used. It is illustrated in Figure 12-10. Here we see that the control variable determines which statement in the list is selected. If I% is 1, then the first statement is selected; if 2, then the second statement; and so on. Upon execution of the subroutine, encountering the **RETURN** will cause execution to continue at line 470.

If the control variable (or expression) is floating point, it will be truncated to yield an integer. If the control variable is not, in this case, in the range of 1–5 (since there are five line numbers in the list), error 58 will occur:

```
?ON STATEMENT OUT OF RANGE AT LINE 460
```

Figure 12-10
The ON-GOSUB
statement

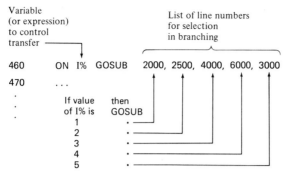

Variable
(or expression)
to control
transfer

List of line numbers
for selection
in branching

460   ON I% GOSUB   2000, 2500, 4000, 6000, 3000
470   . . .

If value   then
of I% is   GOSUB
1
2
3
4
5

For this reason, whenever there is any doubt a test should be made prior to the **ON-GOSUB** (line 450 of Figure 12-9).

Sometimes we want to enter a single subroutine at different points within the subroutine. (The point at which entry to a subroutine is made is called the *entry point*.) For instance, let us assume that we have a subroutine that begins at line 20000 and ends at line 20370. Furthermore, it has three entry points: 20000, 20060, and 20120. The **ON-GOSUB** in Figure 12-11 causes a selection of the entry point according to the value of the variable R% (1, 2, or 3).

Figure 12-11
Multiple entry points
in a subroutine

```
480        ON R% GOSUB 20000, 20060, 20120
   .
   .
   .
20000 ! SUBROUTINE XYZ...
   .
   .
20060 ! ENTRY POINT 2
   .
   .
20120 ! ENTRY POINT 3
   .
   .
20370    RETURN
20380 ! END OF SUBROUTINE XYZ
```

Exercise 12-4 Write an **ON-GOSUB** statement (and whatever else is necessary) to select the subroutine to be executed based on the variable A% as follows:

VALUE OF A%	LINE
1	1000
2	1700
4	2500
6	3000
7	4000
8	3000

Menu Control

Let us assume that our employer wishes us to design a system for handling special data files. The programs required for the file handling system are: (1) create a new file; (2) kill an existing file; (3) add records to an existing file; (4) delete records from an existing file; and (5) make corrections to records of an existing file. There are basically two ways to approach this: one would be to prepare five independent programs; the other would be to write one large program with each of the functions modularized. With the latter approach the user must deal with but one program. The selection of which function is to be performed is commonly handled by use of a *menu*. A menu is simply a list from which the user can make a desired selection. A menu approach to this problem is illustrated in Figure 12-12, which also includes a sample dialog. The key to this solution is use of the **ON-GOTO** statement in line 420. Note that this statement works in exactly the same way as the **ON-GOSUB**. The difference is, of course, that there no automatic return is involved.

Menu control of access to various components of a program is a commonly used technique. It is a convenient method for providing easy-to-remember access to numerous operations, and is often used to control and/or limit access among users to particular operations.

Exercise 12-5 What would occur in Figure 12-12 if line 410 were omitted and a user entered 6 at line 400?

MULTIPLE PROGRAM SYSTEMS

The CHAIN Statement

The approach used in Figure 12-12 to consolidate several programs as components of a single large program and then operate from a menu is often very convenient. However, in some cases it is not possible because the resulting program is too large for the computer. Sometimes even a single program is too large for the system. In cases of this type it is necessary to segment the program into relatively independent component programs, each of which may be called into memory when needed. For example, let us assume that we have prepared a very large program named STAT.BAS, which performs an extensive statistical analysis. Much to our disappointment, we find that it is too large for the computer. Hence we carefully examine it and break it down into two components. PREP.BAS reads the raw data, validates it, performs preliminary calculations, and writes the processed data to a file. From there ANAL.BAS performs the required statistical analyses on the processed data. Then we could simply run PREP, and when it is completed, run ANAL. Actually, this process is simplified by means of the CHAIN statement, which allows one program to call another into memory for execution (thus

Figure 12-12

A menu program

```
      .        Open files and perform
      .        other operations common
      .        to all functions.
300 !    MENU SCHEDULE
310         PRINT "THIS IS THE FILE MAINTENANCE PROGRAM.
320         INPUT "DO YOU WISH TO CONTINUE";Q$
330         IF Q$<>"YES"              &
            THEN                       &
              CLOSE ...           \ &
            GOTO 32767
340         PRINT "THIS IS THE FILE MAINTENANCE PROGRAM."
350         PRINT "THE OPTIONS AVAILABLE TO YOU ARE:"
360         PRINT "  1 - CREATE A NEW FILE"
360         PRINT "  2 - KILL AN EXISTING FILE"
370         PRINT "  3 - ADD RECORDS TO A FILE"
380         PRINT "  4 - DELETE RECORDS FROM A FILE"
390         PRINT "  5 - CORRECT AN EXISTING RECORD"
400         INPUT "WHICH OPTION DO YOU WANT (1,2,...)";Q%
410         IF Q%<1% OR Q%>5%                          &
            THEN                                        &
              PRINT "OPTION MUST BE BETWEEN 1 & 5."  \ &
            GOTO 400
420         ON Q% GOTO 15000, 16000, 17000, 18000, 19000
      .
      .
      .
15000 ! FILE CREATE ROUTINE
      .
      .
      .
15980    PRINT "FILE CREATION COMPLETED"
15990    GOTO 320
      .
      .
      .
16000 ! FILE KILL ROUTINE
      .
      .
      .
16990    GOTO 320
      .
      .
      .
32767    END


THIS IS THE FILE MAINTENANCE PROGRAM.
DO YOU WISH TO CONTINUE? YES
THE OPTIONS AVAILABLE TO YOU ARE:
  1 - CREATE A NEW FILE
  2 - KILL AN EXISTING FILE
  3 - ADD RECORDS TO A FILE
  4 - DELETE RECORDS FROM A FILE
  5 - CORRECT AN EXISTING RECORD
WHICH OPTION DO YOU WANT (1,2,...)? 1
      .
      .              (Creation dialog)
      .
FILE CREATION COMPLETE
DO YOU WISH TO CONTINUE?
```

"overlaying" itself). To accomplish this, the last executable statement in PREP would contain a statement such as:

```
30000    CHAIN "ANAL"
```

or

```
30000    CHAIN "ANAL" 100
```

Assuming that PREP has been run and has encountered statement 30000, the following would take place.

1. All files opened in PREP would be closed. However, this is accomplished with a so-called "fast close" and some data will probably be lost for output files. Thus opened files should be closed with a CLOSE statement prior to chaining.

2. The program named ANAL will be loaded into memory.

3. Execution of ANAL will begin. In the first version of statement 30000 execution will begin at the first line of the program. In the second, it will begin at line 100 as designated in the CHAIN statement. (*Note*: Chaining to a designated line number will lose privilege for a privileged program; the concept of privileged programs is not discussed in this book.)

4. If desired, ANAL can also chain to another program. There is no limit in this respect.

Communication Using Core Common

Since chaining from program A to program B causes B to replace A, all variables in A are lost. If a large number of values are to be carried over, then they must be written to a file. However, if a small amount (up to 127 characters or bytes) is to be transmitted, then a specially reserved area of storage can be used. This area, called *core common,* consists of 127 positions and is not changed when one program replaces another. However, the programmer has access to it through special system functions. Although a large number of system functions are available to the programmer, only two are covered in this book: that to put information into core common and that to get it out. These two functions are illustrated in Figure 12-13. In statement 200, 32 characters of information are placed in core common. In statement 300 (which would most likely be in a chained program) the data in core common would be accessed and placed in the string variable X$. Let us consider how chaining and use of core common can be combined to provide a powerful menu control capability.

Using a Menu Program

Referring to the menu application of Figure 12-12, let us make the following assumptions. (1) Each of the five options represents large sections of code and

Figure 12-13
Core common
system functions

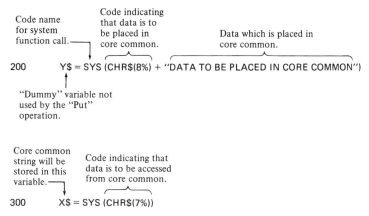

Code name
for system
function call.

Code indicating
that data is to
be placed in
core common.

Data which is placed in
core common.

200   Y$ = SYS (CHR$(8%) + "DATA TO BE PLACED IN CORE COMMON")

"Dummy" variable not
used by the "Put"
operation.

Core common
string will be
stored in this
variable.

Code indicating that
data is to be accessed
from core common.

300   X$ = SYS (CHR$(7%))

must be written as an independent program. The programs will be named **CREATE, KILL, ADD, DELETE,** and **CORREC.** (2) Access to them must be *only* by way of a menu program that chains into the selected program. Thus **MENU** represents the controlling program that provides access to each of the five component programs of the system. This concept is illustrated in Figure 12-14.

Figure 12-15 includes the menu program itself and relevant portions of the **CREATE** and **KILL** programs. The following commentary describes important aspects of this example.

1. Access to the system is via running menu.

2. Menu places the name of the program selected into core common (line 240) before chaining to the appropriate program (line 250). Although the information transmitted is the program name, it could be any desired sequence of characters.

3. Each of the maintenance programs gets core common (line 110) and then checks to ensure that the proper information is stored (line 120). If the program were entered by the **RUN** command, core common would not be properly loaded and execution would be terminated (**GOTO 32767**).

4. With this menu system the user need not remember the name of each program within the system.

Figure 12-14
Menu control over
several programs

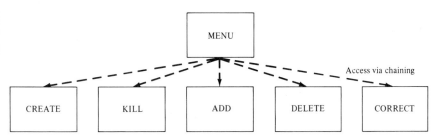

```
Figure 12-15    1      !   FRONT END MENU PROGRAM.                          &
A front-end             !  PROVIDES ACCESS TO CREATE, KILL,                 &
menu program            !  ADD, DELETE AND CORREC.                          &
                        !
              200      PRINT "This is the menu for the file handling system."
              210      PRINT "The options available to you are:"          \ &
                       PRINT "  1 - create a new file"                    \ &
                       PRINT "  2 - kill an existing file"                \ &
                       PRINT "  3 - add records to a file"                \ &
                       PRINT "  4 - delete records from a file"           \ &
                       PRINT "  5 - correct an existing record"           \ &
                       PRINT                                              \ &
                       INPUT "Which option do you want";Q$
              220      OPTION$ = ""
              230      IF Q$ = "1" THEN OPTION$ = "CREATE"        &
                       ELSE                                       &
                       IF Q$ = "2" THEN OPTION$ = "KILL"          &
                       ELSE                                       &
                       IF Q$ = "3" THEN OPTION$ = "ADD"           &
                       ELSE                                       &
                       IF Q$ = "4" THEN OPTION$ = "DELETE"        &
                       ELSE                                       &
                       IF Q$ = "5" THEN OPTION$ = "CORREC"        &
                       ELSE                                       &
                           PRINT "Invalid response - try again"  \ &
                           GOTO 210
              240      Y$ = SYS(CHR$(8%) + OPTION$)
              250      CHAIN OPTION$
            32767      END




              1        !   PROGRAM CREATE ...
              100      !   FIRST GET CORE COMMON
              110        C$ = SYS(CHR$(7%))
              120        IF C$<>"CREATE" THEN GOTO 32767
               .
               .
               .
            32767      END




              1        !   PROGRAM KILL ...
              100      !   FIRST GET CORE COMMON
              110        C$ = SYS(CHR$(7%))
              120        IF C$<>"KILL" THEN GOTO 32767
               .
               .
               .
            32767      END
```

And so on for ADD, DELETE and CORREC.

5. By controlling access to the programs of a system in this way, a number of techniques can be used to establish different security levels for various functions.

   Menu techniques such as these are widely used; they represent a convenient "user friendly" approach to simplifying the use of a system.

Answers to Preceding Exercises

12-1 The payroll calculations box would be further subdivided as follows:

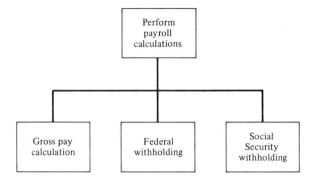

12-2 The end of file will be detected in the read subroutine (executed from line 260). Since the **FOR-NEXT** loop test is not made until the loop is completed, statements 270 and 280 will be executed without a new record being read. Thus the last employee will be processed twice.

12-3 Since all numeric variables are initialized to zero, the line counter would function properly for the first page and print a new set of headings on page 2. However, L% would continue to be incremented beyond 50 and line 5015 would never see another true condition. Thus there would be no more page control.

12-4
```
460      ON A% GOSUB 1000, 1700, 29000, 2500,
         29000, 3000, 4000, 3000
           .
           .
           .
29000    !DUMMY SUBROUTINE
29010       RETURN
```

12-5 Since there are only five line numbers in the list, an error 58 would occur.

Programming Problems

12-1 Programming Problem 9-10 involves reading a data file into a two-dimensional array and processing the data in the array. Write a fully modularized program that includes (but is not limited to) the following modules.

1. File open module. Prints appropriate description at terminal and asks the user for the name of the input data file. If no such data file, then gives appropriate error message. Opens files.

2. Initialization module. Initializes all necessary variables.

3. Heading module. Prints appropriate report headings (including date).

4. Data input module. Reads the data into the array SC.

5. Class average calculation module. Calculates required class average and prints results.

6. Student total module. Calculates and prints total score for each student.

7. Termination module. Prints termination message and closes files.

Ask the user if another processing run is desired upon completion. If yes, then rerun the program; otherwise terminate execution.

12-2 This problem involves sorting and merging two sets of data (see Programming Problems 9-4 and 9-5). The files **A.DTA** and **B.DTA** each contains no more than 50 numeric data values. The data from each of the files is to be read into an in-memory array, printed to an output file, sorted into ascending sequence, and the sorted values printed. (Print 10 data values per line.) In the next step merge the data values into a third array such that the elements of the third array are in ascending sequence. (Note that if the elements from the input arrays are selected properly, the third array elements will be in sequence and will not require sorting.) Print the elements of the third array, 10 per line.

Fully modularize your program.

12-3 An engineering company runs a wide variety of tests on the electronic components it manufactures. For each test run, a record is maintained of the test number and hours before failure of the component. The following information for each test group is stored in a data file.

	FIELD	DESCRIPTION
Header record 1	Test number	4 digits
	Value of zero	
Header record 2	Test number	
	Description	Maximum length = 15
	Date	mmddyy (month, day, year)
Next records	Test number	
	Hours before failure	5 digits, 2 places
		to right of decimal

The data file is composed of a complete test series, which consists of many individual groups as above, each preceded by two header records. The entire file is terminated by a system end of file.

Write a program to compute the average number of hours before failure for each group and the average number of hours for the entire test series. The program should be completely modularized. This problem involves the concept of level breaks, which is described in the next programming problem. Figure 12-16 is a flowchart representation of the logic which, to a limited extent, is applicable to this problem.

12-4 For each budget transaction a company maintains a record in its budget control file with the following information.

Department number (integer)
Budget code (5 characters)
Original budgeted amount (not to exceed 9,999.99)
Expenditures to date (not to exceed 9,999.99)

Each department (department number) will have one record for each budget code which it uses. For instance, department 2219 might include 12 different records, one for each of its 12 budget codes. Data within the file has been sorted in such a way that records for each department are grouped together. Processing the file involves processing each group of records for each department. Printed output for each department must begin on a new page and must include:

1. Appropriate page headings (including the department number) and column headings.

2. One line for each input record, which includes a line count within this department group, the budget code, original budgeted amount, expenditures to date, and budget balance (budgeted amount less expenditures).

3. A summary line that includes totals for all of the figures in item 2.

At the end of the report print grand totals for all three values printed on the detail lines.

Processing of this type is called *level break* processing. It involves following a particular sequence of operations until a change occurs in one of the fields (Department number in this case). Then other action is taken (usually summaries printed) and processing resumes. The overall logic of this solution is illustrated in the flowchart of Figure 12-16. The processing rectangle with double vertical lines is commonly used to indicate a subroutine. Note that three of the subroutines are executed from two different places in the flowchart representation. Modularization of this program should follow the lines suggested by the flowchart.

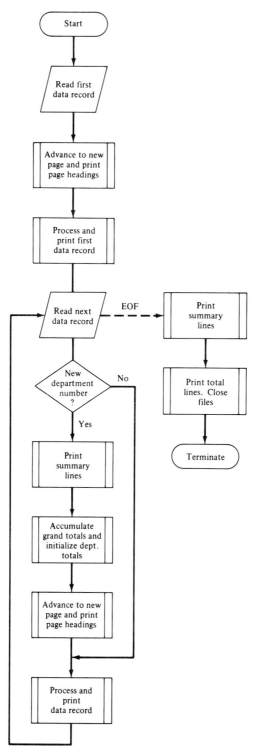

Figure 12-16
Flowchart for
Problem 12-3

Start

Read first
data record

Advance to new
page and print
page headings

Process and
print first
data record

Read next
data record — EOF → Print
summary
lines

New
department
number
? — No →

Yes

Print total
lines. Close
files

Print
summary
lines

Terminate

Accumulate
grand totals and
initialize dept.
totals

Advance to new
page and print
page headings

Process and
print
data record

User-Defined Functions

SINGLE-LINE FUNCTIONS

The built-in functions available in Basic provide a convenient and powerful tool. The Basic language is further enhanced by the provision for the user to define functions. There are two broad categories of user-defined functions: those consisting of one line and those consisting of multiple lines. Let us first consider single-line functions.

Assume that we have a program to calculate accumulated interest in several different places using the formula:

$$I = P(1 + r/100)^t - P$$

where P = principal
r = interest rate, in percent
t = time, in years

This is a natural situation for a subroutine in which we can transmit to the routine the values of P, r, and t and get back the value of I. The function gives us that ability. Every user-defined function must be identified as a function by the letters FN followed by the function name (any valid variable name). For instance, the following are valid function names.

> FNA%—user-defined integer function named A%
> FNINTR—user-defined floating-point function named INTR

Definition of the function requires the word DEF (define function), followed by the name and the arguments, followed by the definition of the operations. For instance, the desired interest function could be defined as shown in Figure 13-1. It is important to recognize that this definition represents a model of the function that indicates the operations to be performed. In itself, *it does not cause any calculations to occur*. For this, it must be used just as any other function such as SQR. For instance, let us assume that in two different places in a program we must calculate the interest. At line 500 the principal, interest rate, time, and interest amount must be printed (the "input" values are stored in the variables PR, RATE, and T2). At line 820 the interest must be calculated for the principle A, rate IR, and time TM. The result is to be multiplied by 2 and stored in the variable TI. This is illustrated in Figure 13-2. Here it is *imperative* to recognize that the variables P, R, and T in the

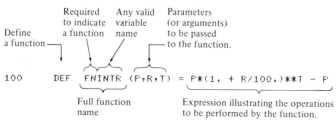

Figure 13-1
Single-line function definition

Figure 13-2
A user-defined
function

```
100    DEF FNINTR(P,R,T) = P*(1. + R/100.)**T - P
  :
  :
500    PRINT PR, RATE, T2, FNINTR(PR,RATE,T2)
  .
  .
  .
820    TI = 2.0*FNINTR(A,IR,TM)
```

function definition (line 100) are *dummy* variables (also called *formal* parameters). They are used to indicate the relationship between the argument list and the variables in the expression. That is, when statement 500 is executed, PR, RATE, and T2 will effectively be substituted for P, R, and T in the function definition. (PR, RATE, and T2 are commonly called *actual* variables.) Similarly, when statement 820 is executed A, IR, and TM will be substituted.

Further points relating to user-defined functions are as follows: First, the number of arguments that can be used can range from zero to five. However, any call to a function must include the exact number of arguments as shown in the definition. Second, the function can be integer, floating point, or string, as required by the programmer. That choice must be reflected in the function name selected.

Exercises 13-1 In using the interest function defined in Figure 13-1 a programmer became confused about the order of the arguments and wrote:

```
820    TI = 2.0*FNINTR(IR,A,TM)
```

Note that the principal amount and interest rate are switched. Would this result in an error condition? What would happen?

13-2 Define a function which, when given hours, minutes, and seconds, will convert them to seconds. Use integer values throughout. Then write an example program statement to calculate the number of seconds in 4 hours, A% minutes, and B% seconds.

MULTIPLE-LINE FUNCTIONS

Interest Calculation with Error Checking

Although single-line functions are convenient for some applications, operations are commonly required that involve many more than a single line of code. To illustrate, let us assume that the interest calculation of the preceding single line involves several lines of checking to ensure that the data is within allowable limits. The definition would then appear as illustrated by Figure 13-3. Here we see that the function definition line includes only the function name and the argument list. The operations to be performed are defined in subsequent lines. The definition is ended by the FNEND statement.

Figure 13-3
General form of a
multiple-line function
definition

```
DEF   FNINTR(P,R,T)
  .        ⎫ Body of function:
  .        ⎬ statements which comprise
  .        ⎭ operations to be performed.
FNEND
```

Example 13-1 Write a function that will calculate either interest or accumulated amount (principal and interest) using the following formula.

$$I = P(1 + r/100)^t - P$$
$$A = P(1 + r/100)^t$$

The function call must have the form

`FNINTR(T$,P,R,T)`

where **T$** = value of "I" means calculate interest I; any other value
means calculate amount A
P = Principal amount
R = rate, in percent
T = time, in years

If any of the arguments **P, R,** or **T** are negative, return a value of zero.

Characteristics of Multiline Functions

The function definition and two examples of using it are shown in Figure 13-4. The following commentary describes points of note relative to this example and to user-defined functions in general.

1. The function definition may be included at any point in the program. It need *not* be defined before it is used (as we see in Figure 13-4). Many installations have standard line number ranges reserved for functions (for instance, lines 17000–18999).

2. The result is returned to the main program at line 10050 through a **LET** statement in which the value is assigned to the function name (*without* the argument list). This is the proper way to return the result.

3. In the first function call (line 360), values for principle, interest rate, and time, together with the calculated interest, are printed. (Presumably, the input values to the function came from earlier statements in the program.) Note that the first argument is the string value "I." This indicates to the function that interest only is to be calculated (see line 10040).

Figure 13-4

A multiple-line function—Example 13-1

```
360       PRINT PRINC, IRATE, YEARS, FNINTR("I",PRINC,IRATE,YEARS)

450       PRINT "YOU CAN GET THE INTEREST ONLY OR THE TOTAL AMOUNT."
460       INPUT "DO YOU WANT INTEREST ONLY"; Q$
470       IF Q$ = "YES"                        &
             THEN C$="I"                        &
             ELSE C$="A"
480       INPUT "PLEASE ENTER PRINCIPAL, RATE & TIME"; PR, RT, Y
490       S = FNINTR(C$,PR,RT,Y)
500       IF S=0                                            &
          THEN                                              &
             PRINT "PRINCIPAL, INTEREST & RATE MUST BE > ZERO."   \ &
             PRINT "PLEASE REENTER YOUR VALUES."                  \ &
             GOTO 480

10000 ! FUNCTION FOR INTEREST CALCULATION
10010     DEF FNINTR(T$,P,R,T)
10020        IF P<=0 OR R<=0 OR T<=0            &
             THEN                               &
                INTR = 0                     \ &
                GOTO 10050
10030        INTR = P*(1. + R/100.)**T
10040        IF T$="I"                          &
                THEN INTR = INTR - P
10050        FNINTR = INTR !   RETURN RESULT
10060     FNEND   !    END OF INTEREST FUNCTION

32767     END
```

4. The second function call (line 490) involves an interactive situation. Here the user is allowed to key in the type of calculation required (interest only or total amount) and the principal, rate, and time. Line 500 checks the value returned to ensure that all values entered were valid.

5. The dummy arguments defined in the function (T$, etc., in this example) are meaningful only within the function. If one or more are modified in the function body, it will have no influence on the equivalent variable in the call. For instance, the statement

```
10005    T=T+1.0
```

in the function of Figure 13-4 would increase the value of T by 1.0 for calculation in the function. However, it would not change the value of YEARS (line 360) or of Y (line 490) in the main program.

6. Any variable used in the function body that is not defined as a dummy argument is treated as simply another variable in the program. For example, assume that in the main program of Figure 13-4 the variable INTR is used to represent some type of interval that is incremented as follows:

```
810    INTR=INTR+0.1
```

This is an unfortunate choice of names because INTR is used as a working variable in the function (line 10030). Upon execution of the function, the value from line 810 would be destroyed. Obviously, care must be taken in selecting working variable names within the function that are not likely to be used in the main program.

7. The function may be floating point, integer, or string, as determined by the selection of the function name. The arguments may also be floating point, integer, and/or string, and are totally independent of the function mode.

8. The main program should never branch into a function; execution must always be from the normal function call (as in statement 490). Similarly, exit from a function must always be via the FNEND; do not simply GOTO a statement outside the function in order to exit from it.

Exercise 13-3 A utility bills on the basis of usage and type of customer. Types A and B are charged a flat $20. All others are charged as follows:

> 1.80 × units used, if units used are less than 10.
> 2.12 × units used, if units used are equal to or greater than 10.

Write a function that uses customer type and units use as arguments and returns the charge.

Answers to Preceding Exercises **13-1** The computer knows only by position. Thus, the first argument, which is the interest rate IR, would be used as the principal amount and the principal, which is A, would be used as the interest rate. There would be no error but the results would likely be quite incorrect.

```
13-2 100    DEF FNSEC%(H%,M%,S%)=3600%*H% + 60%*M% + S%

     300    T%=FNSEC%(4%,A%,B%)


13-3 100    DEF FNCHARGE(T$,U)
     110    IF T$='A' OR T$='B'              &
               THEN C=20                     &
               ELSE                          &
                 IF U<10                     &
                   THEN C=1.8*U              &
                   ELSE C=2.12*U
     120    FNCHARGE=C
     130    FNEND
```

Programming Problems

13-1 Basic-Plus includes a string function (INSTR) to search a string and determine whether or not the string includes a particular sequence of characters. For instance, we might wish to know if the three-character sequence "PQR" is contained in the string F$. The problem involves writing a function to search a string to determine if it includes a particular combination of characters (a substring). Following are two examples of the function call.

```
A% = FNSEARCH%(F$,B$)

B% = FNSEARCH%(L$,"@@")
```

In the first, F$ will be searched to determine whether or not it includes the value of B$. In the second, L$ will be searched to determine whether or not it contains two consecutive @ characters. The value returned from the function is to be zero if the search is unsuccessful and equal to the number of the character position at which the search is successful. For instance, if L$ were

```
ABC429@@7XYZ
```

the value returned in the second example of the function call would be 7.

Do not use the INSTR function; use only the string functions of Chapter 8. Also, write a test program to test your function.

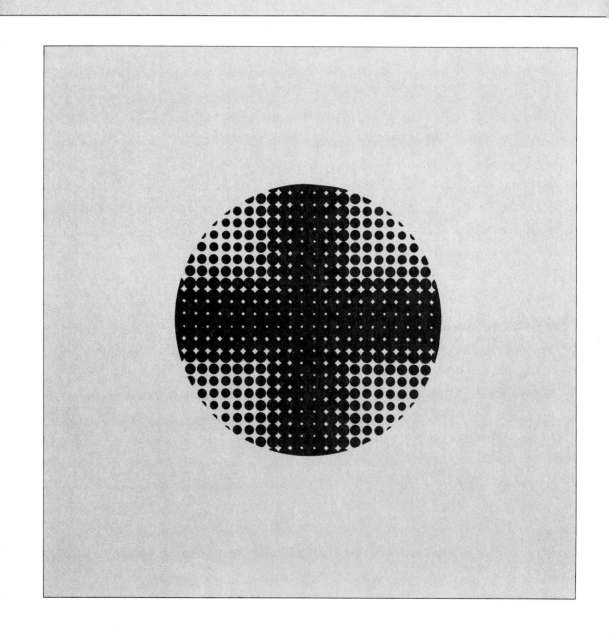

14

Advanced String Operations

BASIC CONCEPT OF ASCII CHARACTERS

The ASCII Character Set

To this point our interest in string data has been fairly superficial. As we know, a string field can be whatever length the program requires. In dealing with a particular value, for example,

```
B$ = "EXAMPLE STRING FIELD"
```

we see it as written and recognize that it has a length of 20. We have given no consideration to the internal form in which it is stored. In Chapter 8 reference was made to the character set in Appendix II. This character set is commonly referred to as the *ASCII* (*A*merican *S*tandard *C*ode for *I*nformation *I*nterchange) character set and represents the internal coding that is used. The ASCII set is a 7 binary-digit code with values that range from binary 0000000 to binary 1111111. The decimal equivalents of these values are 0 and 127. Thus the ASCII set consists of 128 characters.

The first 32 ASCII characters are special control characters, some of which are discussed later in this chapter. The rest are printable characters with which we are familiar: special characters, digits, uppercase letters, and lowercase letters. The decimal equivalent of the binary representation for each character is given in the ASCII table. For instance, the binary coding for the letter A (which is 1000001) has the decimal equivalent of 65. Although for most applications the programmer need not be concerned with these values, some operations do require reference to them.

Exercises **14-1** What is the decimal equivalent of each character in "PDP 11/70"?

14-2 What does the following ASCII coding represent?

66 97 115 105 99 45 80 108 117 115

The CHR$ and ASCII Functions

For certain operations it is convenient to be able to convert a numeric value to its ASCII character or to obtain the decimal value of an ASCII character. The former is done with the CHR$ function and the latter with the ASCII function. Both of these functions operate on a single character of data. For instance, Figure 14-1 illustrates the CHR$ function. Line 200 creates a single character whose ASCII value is 67 (the letter C), then stores it in the string variable A$. The result of printing A$ is shown at the right. The other three examples involve concatenating characters one at a time with the results shown. The reader should study each of these carefully to ensure a good understanding.

The opposite operation is performed by the ASCII function as is illustrated in Figure 14-2. At lines 600 and 710 the ASCII value of the letter C (67) is stored in

Figure 14-1

The CHR$ function

	Statement(s) executed	Then the statement PRINT A$ would yield:
200	A$ = CHR$(67%)	C
300	A$ = CHR$(74%) + CHR$(47%) + CHR$(52%)	J/4
400	A$ = " "	
410	A$ = A$ + CHR$(I%) FOR I% = 97% TO 104%	abcdefgh
500	A$ = " "	
510	A$ = A$ + "+" FOR I% = 1% TO 9%	+++++++++

Figure 14-2

The ASCII function

	Statement(s) executed	Then the statement PRINT A% would yield:
600	A% = ASCII("C")	67
700	A$ = "C"	
710	A% = ASCII(A$)	67
800	A$ = "ABCDE"	
810	A% = ASCII(MID(A$,4%,1%))	68
900	A$ = "ABCDE"	
910	A% = ASCII(A$)	65

A%. At line 810 the ASCII function uses the MID function as an argument, which, in turn, refers to the fourth character (D) in A$. At line 910 we see that A$ has a length of 5. Since the ASCII function operates only on a single character, it uses the first one (A) in A$.

Exercises **14-3** What will be stored in Z$ after execution of the following statements?

```
X$ = "R"
Z$ = CHR$(ASCII(X$) + 32%)
```

14-4 Assuming that X$ contains only letters A–Z, what will be stored in Z$ after execution of the following statements? Explain what happens.

```
Z$ = " "
Z$ = Z$ + CHR$(ASCII(MID(X$,I%,1%)+32%))
     FOR I%=1% TO LEN(X$)
```

CONTROL CHARACTERS

Imbedding a Control Character in a String Field

Consider the string formed by the following statement.

```
A$ = CHR$(68%)+CHR$(45%)+CHR$(52%)+CHR$(54%)
```

We recognize A$ as being composed of the four characters D-46 and as having a length of 4. We can print A$, operate on it with the LEFT, MID, and RIGHT functions, use the LEN function to obtain its length, and concatenate other strings to it with predictable results. However, what if we build a string that includes control functions? For instance, consider:

```
B$ = CHR$(68%)+CHR$(10%)+CHR$(52%)+CHR$(54%)
```

As with A$, the length of B$ is 4 but what about the second character in the string? Referring to the ASCII table, we see that it is defined as the LINE FEED character. It is important to recognize that within storage the computer does not "see" a control character as being different from any other character. Thus we can operate on B$ in exactly the same way as we operate on A$.

Now, the question is, "What happens if we attempt to print B$?" For the answer to this, let us consider how a serial printing device such as a terminal printer works. (Terminals are called *serial* because they handle characters one at a time as they are transmitted from the computer.) If our program says

```
PRINT B$
```

then the characters that make up B$ are transmitted to the terminal one at a time. When the code 68 (the first character of B$) is transmitted, the terminal's internal circuitry causes it to perform a particular operation. This operation, of course, is to print (or display) the letter D. Then the next character, which is code 10, is transmitted and the internal circuitry performs the operation indicated by a 10. Rather than displaying a letter or some other character, the code 10 causes a "line feed" operation to take place. In other words, the terminal skips to the next line. Note that it does *not* also perform a carriage return (that operation is a code 13). Then transmission of the third and fourth characters causes the 4 and 6 to be displayed: This concept is illustrated in Figure 14-3. The result of printing A$ is rather obvious. The result of printing B$ is also obvious—that is, once we understand just how the output devices interpret control characters. Although four characters were transmitted to the terminal, only three characters were printed. One of them (the second) caused the line feed operation to occur with the results we see in Figure 14-3.

Exercise 14-5 Show what you would anticipate the output to be if the following X$ were printed on a terminal.

```
X$ = CHR$(49%)+CHR$(50%)+CHR$(10%)+CHR$(8%)+CHR$(51%)+CHR$(52%)
```

Figure 14-3
(a) Displaying print-
able information.
(b) The effect of an
imbedded
control character

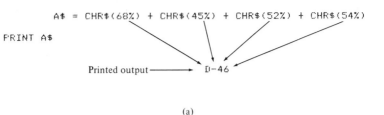

(a)

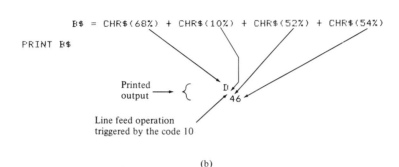

(b)

OTHER CONTROL CHARACTERS AND THEIR USES

Although ASCII includes 32 control characters, only a handful are commonly used in most programming applications. Those we study here (in addition to those of the preceding chapter) are: NULL (0), BELL (7), FORM FEED (12), and CARRIAGE RETURN (13).

The BELL Character

Chapter 13 covers the concept of errors and error recovery. As pointed out, interactive programs involve extensive error checking. In general, the greatest source of erroneous data comes when it is entered into the computer. Therefore every effort should be made to check accuracy. For instance, let us assume that we have a data entry program that accepts personnel information. Each field involves special checks. The Social Security number, for example, might be checked to ensure that it has a length of nine and consists only of digits. If it is not, then the program must alert the operator. Simply displaying an error message will usually be insufficient since a good data entry operator is looking at the source document rather than the screen. The BELL character (7) provides an audio alarm in the form of a buzzer or bell that is built into most terminals. Its use is illustrated in Figure 14-4. Here we see use of a function to perform error checking. If an error is detected, the function FNSSN.ERR% is given a value of true, which is tested at line 660. The true condition causes the value of BELL$ [which is CHR$(7)] to be transmitted to the terminal preceding the message. This causes the terminal bell (or buzzer) to be sounded, thus alerting the operator.

Figure 14-4

An error routine to
alert the operator

```
110    ┌─ BELL$ = CHR$(7%)    !    DEFINE THE BELL CHARA AS BELL$
  .     │
  .     │
  .     │
650     │ INPUT "SOCIAL SECURITY NUMBER"; SSN$
660     │ IF FNSSN.ERR%(SSN$)                               &
        │ THEN                                              &
Causes terminal ─── PRINT BELL$; "BAD SS NUMBER -- TRY AGAIN"   \ &
bell to ring        GOTO 650
  .
  .
  .
19300   ! SOCIAL SECURITY NUMBER CHECK FUNCTION

19310   DEF FNSSN.ERR%(SSN$)
19320      X% = 0%         ! INITIALLY SET ERROR TO FALSE
19330      IF LEN(SSN$)<>9%                      &
           THEN                                  &
              X% = -1%                           \ &
              GOTO 19380
19340      FOR ISSN% = 1% TO 9%
19350         ISSN$ = MID(SSN$,ISSN%,1%)
19360         IF ISSN$<"0" OR ISSN$>"9"          &
              THEN                               &
                 X% = -1%                        \ &
                 GOTO 19380
19370      NEXT ISSN%
19380      FNSSN.ERR% = X%
19390   FNEND
19399   ! END OF SS NUMBER CHECK
  .
  .
  .
```

The FORM FEED Character

Example 14-2 involves the concept of page control: that is, when a printed page is filled, the printer advances to a new page. Some hard copy terminals and most line printers include a built-in feature that allows for page control. On most of these devices a selector switch can be set to correspond to the length of the printed form (usually 8½ or 11 inches). Then by properly positioning the paper relative to the control unit of the printer, detection of a form feed character will cause the paper carrier to position to the top of the next page. A common means of including this in a program is to define the CHR$(12)—the form feed character—as a variable such as illustrated in Figure 14-5. When the form feed character is transmitted, it causes the paper carrier to advance to the top of the next page and then perform the required printing operation. If this code is transmitted to a CRT or a printer that does not include forms control capability, the result will depend upon the particular machine. Usually a few lines are skipped.

The CARRIAGE RETURN Character

In general, our concept of the carriage return key relates to what we see occurring, whether on a typewriter or on a terminal. We depress the return key and the printing element (or cursor) returns to the left-most position and progresses to a new line. Technically speaking, the return key on a terminal transmits only a

Figure 14-5
Using the form
feed character

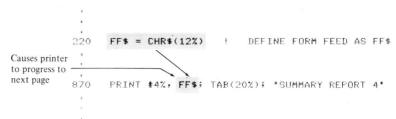

Causes printer
to progress to
next page

```
220   FF$ = CHR$(12%)   !   DEFINE FORM FEED AS FF$


870    PRINT #4%, FF$; TAB(20%); "SUMMARY REPORT 4"
```

CARRIAGE RETURN character (13); the computer appends a LINE FEED character. The carriage return and line feed are generally used as a pair. (In another section of this chapter we see how these two characters mark the end of a line.) It is sometimes convenient to use the carriage return/line feed combination within a print statement as shown in Figure 14-6.

Exercise 14-6 The first statement 620 in Figure 14-6 includes two occurrences of CRLF$. Why does it not cause two blank lines to be printed instead of one (as illustrated by the equivalent statement 620)?

The NULL Character

In some special instances it is necessary to transmit characters to the terminal that cause it to do nothing. For instance, assume that we have a portable terminal that is printing out a program listing. The characters that comprise the lines of the program are being transmitted in a continuous stream with no pause between lines (as indicated by imbedded carriage return and line feed characters). Now, what happens when the terminal performs the physical operation of carriage return while the characters are still being transmitted? Some terminals include a buffer storage into which they can be stored; then the terminal prints at a higher speed to catch up. On unbuffered terminals they will simply be lost. This can be compensated for by preceding each line in the code being transmitted to the terminal with a series of NULL characters that will provide time for the physical return operation. If the terminal is ready to continue printing and null characters are still being transmitted, they will be ignored.

Figure 14-6
Using the carriage
return line feed
combination

```
230    CRLF$ = CHR$(13%) + CHR$(10%)   !   DEFINE CR AND LF
  .
  .
  .
620    PRINT BELL$; "!!WARNING!!"; CRLF$; CRLF$; "VALUES TOO LARGE"

     is equivalent to

620    PRINT BELL$; "!!WARNING!!"           \ &
       PRINT                                \ &
       PRINT "VALUES TOO LARGE"
```

CURSOR CONTROL

The CRT terminal provides the programmer with considerable versatility in controlling the position of the cursor. This section deals with the relatively basic cursor control capabilities found in most CRT terminals. They are: cursor movement (left, right, up, and down), home the cursor, clear a line, clear the screen, and direct cursor addressing. Unfortunately codes to perform cursor functions are not standardized within the industry. In other words, those that will work with one make of terminal might not work on a terminal of another manufacturer. Examples in this section are written for the DEC VT52.

The Concept of an Escape Character

Escape characters are commonly used in communications equipment to modify the meaning of a character. When an escape is detected, the character immediately following it will be interpreted to mean something entirely different from its normal meaning. For instance, if the code 74 is transmitted to a CRT terminal, it will cause the terminal to display the letter J. However, if the code 74 is preceded by an escape character, it will not display a J but will perform some other action (which depends upon the make of the terminal). In Basic-Plus the escape is coded for the computer as a CHR$(155%). Cursor control operations require use of the escape.

The Home and Clear Operation

In many applications, such as menu display, it is convenient to *home* the cursor (position it in the upper left corner) and clear the screen before beginning printing. This is done in two steps: home and clear.

OPERATION	REQUIRED CODE	GENERATED WITH
Home	Escape followed by "H"	CHR$(155%) + "H"
Clear to end of screen	Escape followed by "J"	CHR$(155%) + "J"

Use of the home and clear is shown in Figure 14-7. Note that the clear operation clears from the cursor to the end of the screen. Anything preceding the cursor, on the same or another line, is left unchanged.

Exercise 14-7 Would it make any difference in the home and clear operation if HOME.CLEAR$ were defined as follows? Explain your answer.

```
210    HOME.CLEAR$ = CHR$(155%) + "J" + CHR$(155%) + "H"
```

Figure 14-7

The home and
clear operation

```
                                                                 Clear the screen
                                                                 from the cursor to
                                              Home the cursor.    the end of the screen.
    210    HOME.CLEAR$ = CHR$(155%) + "H" + CHR$(155%) + "J"


    360    PRINT HOME.CLEAR$; "THIS IS THE FILE MAINT...
```

Transmission of this string of four characters causes the home and clear.

This message is printed beginning the upper left corner of the screen.

Cursor Movement and Line Clear

It is possible to move the cursor one position at a time up, down, right, or left without destroying the information over which it moves by using the following.

OPERATION	REQUIRED CODE	GENERATED WITH
Cursor up	Escape followed by "A"	`CHR$(155%) + "A"`
Cursor down	Escape followed by "B"	`CHR$(155%) + "B"`
Cursor right	Escape followed by "C"	`CHR$(155%) + "C"`
Cursor left	Escape followed by "D"	`CHR$(155%) + "D"`

For instance, a common operation is to move the cursor back a certain number of positions, and then clear the rest of the line (from the new cursor position). This operation is illustrated in Figure 14-8. In this example the cursor is moved left 10 positions (line 440) and the line is cleared (line 450). Then the question mark for the INPUT statement appears at the position to which the cursor was moved. Presumably a prompt message precedes it on the line.

Exercise 14-8 Why are semicolons used in lines 440 and 450 of Figure 14-8?

Figure 14-8

Cursor positioning
and line clear

```
220    CUR.LEFT$ = CHR$(155%) + "D"    !  CURSOR LEFT
230    CLEAR.LINE$ = CHR$(155%) + "K"  !  CLEAR TO END OF LINE


440    PRINT CUR.LEFT$; FOR I% = 1% TO 10%  !  MOVE LEFT 10
450    PRINT CLEAR.LINE$;                   !  CLEAR TO END OF LINE
460    INPUT Q$
```

Direct Cursor Addressing

Most CRTs now available provide for *direct cursor addressing*. That is, the cursor position can be specified by the desired line number and column number. However, in addition to the escape character and a code (the letter "Y" for the VT52), a line number code and a column number code (up to 24 and 80, respectively, for most terminals) are also required. An example of the use of direct cursor addressing is shown in Figure 14-9. Note that direct positioning requires a four-position string for the control operation.

Exercise 14-9 A common operation in an interactive system is to print instructions or some type of menu on the upper portion of the screen and then use the lower half (lines 13–24) for user "conversation." The idea is to leave the instructions on the screen at all times. Write a control string (call it MID.CLEAR$) to position the cursor beginning at line 13 and clear the lower half.

PROCESSING A FIXED FORMAT SEQUENTIAL FILE

Records in a Sequential File

Whenever a record is printed to a sequential file, the computer converts all numeric quantities to ASCII, inserts appropriate spacing, adds the carriage return (13) and line feed (10) characters to the end, and writes it to the output device. Thus a file on disk would appear as illustrated in Figure 14-10. This example illustrates four numeric fields in the record shown. If these are to be read by an input statement such as

```
INPUT #4%, A,B,C,D
```

then they must be stored as shown, *including* the commas that separate fields. (This is identical to the manner in which we would enter them from the keyboard.) The significance of the line terminator becomes apparent if the subject record is read by the following.

```
INPUT #4%, A,B,C
```

Here the values read would be

    A—13.1
    B—16.2
    C—1.9

Since the input list includes only three variable names, the value 3.311 would be ignored. The system searches for the line terminator in order to be ready to start on the next record when another INPUT statement is executed.

Figure 14-9

Direct cursor positioning

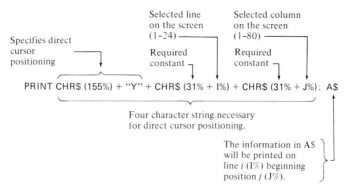

Specifies direct cursor positioning

Selected line on the screen (1–24)

Selected column on the screen (1–80)

Required constant

Required constant

PRINT CHR$ (155%) + "Y" + CHR$ (31% + I%) + CHR$ (31% + J%); A$

Four character string necessary for direct cursor positioning.

The information in A$ will be printed on line *i* (I%) beginning position *j* (J%).

Figure 14-10

Data records in disk storage

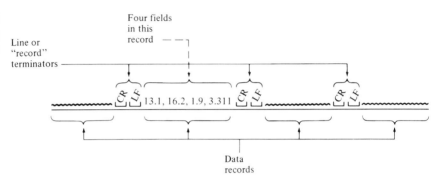

Line or "record" terminators

Four fields in this record

13.1, 16.2, 1.9, 3.311

CR LF

CR LF

CR LF

Data records

To write a sequential file that is to be used as later input is a clumsy procedure because field separating commas must be used. Furthermore, if a string field contains the comma character, it will be interpreted as a delimiter, thus ending that field. One means of avoiding this problem is through use of the INPUT LINE statement.

The INPUT LINE Statement

To illustrate the INPUT LINE statement, let us consider the following example.

Example 14-1 Each record of an input file is exactly 32 characters in length and contains the following data.

FIELD	POSITIONS
Inventory number	1–7
Item description	8–28
Quantity on hand	29–32

Because the item description may contain the comma character, it would not be possible to use an ordinary INPUT statement to read. However, the INPUT LINE statement will read the entire record, *including the terminating carriage return and line feed characters,* into a single string quantity. Let us assume that the file of Example 14-1 has been opened on channel 3 and the next record is read by the INPUT statement in Figure 14-11. Execution of the print statements that follow the input illustrates characteristics of the record. We should note that the entire record, including commas and the terminating CR-LF, is read as a single string. The last print statement separates the fields for convenient human consumption.

Exercise 14-10 If the last print statement of Figure 14-11 were repeated (giving two lines as with the second), would there be a blank line between the two lines of output? Explain.

Updating Numeric Quantities—the VAL and NUM1$ Functions

Assuming that L$ contains the data record illustrated in Figure 14-11, then the quantity on hand could be placed in Q$ by the statement

```
Q$ = MID(L$,29%,4%)
```

We should note that it is stored as a string quantity and not as an integer; thus arithmetic operations using ordinary arithmetic operators are not possible. There are two ways of handling this—one uses string arithmetic functions (which are not covered in this book), and the other involves converting it to a numeric form. Conversion is accomplished with the VAL function; examples of its use are given in Figure 14-12.

The NUM1$ function converts the other way, as illustrated in Figure 14-13. The first two examples are reasonably straightforward; the third is more complex.

Figure 14-11
The INPUT LINE statement

```
INPUT LINE #3%, L$ ◄──── Note: Only one string variable in list.

PRINT LEN(L$)
34 ◄───────────────────── L$ includes data (32 characters) and the
                          carriage return and line feed.

PRINT L$ \ PRINT L$
1576339U-BOLT, 13/16, BRONZE0675 ◄─── Printed by first print-statement.
                                 ◄─── Blank line due to CR and LF.
1576339U-BOLT, 13/16, BRONZE0675 ◄─── Printed by second print-statement.
                                 ◄─── Blank line due to CR and LF.


PRINT LEFT(L$,7%);"  ";MID(L$,8%,21%);"  ";MID(L$,29%,4%)
1576339  U-BOLT, 13/16, BRONZE   0675
```

Figure 14-12
The VAL function

```
A$ = "123.456"        String variable with length of 7.
A  = VAL(A$)          Converted to floating point in A.

B% = VAL(A$)          Converted to integer (123) in B%.

C$ = "-95.06"         String variable has length of 6 (including −).
C  = VAL(C$)          Converted to floating point in C.

D$ = "2,387.65"       String variable with length of 8 (including , and . ).
D  = VAL(D$)          Produces an error since the comma, is not
                      allowed in a numeric field.
```

Figure 14-13
The NUM1 function

```
A% = 2107%                      Integer quantity in A%
A$ = NUM1$(A%)                  converted to string with length of 4.

B  = -157.683                   Floating−point quantity in B
B$ = NUM1$(B)                   converted to string with length of 8
                                (includes − and .).

C% = 32%                        Two−digit integer in C% converted
C$ = RIGHT(NUM1$(1000%+C%),2%)  to string with a leading zero (032);
                                length of 3.
```

Frequently, in building an output line to be written as a fixed format record (such as Example 14-1), leading zeros must be included to fill out the field. That is the purpose of the technique in the third example of Figure 14-13.

Now to apply all of this, let us assume that Example 14-1 involves updating the inventory file to take into account additions to and deletions from the file. This will involve reading each record, asking the operator for additions and deletions, performing the calculations, and then writing a new record. In general sequential files are updated by rewriting an entirely new file. Schematically the process for this example would be as illustrated in Figure 14-14. A skeleton program for this operation is shown in Figure 14-15. For the sake of simplicity, no error-checking routines have been included. Overall the operation is reasonably straightforward. Note the form used in statement 570 to ensure that the quantity field is four characters long.

Although the INPUT LINE has been used in reading input from files, it can be used for input from the keyboard as well. In fact, if data to be entered from the keyboard includes punctuation and spaces, and it must be entered into a single string exactly as keyed, then the INPUT LINE should be used.

Figure 14-14
Updating a
sequential file

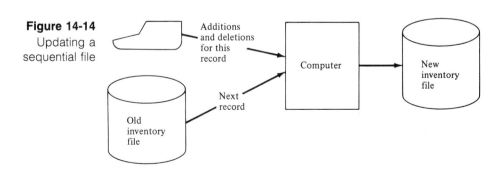

243   PROCESSING A FIXED FORMAT SEQUENTIAL FILE

Figure 14-15

A program segment
to update a sequen-
tial file

```
120   OPEN 'INVEN.OLD' FOR INPUT AS FILE #3%
130   OPEN 'INVEN.NEW' FOR OUTPUT AS FILE #4%
  .
  .
  .
500   INPUT LINE #3%, L$
510   S$ = LEFT(L$,7%)
520   Q% = VAL(MID(L$,29%,4%))
530   PRINT 'NEXT INVENTORY ITEM:'; S$
540   INPUT 'ADDITIONS TO STOCK:'; A%
550   INPUT 'DELETIONS FROM STOCK:'; D%
560   Q% = Q% + A% - D%   ! UPDATE STOCK
570   L$ = LEFT(L$,28%) + RIGHT(NUM1$(10000%+Q%),2%)
580   PRINT #4%, L$
590   GOTO 500
```

Exercises 14-11 A programmer included the following statement in a program and received an error message. Why?

```
340    INPUT LINE A$,B$
```

14-12 In response to the following statement ABCDE was entered at the terminal. What is the length of X$?

```
400    INPUT LINE X$
```

OTHER STRING FUNCTIONS

The CVT$$ Function

The CVT$$ function is a powerful string manipulation feature of Basic-Plus. It performs a wide variety of manipulations on a string to produce a new string. These are summarized in Table 14-1.

For example, a value of 4% can be used to eliminate the CR and LF from an INPUT LINE string as follows:

```
300    INPUT LINE L$
310    L$ = CVT$$(L$,4%)
```

A careful inspection of the codes in Table 14-1 reveals that each is a power of 2. Thus each combination of two or more will give a unique result. As a result they can be used in combination with one another (by adding them together). For instance, the example shown in Figure 14-16 will convert all lowercase to uppercase, except for the characters inside the quotes.

Exercise 14-13 Write a statement to delete leading and trailing spaces and tabs from the field P$ and then add three asterisk characters to the end of it. The result should be in R$.

Table 14-1

A$ = CVT$$(S$,K%)

Converts the source string S$ to a new string (in A$ in this example). The conversion is performed according to the value of the integer represented by K% as follows:

1%	Trim the parity bit.
2%	Discard all spaces and tabs.
4%	Discard excess characters: CR, LF, FF, ESC, RUBOUT, and NULL.
8%	Discard leading spaces and tabs.
16%	Reduce spaces and tabs to one space.
32%	Convert lowercase to uppercase.
64%	Convert [to (and] to).
128%	Discard trailing spaces and tabs.
256%	Do not alter characters inside quotes.

The INSTR Instruction

In string processing a common operation is to search a string for a particular substring. For instance, it might be necessary to determine if a string contains the consecutive letters JR or the single character "=". Basic-Plus includes the powerful INSTR function for this purpose. To illustrate its use, let us assume that we must search the string A$ for a single occurrence of "JR." If found, it must be deleted. Use of the INSTR function to search for JR is illustrated in Figure 14-17. If the value returned to I% is zero, JR was not found and so A$ is left unchanged. The example illustrates what occurs if I% is not zero (meaning JR was found). If the scan must be continued for further occurrences, this can be done within a loop by using a variable as the first argument.

Figure 14-16
The CVT$$ function

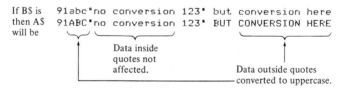

Answers to Preceding Exercises

14-1 80 68 80 32 49 49 47 55 48

14-2 Basic-Plus

14-3 R in X$ is converted to r in Z$.

14-4 The uppercase letters that comprise X$ will be converted to lowercase in Z$. We can see that the MID function provides one character at a time from X$ beginning with the first (I% = 1%) and ending with the last [I% = LEN(X$)].

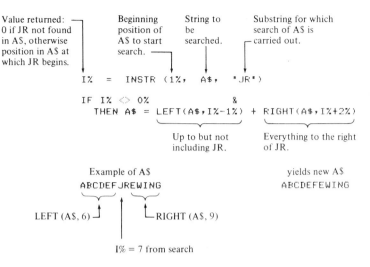

Figure 14-17
The INSTR function

Value returned: 0 if JR not found in A$, otherwise position in A$ at which JR begins.

Beginning position of A$ to start search.

String to be searched.

Substring for which search of A$ is carried out.

```
I% = INSTR (1%, A$, "JR")

IF I% <> 0%                        &
    THEN A$ = LEFT(A$,I%-1%) + RIGHT(A$,I%+2%)
```

Up to but not including JR.

Everything to the right of JR.

Example of A$
ABCDEFJREWING

LEFT (A$, 6)

RIGHT (A$, 9)

yields new A$
ABCDEFEWING

I% = 7 from search

14-5   In this example the line feed is followed by a backspace code (8), which causes the terminal to back up one space before continuing the output.

```
12
 34
```

14-6   The first CRLF$ causes a break in the current line. The second causes a new line where the printing continues. Thus there is only one blank line.

14-7   Yes. It would cause the screen to be cleared from wherever it is positioned to the end of the screen. Anything preceding the cursor would remain on the screen. Then the home operation would take place, leaving the remaining screen display unchanged (as opposed to the entire screen being cleared).

14-8   After a print statement the cursor will be moved to the next line automatically unless the semicolon is included.

14-9

```
MID.CLEAR$ = CHR$(155%) + "Y" + CHR$(44%)       &
    + CHR$(32%) + CHR$(155%) + "J"
```

14-10 No, since the last MID function does not access the CR-LF from L$.

14-11 The INPUT LINE statement may specify only one string variable in its "list."

14-12 The length is 7; X$ includes the CR and LF characters.

14-13 R$ = CVT$$(P$, 136%) + '***'

Programming Problems

14-1   In interactive programs it is quite common to request a user to enter some numeric response in answer to a question. For instance, a menu program might require a numeric entry from 1 to 10; a quizzing program might ask for a question number from

1 to 75; and so on. In such instances two different error conditions commonly arise. First, the quantity entered may not be numeric and, second, the quantity entered may not be within the allowable range. This problem involves writing a function, which is illustrated by the following sequence of code.

```
300   INPUT "PLEASE SELECT AN OPTION BETWEEN 1 AND 9"; N$
310   N% = FNNUM.CHECK%(N$,1%,9%,"Y")
320   IF N% = -32768% THEN GOTO 300
```

The purpose of the function is to check to ensure that the number entered into N$ is (1) numeric and (2) within the allowable range (this is a function option). Referring to the sample call of statement 340, the arguments of the function call are:

> First argument (N$)—numeric quantity to be tested
> Second argument (1%)—smallest allowable value for the number
> Third argument (9%)—largest allowable value for the number
> Fourth argument ("Y")—"Y" for "Yes, the range check is to be performed."
> "N" for "No, the range check is not to be performed"

If the number is valid and within the range (if required in the particular test), then return its numeric value. If invalid, the function should print an appropriate error message and return a value of –32768.

14-2 Keyboard entry of a line of data (with INPUT LINE) is normally signaled to the computer by depressing the RETURN key. However, the LINE FEED and ESCAPE keys can also be used. Where the RETURN key causes the two characters carriage return (13) and line feed (10) to be appended to the line, the other keys involve different characters to be appended. For the first portion of this program you are to write a short program that will show you what these appended characters are.

Then write a program to accept text from the keyboard and write it to an output file. One or more lines from keyboard input are to form one line of output as controlled by terminating an input line with the appropriate key as follows:

> RETURN   To this line it will be necessary to concatenate the next line entered.
> LINE FEED   Concatenate this input line to previous lines (if any) and write to the output file.
> ESCAPE   Concatenate this input line to previous lines (if any), write to the output file, and then write a form feed.
> CONTROL Z   Terminate input (this is the end-of-file indicator for keyboard entry—ERR 11).

The following input and corresponding output illustrate what is to be done.

Input:

THIS TEST (CR)

LINE IS (CR)

SHORT. (LF)

BUT IT (CR)

```
ILLUSTRATES THE POINT.(CR)

OKAY? (ESC)

NEXT PAGE. (LF)
```

control Z

Output:

```
THIS TEST LINE IS SHORT.

BUT IT ILLUSTRATES THE POINT. OKAY?
```

(skip to new page)

```
NEW PAGE.
```

14-3 This problem involves writing a subroutine to allow changes to be made to name and address file. Input to the routine is to be via the following program variables.

N$—person's name (maximum length: 20)
ADDR$—street address (maximum length: 20)
CITY$—city (maximum length: 14)
STATE$—state (length: 2)
ZIP$—Zip code (length: 5)

Figure 14-18
Sample screen displays

```
1)   Name:      Alfred Jones
2)   Address:   123 Okay St.
3)   City:      Oakland
4)   State:     CA
5)   Zip:       94123

Line to be corrected (enter 0 if no more corrections)?▓
```

At this point, user enters 2 and hits RETURN

```
1)   Name:      Alfred Jones
2)   Address:   ▓_____
3)   City:      Oakland
4)   State:     CA
5)   Zip:       94123
```

At this point, user enters new address and hits RETURN

```
1)   Name:      Alfred Jones
2)   Address:   6251 Better Ave.
3)   City:      Oakland
4)   State:     CA
5)   Zip:       94123

Line to be corrected (enter 0 if no more corrections)?▓
```

At this point, user corrects another line or enters 0 to terminate this sequence.

The routine is to display the values and ask if corrections are desired as illustrated by the example screen frames of Figure 14-18. This program is intended to use direct cursor control. The only change to the screen display is to be the requested line change. In that case delete the previous value, fill the line with the underscore character equal in number to the allowable field length, and position the cursor at the beginning.

Output from the subroutine is the same as the input, including corrections made within the subroutine. For any corrections made in N$, ADDR$, or CITY$ the lengths should be 20, 20, and 14 respectively. For any that are less than the required length, pad to the right with spaces in order to make them the maximum length.

14-4 Each record of an address data file contains a person's name, street address, city and state, and Zip code. For instance, the following is a typical record.

`AL JONES/4762 WINDY WAY/SAN FRANCISCO CA/99123`

Notice that fields are separated by the slash character and that the city and state are treated as a single field. The objective of the program is to print mailing labels. For each record, the program must:

1. Access each field from the record.

2. With the exception of the first letter in each word, convert letters to lowercase, except for the state, which is to remain uppercase.

3. Print an address label for each person; for instance, the above would print as follows:
Al Jones
4762 Windy Way
San Francisco CA 99123

Note that the Zip code is separated from the state by two spaces. Assume that the labels on which the addresses are printed are six lines in height.

For a greater challenge, write the program to handle labels that are "three across." This is illustrated in Figure 14-19.

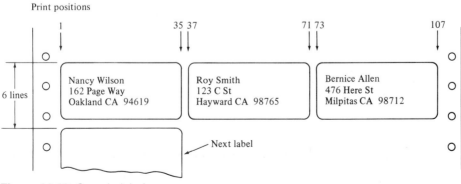

Figure 14-19 Sample labels

15

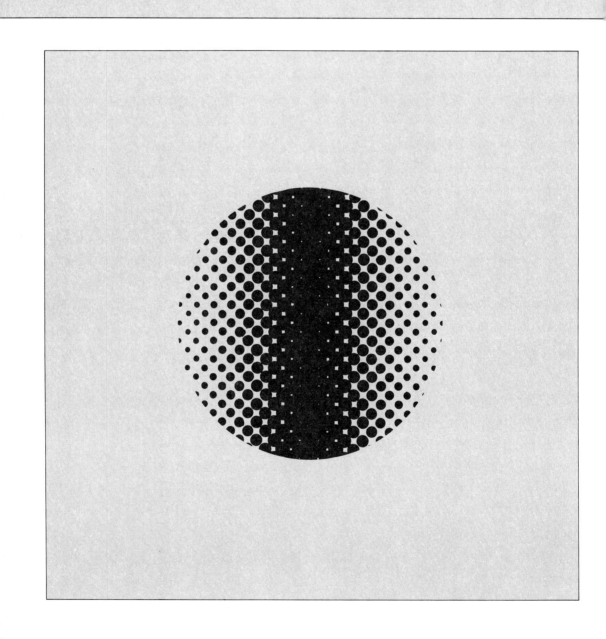

Virtual Array Storage

USING ONE-DIMENSIONAL VIRTUAL ARRAYS

The Concept of Virtual Storage

In Chapter 11 we learned the principles of subscripted variables and arrays. Through the use of subscripts it is possible to have large quantities of data "instantly at our fingertips." However, two problems often crop up when using arrays. The first is that the amount of available memory within a program is limited—which, in turn, limits the size of the array. For instance, a floating-point array consisting of 10,000 elements would simply not fit into memory. The second problem is that when execution of our program is terminated, the array is lost. Remember, the elements of an array are no different from ordinary variables that are held in memory during program execution. Thus if the data in an array is to be saved, it must somehow be written to a file for later reading back and use.

Both of these problems are resolved in Basic-Plus with *virtual array storage*. Virtual storage means that the operating system combines the use of internal memory and disk storage in such a way that the memory size appears to be far greater than it actually is. Thus in the case of virtual array storage the array is actually stored on disk but the programmer operates on it as if it were an ordinary in-memory array. The array can be many times the memory size and, in fact, is limited only by available disk storage. The operating system automatically controls the "swapping" of needed portions of the array into and out of memory as execution of the program progresses. The concept of virtual storage is illustrated in Figure 15-1.

The Virtual Array as a File

Let us assume that we are looking at a program and we spot the statement:

```
470    X = 3.2*A(I%) - 22.1
```

Without looking further it would be impossible to tell whether **A** is an ordinary in-memory array or a virtual array that resides on disk. This is an extremely

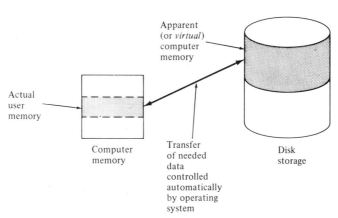

Figure 15-1
The concept of virtual storage

Apparent (or *virtual*) computer memory

Actual user memory

Computer memory

Transfer of needed data controlled automatically by operating system

Disk storage

important factor as it simplifies programming considerably. However, it is important to recognize that the virtual array is indeed a file and must be opened and closed as is the case with any file. This implies then that each virtual array file to be used within a program must be associated with a channel number. To illustrate, let us assume that a virtual array consisting of 5000 floating-point elements is stored on disk as the file EXAMPL.ARY. Figure 15-2 illustrates typical statements that might be found in a program processing this array. Notice that the file open statement does not designate this as a virtual array file; it is simply another file to the system. However, the DIM statement does relate the file EXAMPL.ARY to the program array name A through the channel number.

In dealing with files we normally think in terms of input (INPUT) and output (PRINT). In working with virtual array files the fact that we are dealing with input and output is rather subtle. However, it is helpful in working with virtual arrays to recognize that input and output are, in fact, involved. For example, the statement

```
X = A ( I% )
```

is effectively an input statement since it brings a value from the array file into memory. Similarly, the statement

```
A ( J% ) = Y
```

is effectively an output statement since it places a new value from memory into the file.

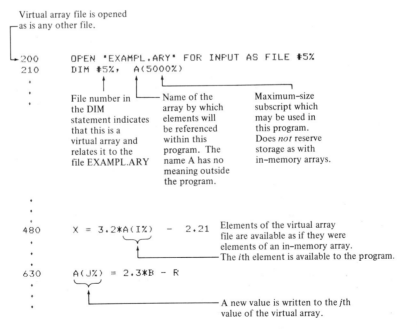

Figure 15-2

The virtual array OPEN and DIM statements

One very important aspect of virtual array files is that data within them may be accessed *randomly*. That is, elements of the file need not be accessed in the order in which they are stored as is the case with sequential files. For instance, the program can process the 789th element, then the 36th element, and so on.

Creating a New Virtual Array File

The following example illustrates many characteristics of virtual array files.

Example 15-1   The sequential file STAT.DAT contains raw statistical data; each record consists of one integer data value. The maximum number of values will be 10,000. A program is required to read each value from STAT.DAT, convert it to "processed form" using a special user-defined function named FNCONVRT%, and write it to the newly created virtual array file STAT.CVT.

For this program, the following assumptions will be made.

1. If an invalid number is encountered in the input file (nonnumeric data), then that value is to be ignored and processing continued.

2. If more than 10,000 input values are encountered, then only the first 10,000 are to be processed and the rest are ignored.

3. If any "unexpected" errors are encountered, the new file should be eliminated and the program terminated with an appropriate error message.

A program to perform this function is shown in Figure 15-3. The following commentary describes the important points of this program.

1. The virtual array file is opened for output on channel 2 as any output file would be opened (line 220).

2. As each data value is read, it is processed by FNCONVRT% and stored in the next element of the virtual array (S%) [line 330]. Note that the index of a FOR-NEXT loop (beginning with 1) is used as the subscript.

3. Normal termination is via detection of the EOF record in STAT.DAT. In the error routine, I% is decremented by one (line 19010) so that it corresponds to the number of data records read.

4. If execution of the FOR-NEXT goes to completion, then 10,000 records have been read, I% contains 10,000, and processing is finished.

5. Within the error routine the EOF condition is handled at line 19010. Any other error resulting from the INPUT statement (line 320) must be a data error, so execution is resumed at the point that will input the next data value.

Figure 15-3

Building a virtual
array file—
Example 15-1

```
100 !    EXAMPLE 15-1
110 !    PROGRAM TO CONVERT RAW STATISTICAL DATA IN STAT.DAT
120 !    TO PROCESSED DATA.  OUTPUT IS TO NEWLY CREATED
130 !    STAT.CVT WHICH IS A VIRTUAL ARRAY FILE.
140 !    CONVERSION IS DONE BY USER WRITTEN FNCONVRT%.
150 !
200      DIM #2%, S%(10000%)
210      OPEN "STAT.DAT" FOR INPUT AS FILE #1%
220      OPEN "STAT.CVT" FOR OUTPUT AS FILE #2%
230      ON ERROR GOTO 19000
300 !    &
    !    MAIN PROCESSING LOOP
310        FOR I% = 1% TO 10000%
320          INPUT #1%, R%
330          S%(I%) = FNCONVRT%(R%)
340        NEXT I%
350 !    END OF MAIN PROCESSING LOOP                          &
    !                                                         &
    !    IF EXECUTION FALLS THROUGH HERE, THERE ARE           &
    !    MORE THAN 10000 DATA VALUES IN INPUT FILE            &
    !      --- USE ONLY THE FIRST 10000.                      &
    !
400 !    FINISH UP AND CLOSE FILES
410        S%(0%) = I%    !  SAVE COUNT IN ELEMENT ZERO.
420        CLOSE #1%, #2%
430        PRINT \ PRINT I%;"DATA POINTS WRITTEN"
440        GOTO 32767
17000 ! &
    ! USER DEFINED FUNCTIONS
17010   DEF FNCONVRT%(A%)
  .          .
  .          .
  .          .
           FNEND

  .
  .
  .
19000 ! &
    ! GENERAL ERROR TRAP
19010     IF ERR=11%                               &
          THEN                                     &
            I% = I% - 1%                       \ &
            RESUME 400   !   END OF FILE
19020     IF ERL = 320                             &
            THEN RESUME !  BAD DATA SO GET NEXT VALUE
19030     PRINT "UNEXPECTED ERROR ENCOUNTERED"            \ &
          PRINT "ERROR ="; ERR; "   LINE ="; ERL          \ &
          PRINT "TERMINATING PROCESSING."                 \ &
          CLOSE #1%                                        \ &
          KILL "STAT.CVT"                                  \ &
          GOTO 32767
32767   END
```

6. Any unanticipated error terminates the program at line 19030. Note the use of the **KILL** statement. Where the **OPEN** (for output) creates a new file, the **KILL** gets rid of an existing file.

7. Note that virtual arrays, as do in-memory arrays, include a zero element. This is commonly used, as it is here, to contain header information. In this case the number of elements in the array is stored in the zero element. Some type of header with an element count or a trailer value is essential with virtual array files since, unlike sequential files, they *do not include an EOF record for automatic termination of processing.*

Figure 15-4

Processing a virtual
array file

```
120      DIM #8%, X%(10000%)
130      OPEN 'STAT.CVT' FOR INPUT AS FILE #8%
140      C% = X%(0%)        !   ACCESS DATA COUNT
150      FOR I% = 1% TO C%   !  PROCESS ENTIRE FILE
160        A% = X%(I%)
          .         .
          .         .
          .         .
         NEXT I%
```

Exercises **15-1** What is meant by virtual storage?

15-2 In looking over someone else's program, you encounter the statement:

```
720    Q = AR(J%)
```

How would you know that AR is a virtual array.

15-3 Why is it necessary in the program of Figure 15-3 to include an element count in S%(0%)?

TECHNICAL ASPECTS OF VIRTUAL ARRAY FILES

The Disk Sector

Throughout this book the emphasis is on the Basic-Plus language and its use as a tool. Very little emphasis has been placed on what occurs inside the computer as a result of program statements. As a rule high-level languages such as Basic are designed to minimize, if not eliminate, the need for the programmer to learn the internal workings of the machine. However, there are a few areas in which a basic insight regarding what is occurring can be very helpful to the end objective—good programs. How virtual arrays function is one of these areas.

To begin, storage of information on disk is different from that in internal memory. Each individual storage area represented by a variable name and containing data can be accessed or written over. On the other hand, information on disk is stored in "blocks"; that is, a number of data values are blocked together and read or written as a unit. The basic block of the PDP 11 disk drives is called a *sector* and consists of 512 bytes. A storage *byte* is a basic character-size storage unit used by most computers. A byte can contain one ASCII character. Two bytes are required to form a PDP-11 word (16 bits) required for an integer variable; similarly, 4 bytes are required for a floating-point variable (8 bytes for double precision).

Thus, whenever a program performs input or output, an entire sector consisting of 512 bytes is transferred. (It may be more, depending upon features of the individual system as defined by the installation.) The fact that the user deals only with variable names, that is, uses simple statements such as

```
200    INPUT #6, A, B, C%
300    A% = X%(I%)
```

is the result of special input/output software that handles the blocking and deblocking operations.

Virtual Array Data on Disk

All data in sequential files is stored on disk in ASCII format. Thus when a statement such as

```
PRINT #3%, A, B%, C$
```

is executed, the binary floating point for A and the binary integer B% must be converted to ASCII. Then they, together with the value of C$, can be printed to the file. When the reverse occurs, that is,

```
INPUT #4, X, Y%
```

the values in ASCII for X and Y% are read from the disk, converted to their binary formats, and stored in X and Y%.

On the other hand, no such code conversion takes place with virtual array files. The data is stored in its binary form. Thus, since integers occupy 2 bytes, 256-integer virtual array elements are stored in one sector. This is illustrated for both integers and floating-point virtual arrays in Figure 15-5.

Figure 15-5

Virtual array layout on disk storage

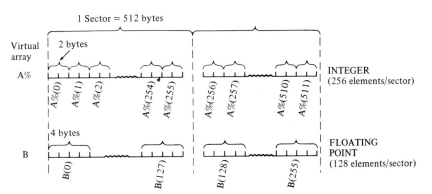

Note: In systems set up to use double-precision floating point, floating-point numbers occupy 8 bytes. Thus a sector can hold only 64 double-precision floating-point elements.

Computer Access to Virtual Arrays

One of the operations performed by the OPEN statement is to set aside an area of storage specifically for handling the sector-size chunks of data that are involved in disk reading and writing. Such an area is called an input/output *buffer*, and is exactly 512 bytes for virtual array files—corresponding to the sector size. (Larger buffers *can* be used for other file types.) Thus whenever a program requests data a full sector is read into the buffer (if it is not already in the buffer) and the needed data is selected from the buffer and made available to the program. Similarly, an output operation involves placing output in the appropriate portion of the buffer. (Actual writing of the data to disk does not occur immediately, but depends on the type of file and operations being performed.)

At this point in our studies it is important to understand the exact functions of the OPEN statement. Whether for INPUT or OUTPUT, an OPEN causes the following:

1. A buffer is set aside for the designated channel number.

2. A "connection" is made between the designated external file and the internal channel number.

3. If FOR INPUT, then the external file must be an existing one; otherwise an OPEN failure occurs. If FOR OUTPUT, then a new one is created. If neither INPUT nor OUTPUT is indicated, then the OPEN is FOR INPUT if the named file is found, and FOR OUTPUT if not found.

4. The system then "forgets" about INPUT or OUTPUT. In other words, *it is possible to write to a file opened as* INPUT. In fact this is a common thing to do with virtual array files.

Since the buffer of a virtual array file is used for reading from and writing to disk, the system must take special care to ensure that elements are properly accessed and/or updated. To keep things straight, the virtual array I/O system maintains, in addition to the buffer, two memory areas. One of them is used to store the sector number of the current sector in the buffer and the other is a flag indicating whether or not any elements in the buffer have been changed. Remember, an element is changed by a statement such as:

```
A%(I%) = X%
```

Let us assume that we have a program that processes an array A% within the following loop.

```
310    X% = A%(I%)
       .
       .
       .
390    A%(I%) = Y%
```

Furthermore, we will assume that the first three passes through this sequence involve values of I% of 312, 258, and 116. The following describes what will take place.

I%	STATEMENT	ACTION BY THE SYSTEM
312	310	Determine that the desired element is in the second sector (the first contains elements 0–255 and the second contains 256–511). Read that sector into the buffer, place the sector number (2) in the sector number memory area, and access element 312, placing it in X%.
312	390	Calculate which sector contains the desired element and compare it with the sector number in the memory area. Since they are equal, write the new value into the buffer and set the flag, indicating that a change has been made.
258	310	Determine that the proper sector is already in the buffer. Access element 258 and place it in X%.
258	390	Repeat the write sequence of element 312 for the current element 258.
116	310	Determine that the desired element is in the first sector, which is not the one in the buffer. Check the change switch; since it is on, write this buffer back onto disk (if the change flag were off, a rewrite would not be necessary). Then read the first sector into the buffer and proceed as before.

Exercises **15-4** How many bytes make up a disk sector? How many integer virtual array elements can be stored in one sector?

15-5 A student remarks about a program: "Since the file was opened FOR INPUT, I cannot write to it." Comment.

VIRTUAL ARRAY STRING STORAGE

Array String Length

The use of virtual array storage is not limited to numeric quantities (integer and floating point) since it is possible to use virtual arrays for storage of string data. In fact virtual array string storage provides the user with a powerful tool for random processing of data files. As we recall, string fields in memory can range in length from zero characters to whatever is necessary. On the other hand, when a string virtual array is defined, the programmer must specify not only the number of elements in the array but also the maximum length. This maximum length, which applies to each element of the array, can range from 2 to 512 bytes (characters). However, in order that a sector contain an integral number of elements, the system operates on the basis of maximum lengths that may be any of the following powers of 2:

2, 4, 8, 16, 32, 64, 128, 256, 512

The array string length is defined, together with the number of elements, in the DIM statement. If, for example, we have an application involving a virtual string array consisting of 500 elements, each with a length of 64 bytes, the DIM statement might appear as follows:

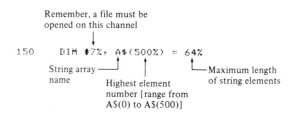

It is important to recognize that each element in the array need *not* be 64 bytes in length. But none can be longer than 64. If a string of fewer than 64 bytes is entered into an array element, the system "remembers" its length.

If the programmer specifies a length that is not a power of 2, the next higher power of 2 will be used automatically. In other words, the statement

```
160    DIM 7%, A$(500%) = 58%
```

is equivalent to the preceding statement 150. If no length is included in the DIM, the system defaults to 16; thus the following statements 170 and 180 are equivalent.

```
170    DIM B$(1000%)
180    DIM B$(1000%) = 16%
```

Exercise 15-6 How many string elements will exist on a disk sector for each of the following arrays?

```
100    DIM #2%, A$(100%) = 64%
110    DIM #2%, B$(50%) = 64%
120    DIM #2%, C$(50%) = 100%
130    DIM #2%, D$(500%)
140    DIM #2%, E$(200%) = 1000%
150    DIM #2%, F$(100%) = 1%
```

Processing Records Randomly

Example 15-1 involves processing fixed format records of a sequential file. Through use of virtual array string files, it is possible to process records in random order. To illustrate this, let us consider the following example.

Example 15-2 Each record of a student information file is 512 bytes in length and includes the following.

FIELD	POSITIONS
Student number	1–5 (<30,000)
Name	6–26
Current units attempted	27–28 (2 digits)
Other data	29–512

Bytes 1–4 of the "zero" record of the array contain, in ASCII, the number of student records currently in the file. The maximum number of student records is 4,000.

Let us assume that our employer needs a program that will allow users to make corrections to any selected record in the file. This is a common need and such programs are referred to as *file maintenance* programs. To illustrate random record accessing, this example will be limited to allowing the user to change the "current units attempted" field. Figure 15-6 includes a program and a sample dialog for this example. Points of note here are as follows:

1. Initial operations include accessing the record count (LAST%) from record zero (line 240).

2. Each request for a student record (R% at line 510) is compared with LAST% (line 530).

3. The heart of the program involves reading and rewriting a record (updating). The record is read at line 540 and rewritten at line 620.

4. A subroutine (at line 18000) is used to break the record down into its component fields.

5. Line 570 illustrates a commonly used technique. The value enclosed in angle brackets is called the *default* value. Depressing only the RETURN signals to the program to use this value (see the test at line 590).

Figure 15-6

Random access vir-
tual array records

```
100 !    EXAMPLE 15-2
110 !    THIS PROGRAM ILLUSTRATES RANDOM ACCESSING OF VIRTUAL RECORDS
120 !
200 !    INITIALIZATION OPERATIONS
210        BELL$ = CHR$(7%)
220        DIM #1%, S$(4000%) = 512%
230        OPEN 'STUDEN.FLE' FOR INPUT AS FILE #1%
240        LAST% = VAL(LEFT(S$(0%),4%))   !  GET RECORD COUNT
250        PRINT 'THIS FILE CONTAINS'; LAST%; 'STUDENT RECORDS.'
260        PRINT 'TO CHANGE THE UNITS ATTEMPTED FIELD, ENTER THE RECORD'   \ &
           PRINT 'NUMBER OF THE DESIRED RECORD.  THE STUDENT ID NUMBER'    \ &
           PRINT 'AND NAME WILL BE DISPLAYED.  THEN YOU WILL BE PROMPTED'  \ &
           PRINT 'FOR THE CORRECTED ENTRY OF UNITS ATTEMPTED.'             \ &
           PRINT 'THE PROMPT WILL INCLUDE THE CURRENT VALUE ENCLOSED'      \ &
           PRINT 'WITHIN ANGLE BRACKETS.  THIS IS THE DEFAULT VALUE;'      \ &
           PRINT 'IF NO CHANGE DESIRED, THEN PRESS THE RETURN KEY.'        \ &
           PRINT '  WHEN NO MORE STUDENTS TO PROCESS, DEPRESS CARRIAGE'    \ &
           PRINT 'RETURN IN RESPONSE TO RECORD NUMBER REQUEST.'
500 !    &
    !    PROCESSING LOOP
510        PRINT \ INPUT 'RECORD NUMBER (RETURN TO TERMINATE)'; R%
520        IF R% = 0%                                 &
               THEN GOTO 800        !  TERMINATE PROCESSING
530        IF R%<1% OR R%>LAST%                        &
               THEN                                    &
                 PRINT BELL$; 'RECORD NUMBER MUST BE BETWEEN 1 AND'; LAST%   \ &
                 GOTO 500
540        R$ = S$(R%)    !  ACCESS THE DESIRED RECORD
550        GOSUB 18000    !  BREAK VIRTUAL ARRAY RECORD INTO FIELDS
560        PRINT                                      \ &
           PRINT 'STUDENT NAME: '; SNAME$             \ &
           PRINT 'STUDENT NUMBER: '; SNUM$
570        PRINT 'UNITS ATTEMPTED <'; U$; '>';        \ &
           INPUT NU$
580 !    IF LENGTH IS ZERO, THEN NO CHANGE TO THE RECORD SO DO NOT'   \ &
    !    REWRITE.  IF LENGTH IS NOT ZERO, THEN THE FUNCTION          &
    !    FNNUM.CHECK IS USED TO ENSURE THAT IT CONTAINS ONLY         &
    !    NUMERIC DATA AND HAS A LENGTH OF 2.
590        IF LEN(NU$) = 0%                           &
               THEN GOTO 640                          &
               ELSE NU$ = FNNUM.CHECK$(NU$,2%)
600        IF NU$ = ''                                &
               THEN                                   &
                 PRINT 'INVALID ENTRY - TRY AGAIN' \ &
                 GOTO 570
610 !    VALID ENTRY SO UPDATE THE RECORD
620        S$(R%) = SNUM$ + SNAME$ + NU$ + RIGHT (S$(R%),29%)
630        PRINT 'RECORD'; R%; 'UPDATED'
640      GOTO 500
650 !    END OF PROCESSING LOOP            &
    !
800 !    CLOSE FILE
810        CLOSE #1%
820        PRINT 'PROCESSING COMPLETE'
830        GOTO 32767
18000 ! &
    ! SUBROUTINE TO BREAK VIRTUAL ARRAY RECORDS INTO FIELDS.   &
    ! INPUT:  R$ - INPUT RECORD                                &
    !                                                          &
    ! OUTPUT: SNUM$ - STUDENT NUMBER                           &
    !         SNAME$ - STUDENT NAME                            &
    !         U$ - UNITS ATTEMPTED                             &
    !
18010      SNUM$ = LEFT(R$,5%)
18020      SNAME$ = MID(R$,6%,21%)
18030      U$ = MID(R$,27%,2%)
18040      RETURN
18050 ! END OF SUBROUTINE
19000 ! &
    ! FUNCTION TO CHECK FOR VALID INTEGER                       &
    !                                                           &
    ! INPUT (ARGUMENTS):                                        &
    !         S$ - INTEGER STRING TO BE CHECKED                 &
    !         N% - NUMBER OF DIGITS                             &
    ! OUTPUT: FNNUM.CHECK$                                      &
    !  VALUE: NULL IF INPUT INVALID                             &
    !         CONTAINS TWO DIGIT STRING (N%) IF VALID           &
    !
```

Figure 15-6
(continued)

```
19010    DEF FNNUM.CHECK$(S$,N%)
19020      IF LEN(S$) > N%                        &
           THEN                                   &
             XS$ = ''                          \ &
             GOTO 19110
19030 !    MAKE THE STRING N% DIGITS IN LENGTH BY PADDING LEFT WITH ZEROS.
19040      IF LEN(S$) < N%                        &
           THEN                                   &
             S$ = '0' + S$                     \ &
             GOTO 19030
19050 !    CHECK EACH CHARACTER TO ENSURE IT IS BETWEEN 0 AND 9 (A DIGIT)
19060      FOR XI% = 1% TO N%
19070        XX$ = MID(X$,XI%,1%)
19080        IF XX$<'0' OR XX$>'9'                &
             THEN                                 &
               XS$ = ''                        \ &
               GOTO 19110
19090      NEXT XI%
19100      XS$ = S$   !  IF EXECUTION FALLS THRU, THEN S$ IS VALID
19110 !    BRANCH-TO POINT IF INVALID
19120      FNNUM.CHECK$ = XS$  !  CHECKS COMPLETE SO RETURN THE RESULT
19130    FNEND
19140 ! END OF FUNCTION FNNUM.CHECK
32767    END
```

```
THIS FILE CONTAINS 2376 STUDENT RECORDS.
TO CHANGE THE UNITS ATTEMPTED FIELD, ENTER THE RECORD
NUMBER OF THE DESIRED RECORD.  THE STUDENT ID NUMBER
AND NAME WILL BE DISPLAYED.  THEN YOU WILL BE PROMPTED
FOR THE CORRECTED ENTRY OF UNITS ATTEMPTED.
THE PROMPT WILL INCLUDE THE CURRENT VALUE ENCLOSED
WITHIN ANGLE BRACKETS.  THIS IS THE DEFAULT VALUE;
IF NO CHANGE DESIRED, THEN PRESS THE RETURN KEY.
   WHEN NO MORE STUDENTS TO PROCESS, DEPRESS CARRIAGE
RETURN IN RESPONSE TO RECORD NUMBER REQUEST.

RECORD NUMBER (RETURN TO TERMINATE)?  2371

STUDENT NAME: JONES   SAM
STUDENT NUMBER: 10863
UNITS ATTEMPTED <15>? 12
RECORD 2371 UPDATED

RECORD NUMBER (RETURN TO TERMINATE)? 3188
RECORD NUMBER MUST BE BETWEEN 1 AND 2376

RECORD NUMBER (RETURN TO TERMINATE)? 318

STUDENT NAME: NEWHOUSE PAT
STUDENT NUMBER: 00979
UNITS ATTEMPTED <16>?

RECORD NUMBER (RETURN TO TERMINATE)? 1701

STUDENT NAME: DICKEY   NANCY
STUDENT NUMBER: 18189
UNITS ATTEMPTED <12>? ID
INVALID ENTRY -- TRY AGAIN
UNITS ATTEMPTED <12>? 16

RECORD NUMBER (RETURN TO TERMINATE)?
PROCESSING COMPLETE
```

6. Referring to the input value for units completed (NU$), since this field is to be 2 digits when stored in the record, a one-digit number must be padded with a leading zero. Also, any nonnumeric entries must be rejected. These operations are performed in the generalized function **FNNUM.CHECK$**. As written (line 19000), it could be used to check a string field of digits of any length.

7. Termination of the program is achieved by depressing the RETURN key without entering a student number (numeric value of zero) at line 510.

A sample dialog follows the program listing. The reader should correlate this with the program.

Exercise 15-7 Write one or more statements to verify that the student number (refer to line 18010 in Figure 15-6) consists only of digits. Print an error message if it is not.

FILE PROCESSING USING TABLES

Building a Table as an Initialization Procedure

A major drawback to the program of Figure 15-6 is that the user must know the record number of the desired student. In most applications the actual record number is of little significance to the end user. Of much greater importance is the student number. As a rule access to records in a random file is by a particular meaningful field of the record. In the student file it most likely would be the student number field since requests would be via that field rather than by the record number. A field treated in this fashion is commonly called a *key field* and, in essence, forms the "key" to accessing records in the file.

Now, what would be involved if the user entered the student number instead of the record number? A brute force approach would be to search the file, record by record, until the desired record was found. This modification to the program of Figure 15-6 is shown in Figure 15-7. Conceptually, this process is quite simple; statement 531 compares successive student numbers from the file with the desired student number. In reality the process can be a disaster. Remember that S$ represents a disk storage *file* array. Since the record is a full sector in length, each execution of line 531 involves a disk read operation. With several thousand records in a file, this could involve a thousand or more disk reads. As disk input/output is relatively slow (a snail's pace when compared with internal operations), most applications are designed to minimize disk accessing.

A simple solution in this particular example might be, depending upon other needs of the program, to read the entire file and store the student numbers as an

Figure 15-7
Searching a file on
a key field

```
500 !    &
    !    PROCESSING LOOP
510      PRINT \ INPUT "RECORD NUMBER (RETURN TO TERMINATE)"; SN%
520      IF SN% = 0%                               &
         THEN GOTO 800        !   TERMINATE PROCESSING
530      FOR I% = 1% TO LAST%
531        IF SN% = VAL(LEFT(S$(I%),5%))           &
           THEN GOTO 540   !  RECORD FOUND
532      NEXT I%
533 !      IF EXECUTION FALLS THRU THEN RECORD NOT FOUND
534        PRINT BELL$; "STUDENT NUMBER"; SN%; "NOT IN FILE" \ &
           GOTO 500
540      R$ = S$(I%)    !   ACCESS THE DESIRED RECORD
```

Figure 15-8

Building an
in-memory table

```
205         DIM TABLE%(4000%)
     .
     .
     .
400 !       LOAD THE STUDENT NUMBERS INTO TABLE%
410         TABLE%(I%) = VAL(LEFT(S$(I%),5%)) FOR I% = 1% TO LAST%
     .
     .
530         FOR I% = 1% TO LAST%
531            IF SN% = TABLE%(I%)                              &
                  THEN GOTO 540  !  RECORD FOUND
532         NEXT I%
533 !          IF EXECUTION FALLS THRU THEN RECORD NOT FOUND
534            PRINT "STUDENT NUMBER"; SN%; "NOT IN FILE" \ &
               GOTO 500
540         R$ = S$(I%)    !  ACCESS THE DESIRED RECORD
```

in-memory array. In Figure 15-8 we see a modification to Figures 15-6 and 15-7
that uses this approach. At line 410 the entire file is read, and each student number
is converted to an integer and stored in the in-memory array **TABLE%**. The search
at lines 530–532 is through the in-memory array of **TABLE%**, which has a
one-to-one correspondence with the records of **S$**. Since no disk input is involved
at this stage, the search is far faster.

Storing the Table in a File

Depending upon the circumstances, building the table each time the program is run
(line 410) may not be practical. One solution is to maintain the table as a separate
virtual array. This approach can involve a separate file, or both arrays making up
the same file. If we assume that the file was originally built to incorporate both the
file and the table arrays, then the processing modification to Figure 15-8 will be as
shown in Figure 15-9. When two or more virtual arrays are defined in a single file
(as in line 200), the file will be arranged with all the elements of the first array
followed by all the elements of the next array, and so on. The advantage of this
approach over that of Figure 15-8 relates to the speed with which the table can be
loaded. In Figure 15-8 one disk read is required for each table entry. In Figure 15-9
each disk read yields 256 table entries. The table will be loaded much more quickly
in this case.

Figure 15-9

Multiple arrays in
a single file

```
200         DIM #1%, I%(4000%), S$(4000%)=512%
205         DIM TABLE%(4000%)
     .
     .
     .
400 !       LOAD THE STUDENT NUMBERS INTO TABLE%
410         TABLE%(I%) = I%(I%)  FOR I% = 1% TO LAST%
     .
     .
     .
```

Exercise 15-8 Internal operation speeds of modern computers are measured in microseconds
(0.000001 second) and nanoseconds (0.000000001 second). The typical time re-

quired to locate and access a record from disk might be of the order of 100 milliseconds (1 millisecond = 0.001 second). Assume that, on the average, access to a student record in a file of 4,000 records involves searching 2,000 records (half the file). How much disk time would be required, on the average, to process each record using the file search approach of Figure 15-7? If that figure does not sound too bad, how much time would be required if a clerk had 120 records to correct?

Using a Table for Sequential Processing

Actually, file processing is a subject in itself and a complete study is well beyond the scope of this book. However, these examples illustrate some of the basic principles that the programmer encounters. Fortunately, many sophisticated data management systems are available that handle many of the functions described in the preceding sections. Among the tools commonly used are *pointers,* which provide flexible access to data in randomly arranged files. To illustrate this concept, let us consider a further variation on Example 15-2. We will assume, as is commonly the case, that the records in the file are stored in no particular sequence—simply as they were loaded. Now, what if it is desired to process the file in sequence on student number (beginning with the lowest number and proceeding through the highest)? The solution is to sort the file. However, in many applications maintaining the entire file in sorted sequence is simply not practical. The solution then is to perform a sorting operation that builds a table directory listing the records in the desired sequence. This concept is illustrated in Figure 15-10. Here we see that element 1 of the table TABLE% contains the record number of the first sequential record (based on the key field) of the file S$. If in our program we load the virtual array T% into the in-memory array TABLE%, then the statement

```
R$ = S$(TABLE%(1%))
```

we will get the first sequential record. Similarly, successive entries in TABLE% contain the record number of the next sequential record in the file. Although both of the virtual arrays T% and S$ can be combined into a single file, generally more overall versatility is introduced by defining them as separate files. (Files of the type illustrated by T% are commonly called *pointer* files for obvious reasons.)

Figure 15-10
The concept of pointers

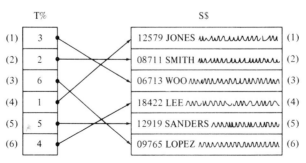

Figure 15-11

Sequential proces-
sing using pointers

```
200     DIM #1%, S$(4000%) = 512%
202     DIM #2%, T%(4000%)
205     DIM TABLE%(4000%)
210     OPEN "STUDEN.FLE" FOR INPUT AS FILE #1%
215     OPEN "STUDEN.SEQ" FOR INPUT AS FILE #2%
  .
  .
  .
410     TABLE%(I%) = T%(I%) FOR I% = 1% TO LAST%   !  LOAD TABLE
  .
  .
  .
500 !    &
    !    PROCESSING LOOP
510        FOR I% = 1% TO LAST%
520          R$ = S$(TABLE%(I%))
  .            .
  .            .     Processing sequence
  .            .
  .          NEXT I%
  .
```

Assuming that the table is stored in the file STUDEN.SEQ, then the program segment of Figure 15-11 shows how the records of the file would be processed in ascending order (based on student number). The notion of using a subscripted variable (TABLE%) as the subscript of the virtual array S$ is usually confusing upon first seeing it. Reference to Figure 15-10 will help to clarify what is happening.

One of the beauties of pointer files is that a system can include as many as desired. For instance, what if another processing application requires that the records be processed in alphabetic sequence based on the student name? The answer is simple—create another pointer file that lists the records in alphabetic sequence. Needless to say, the sorting problem is not a simple one. Many sophisticated and highly efficient sorting algorithms exist for building these pointer tables.

Exercise 15-9 Construct a pointer table similar to T% (Figure 15-10) that would produce an alphabetic sequence on name for the students in S$ of that figure.

ON EFFICIENCY IN USING VIRTUAL ARRAYS

Two-Dimensional Arrays

The virtual array file concept is a powerful and useful tool for many types of file processing applications. However, if used incorrectly, files consisting of two or more virtual arrays, or files involving two-dimensional virtual arrays, can be extremely inefficient. The problem relates to the order in which elements are stored in the file and the sequence in which they are processed. The following example illustrates this concept.

Example 15-3 Points of particular importance in a surveyor's grid are identified by their X and Y locations on the grid. The database representing these points can consist of up to 2,048 pairs. The pairs are to be stored in a virtual array file for processing.

Basically there are three ways to define the array storage for this data:

```
100    DIM #1%, X(2047%), Y(2047%)
110    DIM #1%, XY(1%, 2047%)
120    DIM #1%, XY(2047%, 1%)
```

They will all reserve space for **4096%** elements (including the zero elements): statement 100 in two different arrays and statements 110 and 120 in one two-dimensional array. For instance, the 127th data pair would be stored as follows:

STATEMENT	ELEMENT CONTAINING X	ELEMENT CONTAINING Y
100	X(126)	Y(126)
110	XY(0,126)	XY(1,126)

Does it make any difference as to which of the above is used? The answer is a resounding *yes*. To gain an insight refer to Figure 15-12. Here we see that in the layouts resulting from both statements 100 and 110, corresponding coordinate

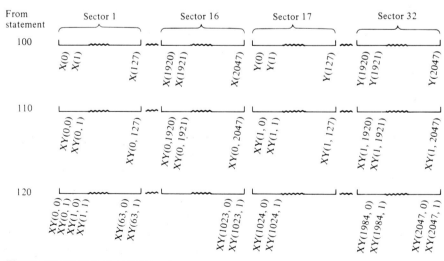

Figure 15-12 Virtual arrays in storage

elements *X* and *Y* are in *different sectors*. (Virtual arrays such as in-memory arrays are arranged in storage with the second subscript varying most rapidly.) Thus to process a set of points two disk reads are required. For instance, the set X(126) and Y(126) will be found in sectors 1 and 17 respectively. [The corresponding elements from statement 110 would be XY(0,126) and XY(1,126).]

On the other hand, we see that the DIM statement of line 120 results in *X* and *Y* pairs being located adjacent to one another. For instance, XY(63,0) and XY(63,1)—which are the 64th *X* and *Y* pair—are both stored in sector 1. Thus a single read will access both of them. The difference in processing time can be quite significant, as illustrated by the two programs in Figure 15-13. The elapsed time for simply accessing each pair of elements in the arrays speaks for itself.

Other Considerations

When a virtual array file is first allocated (by an OPEN FOR OUTPUT statement), *no* space on disk is reserved for it. This is unlike in-memory arrays for which the DIM statement defines the amount of storage to be allocated. Instead,

Figure 15-13
(a) An inefficient use of a virtual array file. (b) An efficient use of a virtual array file

```
LISTNH
100      OPEN "ARRAY1.DAT" AS FILE #1%
110      DIM #1%, XY(1%,2047%)
120      T1 = TIME(0%)   ! GET STARTING TIME FROM SYSTEM
130      FOR J% = 0% TO 2047%
140         X = XY(0%,J%)             ! GET AN
150         Y = XY(1%,J%)             !     X-Y PAIR
160      NEXT J%
170 !    END OF ACCESSING LOOP
180      T2 = TIME(0%)   ! GET FINISHING TIME
190      PRINT "ACCESSING TIME WAS"; T2-T1; "SECONDS"
200      CLOSE #1%
32767    END

Ready

RUNNH
ACCESSING TIME WAS 12 SECONDS

Ready

LISTNH
100      OPEN "ARRAY1.DAT" AS FILE #1%
110      DIM #1%, XY(2047%,1%)
120      T1 = TIME(0%)   ! GET STARTING TIME FROM SYSTEM
130      FOR I% = 0% TO 2047%
140         X = XY(I%,0%)             ! GET AN
150         Y = XY(I%,1%)             !     X-Y PAIR
160      NEXT I%
170 !    END OF ACCESSING LOOP
180      T2 = TIME(0%)   ! GET FINISHING TIME
190      PRINT "ACCESSING TIME WAS"; T2-T1; "SECONDS"
200      CLOSE #1%
32767    END

Ready

RUNNH
ACCESSING TIME WAS 2 SECONDS

Ready
```

for virtual array files the DIM statement merely sets the maximum allowable values of the subscripts. Sectors of disk storage are set aside only as values are written to the array. If, for instance, an array is being loaded sequentially, each additional block will cause the file to be extended in length when that block is written.

If a file is to be loaded to its full capacity immediately, then it is more efficient to require the system to extend it to its full size in a single action rather than block by block as it is written. This is easily done by writing to the last element in the file as illustrated in Figure 15-14. Elements are arranged one after the other, which causes the system to allocate space for element 10000 as well as for all of those preceding it. However, it is important to recognize that elements 0–9999 will *not* be initialized to zero as is the case with in-memory arrays. The virtual array file will contain whatever "garbage" was left over from previous processing. If they must be zeroed, this is easily done with a FOR statement modifier or the MAT ZER statement.

Figure 15-14
Preextending a
virtual array

```
100    OPEN "EXAMPL.ARY" FOR OUTPUT AS FILE #1%
110    DIM #1%, X%(10000%)
120    X%(10000%) = 0%
  .
  .
  .
```

Exercise 15-10 How would it be possible to define the virtual arrays X and Y in statement 100 of the earlier example to gain the efficiency of the statement 120 grouping (Figure 15-12)?

Answers to Preceding Exercises

15-1 Virtual storage involves the combined use of internal memory and external disk storage in such a way that the user memory appears to be far greater than it actually is.

15-2 It is not possible to tell by looking at statement 720. You would have to find the corresponding DIM statement to see if it specifies a channel number.

15-3 The end of a virtual array file is not marked with a system EOF. Thus it is up to the program to keep track of where the end is.

15-4 512; 256

15-5 The purpose of the FOR INPUT is to indicate to the system that an existing file must be found and opened. It does *not* control whether input or output operations are performed.

15-6 A$—8; B$—8; C$—4 (size moves up to 128); D$—32 (default size is 16); E$—not valid since maximum length must fall in range 1–512; F$—256 (size moves up to 2).

15-7
```
IF FNNUM.CHECK$(SNUM$,5%) = " "                    &
    THEN PRINT SNUM$; "IS A BAD SS NUMBER."
```

15-8 0.100 second × 2,000 records = 200 seconds/search
200 seconds/search × 120 records = 400 minutes

15-9 The entries in the alphabetic sequence pointer table would be: 1, 4, 6, 5, 2, 3.

15-10 It would be necessary to define two separate virtual array files, for example:

```
DIM #1, X(2047%)
DIM #2, Y(2047%)
```

This results in a separate buffer being defined for each of the two array files.

Programming Problem *Note*: Several random file processing programming problems are included following Chapter 17. These problems can be programmed using either the virtual array files described in this chapter or record I/O files described in Chapter 17.

15-1 Two virtual array files (TEST.DAT and TEST2.DAT) contain statistical data (integer) stored one data value per record (line). The zero element of each file contains a count of the number of elements in each file. The data in each of these files is in ascending sequence. These files are to be read and the data values merged and written to an integer virtual array file. Merging is to be done in such a way that the resulting virtual array file contains the data from the two input files in ascending sequence. The zero element of the virtual array must contain the count of the number of data values stored in the array.

Print the elements of the virtual array and check to ensure that they are indeed in the proper sequence.

16

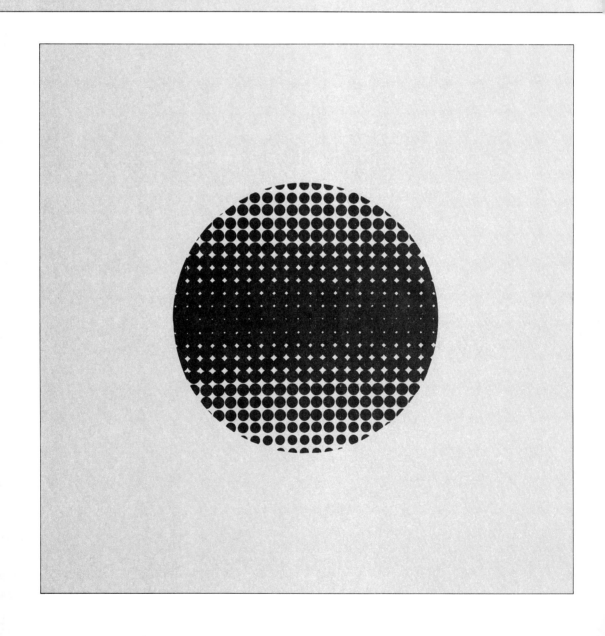

String Storage & Buffer Techniques

INTERNAL STORAGE OF DATA

Numeric Data

In Chapter 7 we learned how the system handles numeric variables in a program. To review, consider the following segment of a program that has been entered and stored on disk.

```
100     INPUT A, B, I%
110     C = A
  .
  .
  .
230     INPUT X$
  .       .
  .       .
  .       .
        GOTO 100
```

If we issue an OLD command to load this program, one of the things the system does is to reserve space for each new variable name that it encounters in the program. Upon encountering A, 4 bytes (two words) would be reserved since this is a floating-point quantity; the same would be true of B. The integer variable I% would cause 2 bytes (one word) to be set aside, and so on. The end result in memory would be as shown in Figure 16-1.

It is important to recognize that, for this program, these are fixed locations in memory and are reserved specifically for the indicated variables. (Also note that string variable X$ is being ignored for the moment.) Whenever a new value is entered or calculated for one of the variables, it replaces the previous contents of that area. For instance, let us consider how these memory contents change with execution of the program as illustrated in Figure 16-2. Of importance to us in this chapter is the manner in which the field A is copied into C by the LET statement. In essence we can think of this form of the LET as a "copy and move operation." That is, data is "moved" into a designated memory area.

At this stage of the game this topic might appear pretty elementary. However, its clear understanding is important in order to distinguish how string data is handled within memory.

String Data

First, the system cannot reserve memory for each string variable in a program when the program is loaded. Where numeric quantities are fixed in size, strings can "grow" and "shrink" within the program as it is executed. For instance, X$ in statement 230 of the above example might accept a 13-character field the first time through the loop. However, the next execution might find a 217-character field entered. Remember, the system does not impose any limits on the size of a string.

Figure 16-1
Storage layout

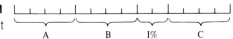

A　　　B　　　I%　　　C

Figure 16-2

Changing memory
contents with pro-
gram execution

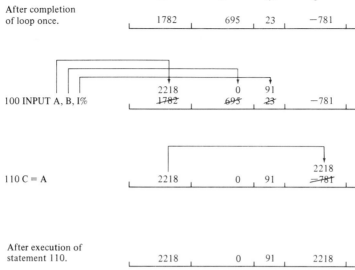

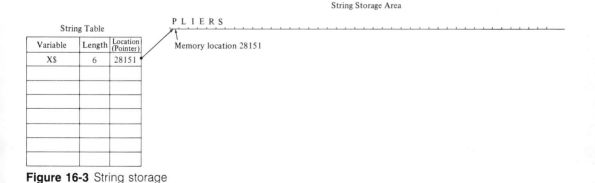

Thus the *only* time that the system knows how much memory to reserve for a string is when the string is actually entered or generated. As a result the system is designed to *dynamically allocate* memory for string variables. An understanding of how this works is critical to efficient string operations and certain types of input/output operations.

Let us assume that statement 230 of the earlier program segment has been executed and that PLIERS has been entered and stored as **X$**. When placing this in memory for later recall, the system must "remember" two pieces of information about it:

1. Where in memory it has been stored.
2. Its length.

This is done by placing the string variable name, the length of the field, and the memory address of the beginning of the field in a memory table. This concept is illustrated in Figure 16-3. Then whenever the "value" of **X$** is required by the

Figure 16-3 String storage

program (for example, the program might PRINT X$), it is only necessary to locate the table entry for X$, which in turn says where the data is located and of how many characters it consists. (For all examples that follow, the concept of the pointer rather than address location will be used in both descriptions and illustrations. However, the "pointer" is, in all cases, the memory address of the stored data as illustrated in Figure 16-3.)

Exercise 16-1 How much memory is reserved for each integer, floating-point, and string variable when the program is first loaded into memory?

Creating New String Values

Let us next consider the execution of another statement that involves a string variable:

```
240    P$ = "ABC"
```

The result shown in Figure 16-4 should be predictable for us now. Note that another table entry is made and the new string is placed in memory at the next "available" position.

Whenever a new string is created, the system handles it in this fashion—even if the new one is a portion of an "old" one, as illustrated by use of the MID function in Figure 16-5. Here we see that an R$ consisting of a midportion of A$ has been created and placed at the end of the string area. In other words, a portion of A$ has been duplicated and stored in a separate area.

Repetition of the loop (and execution of statement 230 again) produces an interesting situation. What happens when a new value is entered for a variable that is already in memory (X$ in this example)? The answer is illustrated in Figure 16-6, in which the word DRILL has been entered through the keyboard. Note that the new value is placed at the next available position of the string area and that the

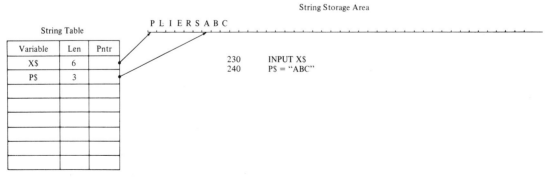

Figure 16-4 Addition of another string value

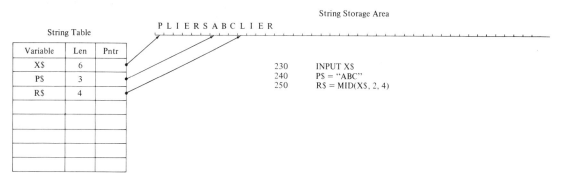

Figure 16-5 Generating a new string with the MID function

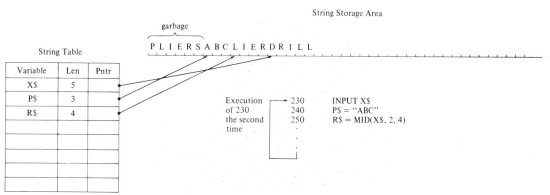

Figure 16-6 Generating a new value for an existing string variable

length and pointer for **X$** are changed accordingly. The previous value of **X$** now has no pointer referring to it, so it is considered *garbage*. We can see that the system makes no attempt to "squeeze" the new value into the same area occupied by the previous value. It simply adds new ones onto the end.

Obviously, as a program progresses and string quantities are INPUT and/or generated within a loop, the string area is going to fill up—and fast. When this happens, a special routine is called that moves everything in the string area up, thus eliminating the "gaps." Pointers in the table are adjusted accordingly. In earlier versions of the operating system this subroutine was called the Garbage Collector—quite an appropriate name. Apparently the search for status reaches everywhere, and current versions of the operating system refer to it as the Core Recycler.

Exercise 16-2 Sketch the string table and string storage area that would result from execution of the following statements.

```
500    A$ = "1234567"
510    B$ = "ABC"
520    C$ = B$ + "XY"
530    A$ = A$ + B$
```

Equating Strings

We know what happens in memory when we equate one numeric quantity to another (Figure 16-2); information is copied and moved. But what happens when a statement such as

```
260    X$ = R$
```

is executed? It neither creates a new string (as with previous examples), nor does it copy and move (as with numeric quantities). The effect of this is to make the string table entry for X$ point to the *same* data field in the string area as the string table entry for R$. This is illustrated in Figure 16-7 (assume that the progression is from Figure 16-5 to Figure 16-7). It is important to recognize that this type of operation occurs *only* when a single string variable appears to the right of the equal sign in the LET statement. For instance, the statement

```
260    X$ = R$ + " "
```

would *not* produce the result shown in Figure 16-7. In fact, any function or concatenation operation causes a new string to be created and stored as with the previous examples. In statement 260, X$ and R$ would be identical (since a null string is added to R$) but they would be two different strings.

Let us refer again to Figure 16-7, in which both X$ and R$ refer to the same information in memory. If a new value is created for R$, either through INPUT or LET, will this change the value of X$ since they refer to the same area of storage? The answer is no, because the operation will create a new value for R$ and leave the previous area unchanged. For instance, in progressing from Figure 16-7 to Figure 16-8 we see what occurs with execution of statement 270, which creates a new value for R$. We see that the string field LIER has not been classified as garbage because it still is referred to by a pointer in the string table (X$).

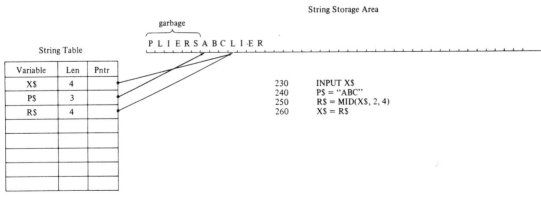

Figure 16-7 Equating two strings

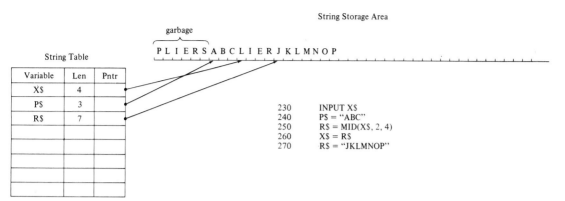

Figure 16-8 Establishing a new value for R$

In summary then, the **LET** statement, when operating on string data, always causes an adjustment to the string table pointer for that variable, and a length adjustment if appropriate. In addition, a new string field is placed in the string area, except for the special case illustrated in Figure 16-7.

Exercise 16-3 Sketch the string table and string storage area contents of Figure 16-7 if statement 260 were

```
260    X$ = R$ + " "
```

The LSET AND RSET STATEMENTS

Basic Characteristics

When operating with numeric variables the **LET** statement can be used to move data from one area in storage to another. Virtually the same operation is performed on string data by two instructions similar to the **LET**: the **LSET** and **RSET**. Where the **LET** statement can omit the word **LET**, the **LSET** must include the word **LSET**. The general form of the **LSET** is:

LSET *<string variable>* = *<string expression>*

The effect of this statement is to evaluate the string expression on the right, and then copy it into the string variable area on the left. To illustrate, the pair of **LET** statements in Figure 16-9 will result in memory contents as shown. As we know from preceding descriptions, execution of the **LET** statement at line 320 of Figure 16-10 causes changes to be made only to entries in the string table, not to string storage area. By contrast, the **LSET** statement of Figure 16-11 will leave the string

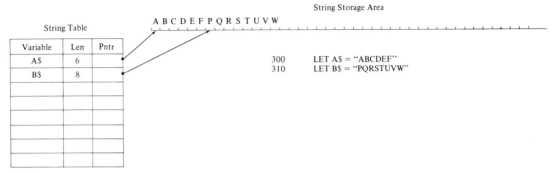

Figure 16-9 Establishing two string values

table unchanged but will duplicate the first six characters of **B$** and move them into the **A$** area. In other words, this is truly a copy and move statement. Important characteristics of the **LSET** are as follows:

1. The variable (or expression) on the right of the equal sign can be thought of as the *transmitting* field and the variable to the left as the *receiving* field.

2. Information is moved from the transmitting field to the receiving field.

3. The length of the receiving field governs the number of characters moved. If the transmitting field is longer, then excess characters are ignored (truncated); for instance, refer to Figure 16-11. If the transmitting field is shorter, then extra positions to the right in the receiving field are filled with the space character.

4. The **LSET** operation *does not change entries in the string table*.

The **RSET** statement, which is infrequently used, works in a similar way. It differs only in regard to positioning when the two fields are of different lengths. If the transmitting field is shorter, the **RSET** causes it to be *right-justified* (posi-

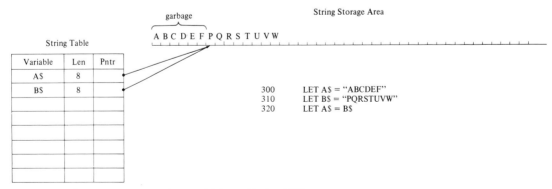

Figure 16-10 Equating two string variables with the LET

String Table

PQRSTUPQRSTUVW

Variable	Len	Pntr
A$	6	
B$	8	

```
300     LET A$ = "ABCDEF"
310     LET B$ = "PQRSTUVW"
320     LSET A$ = B$
```

Figure 16-11 The effect of the LSET statement

tioned to the right) in the receiving field. Needed spaces are inserted to the left. If the transmitting field is longer, then truncation occurs on the left end of the transmitting field.

A Consideration When Using the LSET

When two string quantities are made equivalent through the **LET** statement as illustrated in Figure 16-12, confusing results can occur if an **LSET** is later used. Here we see that **A$** and **B$** point to the same string field. Now if we set **A$** to a different value using a **LET** statement, **B$** and the corresponding memory contents will remain unchanged. However, consider the effect of the **LSET** statement in Figure 16-13. Here the 4-byte field **C$** consisting of PQRS has been copied and moved into the 7-byte area for **A$** (the three positions to the right are padded with spaces). Since the **LSET** *does not affect the string table,* **B$** and **A$** still point to the same area. Thus, even though statement 830 refers only to **A$**, **B$** has also been changed since they refer to the same area. In some situations it is necessary to define **B$** as a physically separate copy of **A$**, so that the problem of Figure 16-13 will not occur. This is easily accomplished by concatenating a null string to **A$** (see Figure 16-14), which forces the generation of a new string in the string storage area.

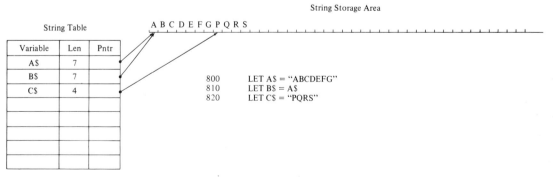

String Storage Area

String Table

ABCDEFGPQRS

Variable	Len	Pntr
A$	7	
B$	7	
C$	4	

```
800     LET A$ = "ABCDEFG"
810     LET B$ = A$
820     LET C$ = "PQRS"
```

Figure 16-12 Equivalencing two string variables

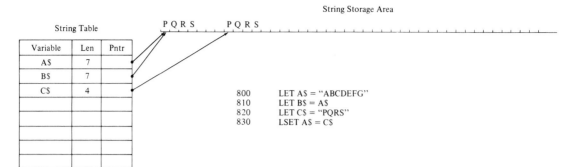

Figure 16-13 Changing the value of two variables using the LSET

As we can see, the data in **A$** has been copied into another area that is pointed to by **B$**. The value of this process will become important in the discussion later in this chapter of moving data into and out of buffers.

Exercise 16-4 A programmer has a 5-byte string field in the variable **L$**. In order to save it for later use, since **L$** will be used for something else, the programmer writes the following statement to save **L$**.

LSET S$ = L$

This is the first time that **S$** has appeared in the program. Explain what will take place.

PROCESSING FIELDS IN A RECORD

Record Definition

With this newly acquired "expertise" in string handling, we can better appreciate what occurs when a fixed format record (either from an **INPUT LINE** or a virtual

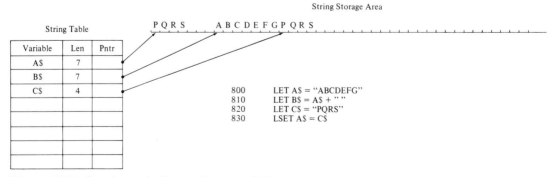

Figure 16-14 Creating a duplicate of a string field

string array) must be broken down into component fields. For instance, let us assume that we are dealing with the record defined in Example 16-1.

Example 16-1 Each record of an input file includes the following information.

FIELD	POSITIONS	VARIABLE NAME
Accounting code	1–3	C$
Location	4–7	L$
Division	8–11	D$
Activity	12–16	A$
Budgeted amount	17–24	B$
Expenditures	25–32	EX$
Encumberances	33–40	EN$

Upon reading this record, one of the first operations would probably be to break it into component fields as shown in Figure 16-15. We should note that each time a record is read, the string value of **L$** will be entered into the string area and the pointer for **L$** will be adjusted accordingly. Similarly, each **LET** statement that breaks out an individual field will cause the same thing to occur. This is an inefficient process. A much more efficient approach would be somehow to define a special area that conforms to record format. Then the record could be **LSET** into the predefined area. This concept is illustrated in Figure 16-16. Execution of statement 510 copies the record from **R$** into **M$**. Since **M$** is "overlayed" with component field definitions, the desired fields automatically will have their appropriate values. This is much more efficient than the process of Figure 16-15, as it does not require repetitive execution of string functions. Furthermore, since an entirely new set of fields need not be created for each record, the garbage collector will be required less frequently. To perform this type of operation we must be able to:

1. Set up a reserved area of storage of a required length which will not be used by the system for other string quantities.

Figure 16-15

Breaking a record into component fields

```
400     INPUT LINE #1%, R$
410     C$ = LEFT(R$,3%)          \ &
        L$ = MID(R$,4%,4%)        \ &
        D$ = MID(R$,8%,4%)        \ &
        A$ = MID(R$,12%,5%)       \ &
        B$ = MID(R$,17%,8%)       \ &
        EX$ = MID(R$,25%,8%)      \ &
        EN$ = MID(R$,33%,8%)
```

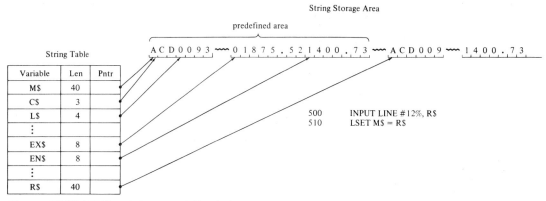

Figure 16-16 LSETing into a predefined storage area

2. Define individual fields within that area to meet the particular needs of a given problem.

In other words, we require the ability to directly manipulate the entries in the string table.

Using an Input/Output Buffer as a String Area

The one means in Basic-Plus for reserving a storage area is by opening a file. For instance, the statement

```
100    OPEN "X.X" AS FILE 12%
```

will create a memory buffer of 512 bytes. Normally we would think of performing input and/or output operations that would make use of the buffer. However, we *could* open a file (thus creating the buffer) solely for the purpose of reserving a storage area. If this is the case, then there should be no need actually to specify a file in the **OPEN** statement. Basic-Plus provides for this by allowing us to refer to a *null file*. A null file is one that does not really exist but allows us to perform an **OPEN** (thus creating the buffer). Use of the **OPEN** with a null file is illustrated in Figure 16-17. Here we see use of the predefined name **NL:** for the file-name. Also, we should note use of the **RECORDSIZE** clause. Where disk file buffers default to 512 bytes (the size of a disk sector), the **NL:** file defaults to a buffer size of 2 bytes. The **RECORDSIZE** overrides the default value and sets the buffer size to 40 bytes, as required by this example. Note that the specified number must be even: If 41% were used in statement 100, the size would be dropped to 40.

Figure 16-17
Opening a null file

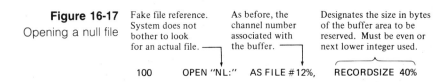

The FIELD Statement

The ability to reserve an area of memory is fine, but how do we access it with a program? The answer is through use of the FIELD statement, which allows us to define string variables that point to the buffer. As we can see in Figure 16-18 the FIELD statement must be associated with a channel number opened by an OPEN statement. It is this channel number that allows the system to correlate to the correct file buffer. As we can see, the FIELD statement specifies the string variable name and length. These values are, in turn, entered into the string table. It is important to recognize that this buffer is completely independent of (and has no influence upon) the normal string storage area. A detailed description of statement 110 and the general format of the FIELD statement are included in Figure 16-19.

In referring to the general description of Figure 16-19, we see that the FIELD statement is not limited to defining a single field within a buffer. Furthermore, being an executable statement, it can dynamically associate string variable names with all or part of a buffer. This is illustrated in Figure 16-20 where M$ is defined as a full 40 positions by statement 110. Then a second FIELD defines each record in the file. It is important to note that each execution of a FIELD statement causes

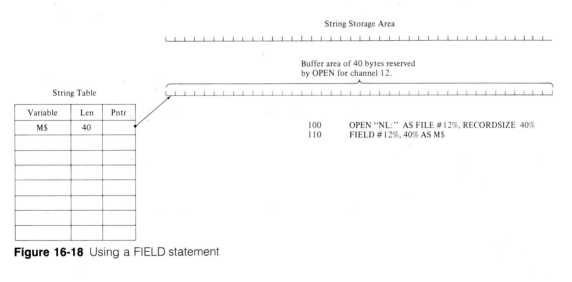

Figure 16-18 Using a FIELD statement

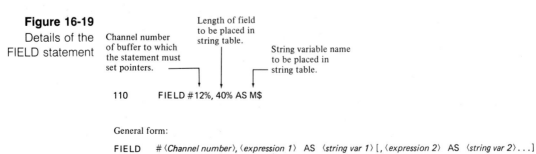

Figure 16-19
Details of the
FIELD statement

General form:

FIELD   # ⟨Channel number⟩, ⟨expression 1⟩ AS ⟨string var 1⟩ [, ⟨expression 2⟩ AS ⟨string var 2⟩ . . .]

String Table

Variable	Len	Pntr.
M$	40	
C$	3	
L$	4	
D$	4	
A$	5	
B$	8	
EX$	8	
EN$	8	

```
100    OPEN "NL:" AS FILE #12%, RECORDSIZE 40%
110    FIELD #12%, 40% AS M$
120    FIELD #12%, 3% AS C$, &
                    4% AS L$, &
                    4% AS D$, &
                    5% AS A$, &
                    8% AS B$, &
                    8% AS EX$, &
                    8% AS EN$
```

Figure 16-20 Defining multiple fields with a FIELD statement

one or more variables to be defined, starting at the beginning of the buffer. Thus both M$ and C$ point to the same place. However, M$ has a length of 40 and C$ a length of 3.

If we now compare Figure 16-20 and Figure 16-16, we see that the former is exactly the form desired. We now effectively can break the input record into its component fields with the single LSET of Figure 16-16, repeated here.

```
500    INPUT LINE #12%,R$

510    LSET M$ = R$
```

Exercise 16-5 A single buffer must be defined with a length of 31 bytes. Three record formats must be defined for this buffer as follows:

FORMAT	VARIABLE	LENGTH
1	R$	31
2	A$	6
	B$	9
	C$	10
3	W$	1
	X$	22
	Y$	3
	Z$	5

Using channel 10, create a buffer and define the required fields.

A PROCESSING EXAMPLE USING FIELD AND LSET

Let us consider the following expansion of Example 16-1, which involves actually putting some of these principles to use.

Example 16-2 A file consisting of records defined by Example 16-1 must be processed. Each record is to be read, updated, and written to a new file. The file of records is to be in sequence based on the "location" field (the second field in the record). That is, the first record should have the smallest location number and the last field the largest. If a sequencing error is detected, terminate processing.

Performance of the sequence check requires that the location field from each record be saved so that it can be compared with the location field from the next record. This and other operations of interest here are illustrated in Figure 16-21. The following commentary describes the important features illustrated by this example.

Figure 16-21

A program segment to update a file—Example 16-2

```
100      OPEN "NL:" AS FILE #12%, RECORDSIZE 40%
110      FIELD #12%, 40% AS M$
120      FIELD #12%,  3% AS C$,              &
                      4% AS L$,              &
                      4% AS D$,              &
                      5% AS A$,              &
                      8% AS B$,              &
                      8% AS EX$,             &
                      8% AS EN$
130      OPEN "BUDGET.FLE" FOR INPUT AS FILE #1%
140      OPEN "BUDGET.NEW" FOR OUTPUT AS FILE #2%
150      ON ERROR GOTO 900
160      LL$ = "    "     !  INITIALIZE LOCATION SAVE AREA TO 4 SPACES
200 !    &
    !    PROCESSING LOOP
210        INPUT LINE #1%, R$
220        LSET M$ = R$
230        IF L$ <= LL$                                              &
           THEN                                                      &
             PRINT "SEQUENCING ERROR AT THE FOLLOWING RECORD:"  \ &
             PRINT M$                                           \ &
             GOTO 900
240 !      ELSE
250          LSET LL$ = L$   !  SAVE LOCATION NUMBER
260          B = VAL(B$)      !  GET BUDGET FIELD & CONVERT TO NUMERIC
     .
     .
     .
470          LSET B$ = ...  !  MOVE NEW VALUE TO B$
     .
     .
     .
900 !      &
    !      CLOSE FILE AND TERMINATE
     .
     .
     .
```

1. In addition to the normal input and output files, the null file requires a third file to be opened.

2. As each input record is read it is LSET into M$. This gives the program access to individual fields defined by FIELD statement 120.

3. The location field (L$) of each record is compared with that of the preceding record (LL$). If L$ is not larger, processing is terminated; otherwise, processing continues.

4. At line 250 the location field of the current record is copied to LL$ for comparison with the next record when the loop is repeated.

5. Accessing fields from M$ for normal processing involves the usual techniques, as illustrated at line 260.

6. Placing a new value into one of the buffer-defined fields requires use of the LSET statement in order to copy the new contents into the buffer-defined field (for instance, see line 470).

As we can see, a certain amount of care must be taken to use LSET at the proper time or trouble results (refer to the following exercises).

Defining fields in this fashion is a valuable tool. This example illustrates a very basic use; it can be used in virtually an identical manner to break virtual array records into component fields. Furthermore, it is a necessary tool when dealing with record I/O files, the topic of the next chapter.

Exercises **16-6** What would happen in the program of Figure 16-21 if statement 250 were as follows?

```
250    LET LL$ = L$
```

What would be required to use a LET instead of an LSET?

16-7 What would happen if statement 470 were as follows?

```
470    LET B$ = ...
```

Answers to **16-1** Each integer variable causes the system to reserve 2 bytes and each floating-point
Preceding   variable 4 bytes (8 bytes for double precision). No storage is reserved for string
Exercises   variables; they are allocated dynamically upon execution of the program.

16-2

String Table

Variable	Len	Pntr
A$	10	
B$	3	
C$	5	

String Storage Area

1 2 3 4 5 6 7 A B C A B C X Y 1 2 3 4 5 6 7 A B C

16-3

String Table

Variable	Len	Pntr
X$	4	
P$	3	
R$	4	

String Storage Area

P L I E R S A B C L I E R L I E R

```
230    INPUT X$
240    P$ = "ABC"
250    R$ = MID(A$, 2, 4)
260    X$ = R$ +  " "
```

16-4 The value of **S$** will be null and thus have a length of zero. Since the receiving field controls the number of characters copied, nothing will be copied from **L$** into **S$**.

16-5
```
100    OPEN "NL:" AS FILE #10%, RECORDSIZE 32%
110    FIELD #10%, 31% AS R$
120    FIELD #10%, 6% AS A$, 9% AS B$, 10% AS C$
130    FIELD #10%, 1% AS W$, 22% AS X$, 3% AS Y$, 5% AS Z$
```

16-6 Use of the **LET** in place of the **LSET** would cause **LL$** to point into the buffer so that **LL$** and **L$** would refer to the identical storage area. The comparison at line 230, upon processing the second record, would give an equal condition and the program would be terminated. If the **LET** statement is used, then concatenation is required as follows:

```
250    LET LL$ = L$ + " "
```

16-7 The **LET** statement influences string pointers so that the desired string would be placed in the general string area, not the designated buffer area. The variable **B$** would no longer point to the buffer area.

Programming **16-1** The purpose of this programming problem is to permit the reader to become familiar
Problem with the FIELD statement and to gain an insight into the efficiency of its use over
corresponding MID functions in some instances. The program is to do the following.

1. Define a string field (L$) in storage consisting of 80 characters using a LET
   statement. Think of this as corresponding to a record consisting of component
   fields that have been read from a file.

2. Using the MID function, break this "record" into 16 component fields of 5 bytes
   each. In order to gain a realistic insight into the time required, repeat the
   breakdown sequence using a FOR-NEXT loop.

3. Preceding the FOR statement, save the system time; following the NEXT
   statement, print the elapsed time. (Refer to the program of Figure 15-13.)

4. For comparison, now open a null file, define the fields with a FIELD statement,
   and perform the breakdown by using an LSET in conjunction with the null file
   buffer.

5. Repeat this process with a FOR-NEXT as in step 3. Do it in two ways: First, place
   only the LSET within the FOR-NEXT loop; second, place both the LSET and
   FIELD statement within the loop.

6. Make the end value in the FOR-NEXT loops variable and experiment with the
   number of executions in order to gain realistic values for execution times.
   Compare the times that result from these tests.

17

Record I/O

BASIC CONCEPTS OF RECORD I/O

General Introduction

As we have learned, all disk input and output involves the use of memory buffers. That is, each OPEN statement causes a 512-byte buffer to be created. Each sector read from or written to disk moves through the buffer. One of the beauties of sequential and virtual array I/O is that all management of the buffer area is handled by the system. For instance, we simply say INPUT and the system gets the fields we list. They may reside in the current buffer load or partially in the current and partially in the next sector. Similarly with virtual arrays, the user need only specify the virtual array subscripted variable. In both cases all buffer management functions are performed by the system and are completely transparent to the user.

By contrast, in the case of record I/O the programmer assumes control over the buffer and is completely responsible for its use. The system reads data and places it in the buffer and writes the buffer contents to disk in response to specific instructions in the program. Furthermore, the transfer of data to and from the buffer is also handled by the user program. Although this imposes a significant burden on the programmer, it is a powerful tool for controlling input/output operations and provides a wide degree of flexibility.

When record I/O is used, input and output are performed by the GET and PUT statements respectively. Each GET causes an entire sector to be read from disk into the buffer. Similarly, each PUT causes the sector in the buffer to be written to disk. (Technically, this is not exactly true since the RECORDSIZE can define buffers as consisting of two or more sectors.) As the reader might suspect, the user gains access to the data record in the buffer through use of the field statement. Data is moved into the buffer for output by use of the LSET operating with fields defined by the FIELD statement.

Every file on disk consists of one or more sectors, which the system recognizes by their numbers. For instance, if a file consisted of 100 sectors, the first one would be sector or record 1, the second, sector or record 2, and so on. By using record I/O it is possible to access any record (sector) of the file by specifying its relative record number. In this respect, record I/O files are similar to virtual array files because records can be accessed in random order.

Building a Record I/O File

To illustrate record I/O concepts, let us assume that we are just starting in business and we wish to maintain a computerized customer mailing list. The first two tasks are to design the file format and enter the data.

Example 17-1 A computerized mailing list is required; following is a record definition table for this system.

FIELD NUMBER	VARIABLE NAME	LENGTH	DESCRIPTION
1	N$	20	Name
2	S$	22	Street address
3	C$	17	City and state
4	Z$	5	Zip code

Total 64

The first 4 bytes of record 1 are to contain, in ASCII, a count of the number of records stored in this file.

Let us first consider a simple program to create this file. Since it will be necessary to include a record count in the first record, we will have to count entries. In order to concentrate on the details of record I/O, the usual editing and error checking are omitted from the program of Figure 17-2 (on next page). General commentary relating to this program is as follows:

1. Two **FIELD** statements are needed. The first one (line 220) defines the 4-byte field to be used as a data record count in record 1. The second defines the fields of the data records.

2. Processing is terminated by entering no data for the name at line 310. However, since the **INPUT LINE** is used, **N$** will contain the carriage return and line feed characters. This explains the test at line 320.

3. The input data strings are stripped of their CR-LF characters prior to being **LSET** into the buffer fields (lines 400–430).

4. The variable I% represents the data record count so it is incremented prior to writing (line 510).

5. The record that has been built in the buffer is written by the **PUT** statement of line 520. This statement is described in more detail in Figure 17-1. During the first pass through the loop I% will be 1 and so the first customer will be written to relative record 2. Remember, record 1 is to be used as a header record.

Figure 17-1
Characteristics of the PUT statement

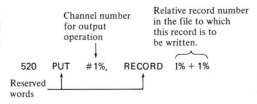

Figure 17-2
Creating and
loading a record
I/O file—
Example 17-1

```
100 !     EXAMPLE 17-1                                                  &
    !     BUILDING A RECORD I/O FILE
200 !     &
    !     INITIAL PROCESSING
210       OPEN "MAIN.FLE" FOR OUTPUT AS FILE #1%
220       FIELD #1%,    4% AS M$   !  FIELD POINTER FOR HEADER RECORD
230       FIELD #1%,   20% AS N$,         &
                       22% AS S$,         &
                       17% AS C$,         &
                        5% AS Z$
240       I% = 0%
300 !     &
    !     PROCESSING LOOP
310       PRINT "NAME (CR TO TERMINATE)";             \ &
          INPUT LINE NI$
320       IF NI$ = CHR$(13%)+CHR$(10%)                  &
             THEN GOTO 600    !  TERMINATE PROCESSING
330       PRINT "STREET ADDRESS";                     \ &
          INPUT LINE SI$
340       PRINT "CITY & STATE";                       \ &
          INPUT LINE CI$
350       PRINT "ZIP CODE";                           \ &
          INPUT LINE ZI$
400       LSET N$ = CVT$$(NI$,4%)   !   DELETE CR & LF
410       LSET S$ = CVT$$(SI$,4%)   !    THEN MOVE THE
420       LSET C$ = CVT$$(CI$,4%)   !     INPUT FIELDS
430       LSET Z$ = CVT$$(ZI$,4%)   !     TO BUFFER
500 !      RECORD BUILT IN BUFFER SO WRITE TO DISK
510       I% = I% + 1%
520       PUT #1%, RECORD I%+1%
530       GOTO 300
600 !     &
    !     TERMINATION SEQUENCE
610       LSET M$ = NUM1$(I%)   !  PREPARE THE HEADER
620       PUT #1%, RECORD 1%    !   AND WRITE IT TO RECORD 1
630       CLOSE #1%
640       PRINT I%; "DATA RECORDS WRITTEN."
32767     END
```

6. When data entry is completed, execution is transferred to line 600. At line 610 the data record count is entered into the buffer, and at line 620 that header record is written to relative record 1 of the file.

Exercise 17-1 Show the changes that would be necessary in the program of Figure 17-2 if I% had been initialized to 1 so that it would represent the relative record number at line 520 rather than the data record count. Do not change the sequencing of any statements.

Sequential Processing a Record I/O File

To illustrate sequential processing of a record I/O file, let us assume that we must simply "dump" the file contents. That is, each record is to be printed on a single line with no formatting. This is a relatively simple task as illustrated by the program of Figure 17-3. Here we can see that the GET statement is used in exactly the same form as the PUT. In line 240 the header record is read to access the data record count, which is, in turn, used to control the FOR-NEXT loop. The output in this case will be the data record number followed by the entire data record (see lines 320 and 330).

Actually, if records of a record I/O file are to be read or written sequentially,

Figure 17-3

Processing a record
I/O file sequentially

```
100  !    EXAMPLE 17-1 -- FILE DUMP
200  !    &
     !    OPEN FILES AND INITIALIZE
210       OPEN "MAIL.FLE" FOR INPUT AS FILE #1%
220       FIELD #1%, 4% AS M$
230       FIELD #1%, 64% AS R$
240       GET #1%, RECORD 1%
250       M% = VAL(M$)   !  GET RECORD COUNT
300  !    &
     !    PROCESSING LOOP
310       FOR I% = 1% TO M%
320          GET #1%, RECORD I%+1%
330          PRINT I%; TAB(8%); R$
340       NEXT I%
500  !    &
     !    TERMINATION
510       PRINT \ PRINT "PROCESSING COMPLETE"
520       CLOSE #1%
32767     END
```

then it is not necessary to designate the desired record number in the **GET** or **PUT**. Thus statements 240 and 320 in Figure 17-3 could be written as follows:

```
240     GET #1%
   .
   .
   .
320     GET #1%
```

Whenever the **RECORD** qualifier is omitted in a **GET** (or **PUT**) the system will access the record that follows the last access to that channel. For instance, if last access to channel 5 involved record 27, the next **GET** or **PUT** without the **RECORD** qualifier would refer to record 28. Thus in our example the first **GET** (line 240) accesses the first record and repeated execution of the second **GET** (line 320) accesses subsequent records. In other words, the program in Figure 17-3 executes exactly the same with or without the **RECORD** qualifiers in the **GET**s.

   With sequential I/O (but *not* virtual array I/O) we used the automatic EOF capabilities to terminate processing. This is also possible with record I/O files, as illustrated by the program of Figure 17-4. Here we can see that the processing is

Figure 17-4

Using the automatic
EOF detection.

```
100  !    EXAMPLE 17-1 -- USING THE EOF
200  !    &
     !    OPEN AND INITIALIZE
210       OPEN "MAIL.FLE" FOR INPUT AS FILE #1%
220       FIELD #1%, 64% AS R$
230       GET #1%
240       ON ERROR GOTO 500
300  !    &
     !    PROCESSING LOOP
310       GET #1%
320       PRINT I%; TAB(8%); R$
330       GOTO 310
500  !    &
     !    TERMINATION
510       IF ERR<>11%                        &
             THEN ON ERROR GOTO 0
520       PRINT \ PRINT "PROCESSING COMPLETE"
530       CLOSE #1%
32767     END
```

identical in concept to processing a sequential file. One might argue that with this capability the record count in a header is not necessary. However, it is important to recognize that we are dealing with random accessing capabilities and that the records will not normally be accessed sequentially. This is illustrated in the next section.

Exercises **17-2** In the program of Figure 17-4, what is the purpose of the GET statement at line 230? What would happen if it were omitted?

17-3 A program requires that records in a file be read, updated, and rewritten. Processing of the file is to be sequential so a programmer decides to omit the RECORD qualifier and includes the following in the processing loop. What will happen?

```
GET #1%  ! GET NEXT RECORD FROM DISK
.
.
.
PUT #1%  ! WRITE CORRECTED RECORD BACK TO DISK
```

Random Processing of a Record I/O File

At this point the method of random processing of this file should be fairly obvious. Let us assume that we require a program that will allow us to display a selected record. This would be done as shown in Figure 17-5. After accessing the data record count (lines 240 and 250), processing merely involves confirming that the requested record number is within the limits of the file, and then accessing that record.

Exercise **17-4** The program of Figure 17-5 involves direct access to a selected record by its location in the file. What would be necessary if the user requested a record by entering the name of the person?

LOGICAL AND PHYSICAL RECORDS

Distinction Between a Physical Record and a Logical Record

In the discussion of Example 17-1 the word record was used in an ambiguous fashion. On one hand, the data record as defined by the FIELD statement (line 230 of Figure 17-1) consists of 64 bytes. Each 64-byte record contains the address information for one customer. On the other hand, each execution of the PUT statement (the GET in Figures 17-3, 17-4, and 17-5) referred to a record that consists of a single disk sector of 512 bytes. This is commonly referred to as a *physical record* and its length, in the case of disk storage, is determined by the

298 RECORD I/O

Figure 17-5

Processing a record
I/O file randomly

```
100 !    EXAMPLE 17-1  ---  RANDOM PROCESSING
200 !    &
    !    OPEN FILE AND INITIALIZE
210      OPEN "MAIL.FLE" FOR INPUT AS FILE #1%
220      FIELD #1%, 4% AS M$
230      FIELD #1%, 64% AS R$
240      GET #1%, RECORD 1%
250      M% = VAL(M$)
300 !    &
    !    PROCESSING LOOP
310      INPUT "WHICH RECORD (CR IF FINISHED)"; R%
320      IF R% = 0%                                          &
             THEN GOTO 500
330      IF R% < 0% OR R% > M%                               &
         THEN                                                &
             PRINT "ENTRY MUST BE BETWEEN 0 AND "; M%    \ &
             GOTO 300
340      GET #1%, RECORD R%+1%
350      PRINT R$
360      GOTO 300
500 !    &
    !    TERMINATION
510      PRINT \ PRINT "PROCESSING COMPLETE"
520      CLOSE #1%
32767    END
```

physical nature of the device. However, the length of the data record depends upon the logic of the program and thus it is commonly called a *logical record*. This concept is illustrated in Figure 17-6. As we can see, there is a great deal of wasted disk storage—in fact, one-eighth of the sector is used and seven-eighths are wasted. The obvious question is; Why not use the entire physical record? This question brings us to the topic of blocked records.

Unblocked and Blocked Records

Files in which each physical record contains only one logical record are said to be *unblocked*. Although unblocked records are convenient to handle, they can waste a lot of disk space. (Of course, if the logical record were 512 bytes in length, unblocked records would be quite satisfactory.) The method of combating this wasted space problem is to store more than one logical record in each physical record.

To illustrate, let us assume that we are working with logical records of 128 bytes in length. Then in Figure 17-7 we see four logical records stored in each physical record. These generally are referred to as *blocked records*. In this case,

Figure 17-6

A physical and a
logical record

Logical record
collection of fields
for one customer—
64 bytes.

Physical record
1 disk sector of
512 bytes.

Figure 17-7
Blocked records

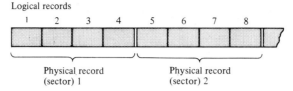

Logical records

where the logical record length divides evenly into the physical record length, there is no wasted space. However, this improvement in disk utilization is accomplished at the expense of program complexity. That is, the disk drive still sees record 2 as the second sector of the file; it does not "know" how we have used blocking. Therefore, if we wish to access logical record 2 or 17 or any other, we must figure out where it is. This is covered later in this chapter.

Partially Filled Blocks and Spanned Records

Obviously, Example 17-1 was contrived to yield a situation in which exactly eight logical records fit into a sector. What can we do if the record length does not divide evenly into 512 (for instance, consider a length of 160)? The easiest answer is to block as many records as possible and not worry about wasted space. In the case of a 160-byte record, we would have three records per block occupying 480 bytes, with 32 bytes left over. The alternative to this is to allow records to *span* blocks; these are referred to as *spanned records*. Both of these approaches are illustrated in Figure 17-8. Although the spanned record concept utilizes disk more efficiently, the programming is more complex. For example, two disk reads would be required to access the spanned logical record number 4 in Figure 17-8. None of the examples in this book deal with spanned records.

Exercises 17-5 Assume that an application uses records that are 120 bytes long. Which method (unblocked, blocked, or spanned) would provide the most efficient use of disk storage? The least efficient? Which would require the least programming effort?

17-6 If an application involved records of 128 bytes, would it be best to use unspanned blocked records or spanned records?

PROCESSING FILES OF BLOCKED RECORDS

Random Accessing of Blocked Records

Access to a record when it is the only one in a block is relatively simple, as we have discovered (Figure 17-5). However, what about accessing a record from a blocked file that has, for example, four records per block? We must keep in mind that the first physical record contains the first four logical records, the second physical record contains the next four logical records, and so on. Perhaps the reader has guessed that integer dividing the logical record number by 4 (the number of logical

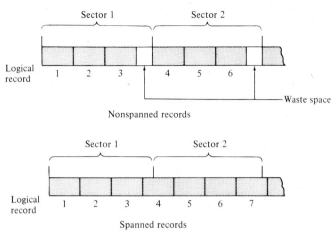

Figure 17-8
Blocked and
spanned records

Sector 1   Sector 2

Logical
record   1   2   3   4   5   6

Waste space

Nonspanned records

Sector 1   Sector 2

Logical
record   1   2   3   4   5   6   7

Spanned records

records in a physical record) would be a good starting point. In fact, this is precisely the procedure that is used. However, a bit of manipulation is required to obtain the desired result, as we can see in Table 17-1. Here P is used to represent the physical record number and L to represent the logical record number.

The last two columns show us the way to finding the desired record. We see that in the next to last column the quotient is always one less than the physical record number. The remainder in the last column gives an indication of which logical record we desire in the given sector. For example, using this approach we could locate the 18th logical record in the file as follows:

$$\frac{18 - 1}{4} = 4 \qquad \text{remainder} = 1$$

Table 17-1

P	L	L − 1	(L − 1)/4	REMAINDER
1	1	0	0	0
	2	1	0	1
	3	2	0	2
	4	3	0	3
2	5	4	1	0
	6	5	1	1
	7	6	1	2
	8	7	1	3
3	9	8	2	0
	10	9	2	1
	11	10	2	2
	12	11	2	3

Thus logical record 18 would be the second logical record in physical record 5. This technique is applied in the program sequence of Figure 17-9. The only way to really understand how this works is to use some sample values and step through it. The method of selecting the proper logical record from the accessed physical record is worthy of note. To illustrate, let us assume that we desire record 7; then from line 520, R% is 2. The result of executing the FIELD statement (line 540) will be as shown in Figure 17-10. Here the remainder R% is used as a multiplier to "push down" R$ so that it points to the correct area. Needless to say, this is the only function of Q$, so it serves merely as a dummy variable (formal parameter). If the remainder is 0, then both Q$ and R$ point to the first position of the buffer. The distance from the beginning of the physical record to the desired logical record (256 bytes in this case) is called the *offset*. The variable R% then is the multiplier to achieve the desired offset.

Exercise 17-7 In Example 17-1 the first logical record is the header record. Thus the first data record would be logical record number 2. What change would be required to the sequence of Figure 17-9 if the request is for a particular data record as opposed to a logical record?

Sequentially Processing a Blocked Record File

Now let us return to the program for dumping the file of Example 17-1. We will assume that this file is as defined earlier, except that it consists of records blocked eight per sector. The first logical record of the first block contains the header consisting of the data record count (*not* the sector count) for the file. A program to perform this dump operation is shown in Figure 17-11. The fact that the first block contains the header followed by seven data records requires special handling. We can see that this sector is read outside of the processing loop (see line 230). The one other item that might require some special attention is the variable REL%. It is the multiplier used to calculate the offset value for accessing the desired logical record from the physical record. We see it used as the multiplier in the FIELD statement (line 320). When REL% is zero, R$ will point to the first logical record in the buffer. When it is seven, it will point to the last. (This is the principle illustrated by Figure 17-10.) It is set to one in processing the first block in order to skip over the header record in the processing loop.

Exercise 17-8 How many times will the FOR-NEXT loop in Figure 17-11 be executed the first time through? The second time? The last time?

Figure 17-9

Accessing a blocked record

```
500        INPUT 'LOGICAL RECORD'; L%
510        P% = (L%-1%)/4%          !  CALCULATE THE QUOTIENT
520        R% = (L%-1%) - 4%*P%     !  GET THE REMAINDER
530        P% = P% + 1%             !  ADJUST QUOTIENT TO PHYS REC NUMBER
540        FIELD #1%,
540        FIELD #1%, 128%*R% AS Q$,        &
                   128% AS R$
550        GET #1%, RECORD P%
560        PRINT R$
```

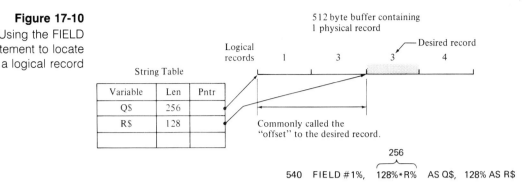

Figure 17-10
Using the FIELD statement to locate a logical record

512 byte buffer containing 1 physical record

Desired record

Logical records   1   3   3   4

String Table

Variable	Len	Pntr
Q$	256	
R$	128	

Commonly called the "offset" to the desired record.

256

540   FIELD #1%,   128%*R%   AS Q$,   128% AS R$

INDEXING A FILE

Simple File Indexing

Although Example 17-1 serves to illustrate basic principles of random files and their processing, it is very limited in scope. For instance, Exercise 17-4 broaches the topic of processing on other than the logical record number. In an actual application each customer probably would be assigned a customer number. This field would be included as part of the record and likely would serve as the key field (the key field concept is described in Chapter 15). Then most of the processing would be based on the key field. Sequential processing would proceed as illustrated in Figure 17-11. However, random processing would now require searching

Figure 17-11
Sequential processing of a file with blocked records

```
100 !    EXAMPLE 17-1  ---  FILE DUMP WITH BLOCKED RECORDS
110 !    VARIABLES USED:                                          &
    !      M% - NUMBER OF DATA RECORDS IN FILE (EXCLUDING HEADER)  &
    !      PHYS% - PHYSICAL RECORD NUMBER                          &
    !      REL% - RELATIVE LOGICAL RECORD NUMBER WITHIN A BLOCK    &
    !      CNT% - COUNT OF DATA RECORDS PROCESSED (NOT TO EXCEED M%) &
    !
200 !    &
    !    OPEN FILE AND INITIALIZE
210      OPEN 'MAIL.FLE' FOR INPUT AS FILE #1%
220      PHYS% = 1%  !  FIRST PHYSICAL RECORD
230      GET #1%, RECORD PHYS%  !  GET FIRST PHYSICAL RECORD
240      FIELD #1%, 4% AS M$    !  GET FIRST LOGICAL RECORD
250      M% = VAL(M$)           !   TO OBTAIN LOGICAL RECORD COUNT
260      REL% = 1%  !  FIRST LOGICAL RECORD (HEADER) ALREADY PROCESSED
300 !    &
    !    PROCESSING LOOP
310      FOR I% = REL% TO 7%
320        FIELD #1%, 64%*REL% AS Q$,  64% AS R$
330        CNT% = CNT% + 1%
340        PRINT CNT%; TAB(8%); R$
350        IF CNT% = M%                                   &
              THEN GOTO 500
360      NEXT I%
370      PHYS% = PHYS% + 1%   !  ACCESS NEXT RECORD
380      GET #1%, RECORD PHYS%
390      REL% = 0%      ! FIRST PASS REL% WAS 1 SINCE FIRST BLOCK CONTAINED  &
                        ! HEADER.  ALL OTHER PASSES REL% = 0.
400      GOTO 300
500 !    &
    !    TERMINATION
510      PRINT \ PRINT 'PROCESSING COMPLETE'
520      CLOSE #1%
32767    END
```

the field to find the desired customer number. It would involve exactly the sequential principles illustrated in Figure 17-11 and would, in fact, take no advantage of the random accessing capabilities of record I/O files. Furthermore, the process would be very slow for large files and totally impractical if numerous requests were to be processed. In this respect we have the same problems illustrated in Chapter 15 for virtual array files. One solution is to create a *directory* or *index* to the file on the basis of the key field. To illustrate different techniques involving key fields, let us consider another example.

Example 17-2 Each record of an employee information file consists of 256 bytes and includes the following information.

FIELD	LENGTH
Social Security number	9
Name	21
Other data	226

Records are blocked two per sector. All processing is to be based on the use of indexes.

The simplest indexing approach is to build a separate index file that has entries in a one-to-one correspondence with those of the data file. This concept is presented in Figure 17-12. To illustrate how the index would be used, let us

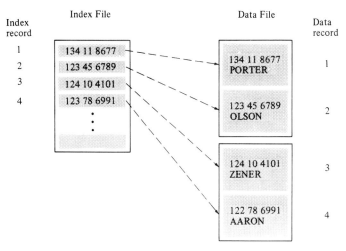

Figure 17-12
Indexing a file

assume that the data record for Social Security number 123 78 6991 is required. The program simply searches the index file until the desired number is found. Upon finding it as entry 4, the desired data record (4) can be directly accessed using the technique of Figure 17-9. However, before processing, the key field within the data record should be compared with the desired key to ensure that they are indeed the same. If they are different, then the file has somehow been corrupted and a new index file can easily be built merely by processing the data file sequentially.

The advantage of searching the index file rather than the data file is that far fewer disk reads will be required. Where each block of the data file contains two logical records, each block of the index contains 56 keys.

Exercise 17-9 Assume that the file of Example 17-2 contains 5,000 records. On the average, to find a record means reading halfway through the file. On this basis, how many disk reads would be required per search without use of the index? How many with use of the index?

Sequenced File Indexing

For relatively small files the index can be loaded into an in-memory array, thus speeding processing considerably (refer to Figure 15-8). However, for most file processing this is not practical. In fact, for very large files the index file itself can be quite large, as illustrated by Exercise 17-9. Many techniques have evolved for handling this problem. One of them is to store in each index entry the key field *and* the record number of the data record. Then the index file can be sorted into an ascending sequence based on Social Security number, which provides the programmer much more flexibility. The concept of a sorted index is illustrated in Figure 17-13. (For the sake of a simple illustration, this is shown as if the file consists of only four records.) At first glance this may appear to buy us nothing.

Figure 17-13
A sequenced index file

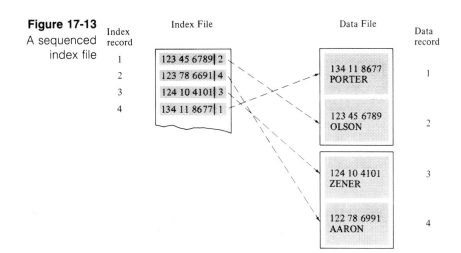

However, we can now create somewhat of a directory to the index. In Figure 17-14 we see a table of the last (highest) Social Security number in each index file block. Since there are 56 records in each block, a file of 5,600 records would consist of 100 blocks and would thus have 100 "highest" entries in the directory. This is quite small and could easily be kept in memory. To illustrate how to use this directory, if we need the record for Social Security number 203 11 9141, the procedure would be as follows:

1. Search the in-memory table for the first entry that exceeds the desired Social Security number. This gives us 203 99 8211, which is the third entry in this table.

2. Read the third block (which contains the desired entry) and search it. When found, access the logical record number of the data record (1638 in this case).

3. Read the disk block containing the desired record.

Although this technique may appear somewhat clumsy, it is actually relatively simple to program. It is certainly efficient since it requires only two disk read operations.

Overall, this process is a powerful technique and one (of many) that is widely used. One very useful feature relates to the ease with which an index can be created. For instance, a particular application might require that processing of the file be based on some other field within the record, such as the person's name. Then a complete index could be created and sorted, and a directory to the index created. This basic principle is used in many data management software systems that are commercially available.

Figure 17-14

A directory to a sequenced index file

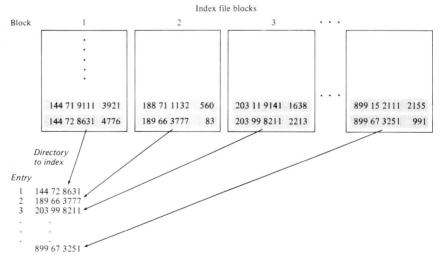

HANDLING NUMERIC QUANTITIES

Mapping Numeric Quantities to String

To this point all data stored in files has been in ASCII format. For instance, if our program includes the quantity K%, which will never be larger than 4 digits, the NUM1$ function will be used to convert it to four ASCII characters. Remember, our access to the I/O buffers is through the string variable table. In some cases it is undesirable to convert numeric quantities back and forth for disk storage. For one thing, these conversions are relatively slow. For another, the above K% occupies 2 bytes as an integer but 4 as a string. If we have a large file consisting of many numeric fields, these factors could be quite significant.

What is needed is a method whereby we can take the 2-byte binary field (which we know as K%) and place it in the string data area (even though it is not truly string data). Then, of course, we need a string variable entry in the string table (with a length of *two*) that points to it. Basic-Plus provides this capability through the CVT functions, which allow both integer and floating-point quantities to be so treated. The CVT%$ function maps an integer quantity into the string area, as illustrated in Figure 17-15. It is important to recognize that "convert" (CVT) is really a misnomer—*no code conversion takes place*; the binary data is simply duplicated into the string area. Needless to say, if we attempted to PRINT K$, we would obtain garbage. The complementary function, that of taking a binary string from the string area and placing it into the data area of the program, is performed by the CVT$% function. For instance,

```
A% = CVT$%(K$)
```

will perform the inverse operation. However, if K$ is longer than 2 bytes, only the first 2 are used. If shorter, one or more null bytes will be appended.

Floating-point numbers can be handled in exactly the same way. However, remember that standard precision floating-point numbers occupy 4 bytes. If the

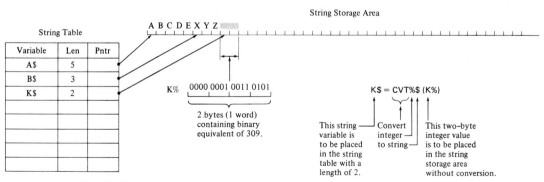

Figure 17-15 The CVT$% function

system uses double precision, then each will occupy 8 bytes. The corresponding floating-point conversions are:

CVTF$—map floating-point quantity to string.
CVT$F—map string to floating point.

Single-Byte Numeric Quantities

Frequently, in programming applications integer fields are used that have relatively small values. For instance, the accumulated sick leave for employees may have the range of 0–200. In ASCII this would require 3 bytes, and as an integer 2 bytes. However, numbers that are in the range 0–255 can be stored, in binary, in a single byte. Conversion from integer to a 1-byte string is done with the CHR$ function; the reverse operation uses the ASCII function. For instance, to store the "small" value integer A% in a buffer, we might write:

```
100    FIELD 5%, 1% AS A$,...

110    LSET A$ = CHR$(A%)
```

Retrieving the value would be done using the ASCII function as follows:

```
300    C% = ASCII(A$)
```

A Sample Application

To illustrate how these functions are used to minimize record size, let us consider a further expansion of the record in Example 17-2. However, before proceeding further, it should be emphasized that use of these techniques introduces further complexity in the program. As computer hardware costs have fallen and programmer costs have increased, less emphasis has been placed on efficient storage use and more on programmer efficiency. As a rule, files that use ASCII format throughout are more desirable than those that use binary techniques illustrated here.

FIELD	LENGTH	DESCRIPTION
Social Security number	9	
Name	21	
Pay code	2	2 digits
Monthly salary	6	6 digits, dollars and cents
Department	4	4 digits
Accumulated sick leave	3	always < 150
Other data		

Table 17-2

FIELD NUMBER	TYPE	VARIABLE NAME	LENGTH	DESCRIPTION
1	String	SSN$	9	Social Security number
2	String	N$	21	Employee name
3	Byte	PC$	1	Pay code
4	Floating point	MS$	4	Monthly salary
5	Integer	D$	2	Department
6	Byte	ASL$	1	Accumulated sick leave
:				
:				

We can see that the numeric fields are well suited to the principles described in the preceding section. For instance, pay code can be stored in a 1-byte field and monthly salary in a 4-byte field (floating point). In any application where these techniques are used, the record format must be carefully defined. This is done in Table 17-2. Notice that this table includes all of the pertinent information regarding each field in the record. The type clearly indicates which category of mapping is required. Setting up this data in an I/O buffer and retrieving it are illustrated in Figure 17-16.

Figure 17-16
Using the functions
to store data
in a record

```
200   FIELD #3%, 9% AS SSN$,        &
                 21% AS N$,         &
                 1% AS PC$,         &
                 4% AS MS$,         &
                 2% AS D$,          &
                 1% AS ASL$
      .
      .
      .
420   LSET PC$ = CHR$(PC%)
430   LSET MS$ = CVTF$(MS)
440   LSET D$ = CVT%$(D%)
450   LSET ASL$ = CHR$(ASL%)
      .
      .
      .
650   C% = ASCII(PC$)
660   SAL = CVT$F(MS$)
670   DEPT% = CVT$%(D$)
680   LEAVE% = ASCII(ASL$)
      .
      .
      .
```

Exercise 17-10 Referring to the data definition for this file (preceding Table 17-2), how many bytes would be required to store the four numeric fields if ASCII formatting were used? How many bytes are used with the technique of Table 17-2?

A CASE STUDY

Definition of the Application

Let us consider a company that manufactures a wide variety of do-it-yourself kits. Each kit is made up of one or more of a number of components. For instance, the components of kits 1 and 2 are illustrated below.

KIT 1		KIT 2	
COMPONENT	QUANTITY	COMPONENT	QUANTITY
A	5	A	5
B	3	D	1
C	1	F	1
D	6	H	9
		N	2

Note that not all kits include the same number of components. In fact, the number of different components (A, B, C, and so on) varies from 2 to 50.

This application is to include two main files: the *raw components file* and the *kit file*.

The Raw Components File

The record format of the raw components file is defined in Table 17-3. We can see that the record length is 39 bytes; thus they can be blocked 13 records per sector.

The Kit File

The record format for the kit file is defined in Table 17-4.

Of particular significance for this file is that records will have different lengths, depending upon the number of basic components comprising the kit. In other words, we are dealing with *variable length records*. An example record that

Table 17-3

FIELD NUMBER	TYPE	VARIABLE NAME	LENGTH	DESCRIPTION
1	String	RP$	5	Part number
2	String	RDESC$	32	Description
3	Integer	RSTOCK$	2	Stock on hand

Table 17-4

FIELD NUMBER	TYPE	VARIABLE NAME	LENGTH	DESCRIPTION
1	Byte	**L$**	1	Number of raw components
2	String	**KP$**	5	Part number
3	String	**KDESC$**	32	Description
4	Integer	**KSTOCK$**	2	Stock on hand
5	Raw component part number and number of units required by this kit. The following pair of fields is repeated once for each component in the kit.			
5.1	String	**KRP$**	5	Raw component part number
5.2	Byte	**KRN$**	1	Quantity required

Note: First 2 bytes of first sector contain the record count in integer.

includes four different components is shown in Figure 17-17. Note that the byte count of the record is included as the first field in the record.

Perhaps the simplest processing operation using the kit and raw components file would be to produce a so-called *parts explosion* report. Such a report would include each kit and a list of its components, for instance:

```
1983B    HAWTHORNE COLLECTOR
         8   R1152   HAWTHORNE BASIC UNIT
         1   R8992   HAWTHORNE CONTROLLER
         3   R2100   MILLSTONE DRIVER
         4   R1161   M4 DETECTION UNIT
```

We can see that all of this information is available from the record of Figure 17-17, *except* for the raw component descriptions. Processing each record of the kit file then involves accessing the record of each raw component listed for the kit.

Figure 17-17
Kit record layout

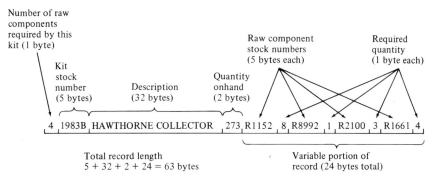

The Index File

Now we might ask ourselves the question: "How many kit records will be stored in each sector?" The answer is that it will be variable and will depend upon the length of the kit records. Because of this, it will be necessary to include an index file in order to gain random access to the kit file. The record format for the index file will be as shown in Table 17-5.

To access a kit record involves:

1. Search the index and find the part number.
2. Access the physical record number and read that record.
3. Use the offset field from the index to gain access to the desired kit record via the FIELD statement.

Building the File

To illustrate basic principles involved with processing a file system of this type, let us consider a program to build the kit file from scratch. We will assume that the raw components file has already been built. All information is to be entered from the keyboard. In order to simplify the example, no error checking is performed. A brief program to perform this function is shown in Figure 17-18. Notice the following facts:

1. The variable L$ is used to build the record as data is entered. Since it is not known whether the record will fit in the current buffer until after the record is built (its length is known), it is not practical to build it in the buffer.

2. The integer variable OFF% (offset) is maintained as a pointer to determine the next available buffer position. It is used to set the pointer for KR$ (the FIELD statement at line 600) for moving the record L$.

3. Whenever a record will not fit into the kit buffer, that buffer is written and OFF% is set to zero (line 580).

4. The variable IC% (index counter) is used to count the number of entries moved into the current buffer. When the buffer is full it is written to disk (line 690).

Table 17-5

FIELD NUMBER	TYPE	VARIABLE NAME	LENGTH	DESCRIPTION
1	String	IP$	5	Part number
2	Integer	IR$	2	Sector number
3	Byte	IO$	1	Offset to record

Note: The first 2 bytes of first record contains the record count (integer).

Figure 17-18

Program to build the
kit and index files

```
100 !    FILE BUILD ROUTINE                                          &
    !    THIS PROGRAM BUILDS THE KIT FILE AND CORRESPONDING INDEX    &
    !    FILE.  KIT INFORMATION IS ENTERED FROM THE KEYBOARD.
200 !    &
    !    OPEN FILES AND INITIALIZE
210      PRINT "THIS PROGRAM BUILDS A NEW KIT FILE."                 \ &
         INPUT "DO YOU WISH TO CONTINUE"; Q$
220      IF LEFT(CVT$$(Q$,32%),1%) <> "Y"                            &
            THEN GOTO 32767
230      OPEN "PART.KIT" FOR OUTPUT AS FILE #1%
240      OPEN "PART.IDX" FOR OUTPUT AS FILE #2%
250      FIELD #1%, 512% AS KIT$
260      FIELD #2%, 512% AS IDX$
270      LSET KIT$ = " "          !    FILL BUFFERS
280      LSET IDX$ = " "          !      WITH SPACES
290      RECCNT% = 0% !   NUMBER OF KIT RECORDS CURRENTLY             &
                      !     WRITTEN TO THE KIT FILE.
300      OFF% = 2%    !   OFFSET TO NEXT AVAILABLE POSITION IN KIT    &
                      !     BUFFER AREA.  INITIALIZED TO 2 SINCE RECORD &
                      !     COUNT OCCUPIES 2 BYTES OF FIRST SECTOR.
310      IC% = 1%     !   COUNTER FOR NUMBER OF INDEX ENTRIES ALREADY &
                      !     MOVED TO INDEX BUFFER.  INITIALIZED TO 1  &
                      !     SINCE RECORD COUNT OCCUPIES FIRST INDEX   &
                      !     RECORD.  MAXIMUM NUMBER OF INDEX ENTRIES  &
                      !     PER SECTOR IS 64.
400 !    &
    !    MAIN PROCESSING LOOP                                        &
    !    ACCEPT ALL DATA FOR A KIT RECORD, BUILD THE RECORD, STORE IT &
    !    IN THE BUFFER (WRITE TO DISK IF BUFFER FULL),               &
    !    AND STORE INDEX ENTRY TO INDEX BUFFER (WRITE IF BUFFER FULL). &
410      L$ = ""
420      INPUT "KIT STOCK NUMBER"; KPI$
430      PRINT "DESCRIPTION";                                        \ &
         INPUT LINE KDESCRI$                                         \ &
         KDESCRI$ = LEFT(CVT$$(KDESCRI$,4%)+SPACE$(32%),32%)
440      INPUT "QUANTITY ONHAND"; K%                                 \ &
         KSTOCKI$ = CVT%$(K%)
450      L$ = KPI$ + KDESCRI$ + KSTOCKI$
460      PRINT "NOW ENTER COMPONENTS"
470      FOR I% = 1% TO 50%
480         INPUT "COMPONENT STOCK NUMBER (CR IF FINISHED)"; KRPI$
490         IF LEN(KRPI$)=0%                                         &
               THEN GOTO 540   !  EXIT THE RAW COMPONENT LOOP
510         INPUT "NUMBER REQUIRED"; K%                              \ &
            KRNI$ = CHR$(K%)
520         L$ = L$ + KRPI$ + KRNI$
530      NEXT I%
540 !    &
    !    RAW COMPONENT ENTRIES COMPLETE SO PREPARE RECORD FOR WRITING
550      L$ = CHR$(I%) + L$  !  PREFIX COMPONENT COUNT TO L$
560      L% = LEN(L$)     !  LENGTH OF THIS RECORD
570 !    &
    !    SEE IF THERE IS ROOM IN CURRENT BUFFER FOR THIS RECORD.     &
    !    IF NOT THEN INCREMENT TO NEXT RECORD AND ZERO THE OFFSET.
580      IF L% + OFF% > 512%                                         &
         THEN                                                        &
           PUT #1%                                                   \ &
           OFF% = 0%                                                 \ &
           LSET KIT$ = ""
590 !    &
    !    MOVE THIS RECORD (L$) INTO THE BUFFER
600      FIELD #1%, OFF% AS Q$, L% AS KR$
620      LSET KR$ = L$
630      RECCNT% = RECCNT% + 1%
640 !    &
    !    NOW WRITE ENTRY TO THE INDEX FILE
650      FIELD #2%, IC% AS Q$,            &
                    5% AS IP$,            &
                    2% AS IR$,            &
                    1% AS IO$
660      LSET IP$ = KPI$                  \ &
         LSET IR$ = CVT%$(SECTNUM%)       \ &
         LSET IO$ = CHR$(OFF%)
670      IC% = IC% + 1%    !  COUNT THIS INDEX ENTRY
```

(continued on next page)

Figure 17-18
(continued)

```
680 !      &
    !      IF BUFFER FULL, THEN WRITE IT TO DESK AND ZERO
690        IF IC% = 64%                              &
           THEN                                      &
             PUT #2%                              \ &
             LSET IDX$ = ' '                      \ &
           IC% = 0%
700        OFF% = OFF% + L%   !  INCREMENT OFFSET
710        PRINT 'KIT ';KPI$;' WRITTEN AS RECORD NUMBER'; RECNUM%    \ &
           INPUT 'DO YOU HAVE MORE ENTRIES'; Q$                      \ &
           IF CVT$$(LEFT(Q$,1%),32%) = 'Y'                             &
             THEN GOTO 900
720        GOTO 400        !  REPEAT THE LOOP
900 !      &
    !      ENTRY COMPLETE SO WRITE HEADERS AND TERMINATE
910        IF OFF% > 0%                                              &
             THEN PUT #1%          !  WRITE PARTIALLY FILLED KIT BUFFER
920        IF IC% > 0%                                               &
             THEN PUT #2%          !  WRITE PARTIALLY FILLED INDEX BUFFER
930 !      &
    !      GET FIRST SECTOR OF KIT FILE IN ORDER TO WRITE            &
    !      RECORD COUNT IN BUFFER
940        GET #1%, RECORD 1%                        \ &
           FIELD #1%, 2% AS C$                        \ &
           LSET C$ = CVT%$(RECCNT%)                   \ &
           PUT #1%, RECORD 1%
950 !      DITTO FOR INDEX FILE
960        GET #2%, RECORD 1%                        \ &
           FIELD #2%, 2% AS C$                        \ &
           LSET C$ = CVT%$(RECCNT%)                   \ &
           PUT #2%, RECORD 1%
970        CLOSE #1%, #2%
980        PRINT \ PRINT 'PROCESSING COMPLETE'
32767      END
```

5. When processing is complete the first records from each of the files are read, the count header field updated, and the records rewritten (lines 930–960).

This program has been kept relatively simple in order to illustrate basic techniques. It does, however, demonstrate the powerful file processing capabilities that record I/O places at our disposal.

Answers to
Preceding
Exercises

17-1 Changes to the following statements would be required as shown.

```
220    I% = 1%

520    PUT 1%, RECORD I%

610    LSET M$ = NUMI$(I%-1%)
```

17-2 The first record is the header and it is read (and ignored) by the GET statement of line 230. If this statement were omitted, the header would be listed at line 320 and the value of I% would not correspond to the data record number.

17-3 The GET statement will access the next record since it has no RECORD qualifier. Then the next access to channel 1 will be to the record that follows. For instance, if the GET accesses record 13, it should be updated and written back to sector 13. However, next access to this channel is to record 14 so the updated information will be PUT to the wrong place.

17-4   Access to a record based on the name field would require that the file be searched beginning with the first record and progressing until the desired one is found. A more realistic approach would involve using a key field such as a customer number and maintaining a key field directory to the file. This approach is described in this chapter.

17-5   Most efficient use of disk is with spanned records; least is with unblocked. Unblocked records would require the least programming effort.

17-6   The record length 128 divides evenly into 512 so the records could not span blocks.

17-7   Since data record 1 is logical record 2, data record 2 is logical record 3, and so on, it will be necessary to add 1 to the data record number requested. This could be done with the following modification.

```
500    INPUT "DATA RECORD NUMBER"; D%
505    L% = L% + 1%
```

17-8   The first execution, REL%, will have a value of 1. Thus it will be executed seven times. All others, except the last, will be executed eight times since REL% will have a value of zero. Termination of processing occurs when an equal condition occurs at line 350. The number of passes through the loop during the last execution will be equal to the number of logical records in the last physical record.

17-9   Without an index means that, on an average, 2,500 logical records will be inspected. This requires 1,250 disk reads (two records per block). The index file will consist of 5000/56, or 90 blocks. Thus 45 index file reads plus 1 data file read gives a total of 46.

17-10   Storing the four numeric fields in ASCII would require $2 + 7 + 4 + 3 = 16$ bytes. (Remember, the decimal point would occupy 1 byte for the salary.) From Table 17-2 these same four fields occupy 8 bytes. Such a saving could be significant in some instances (large applications on small computers). However, as a rule in commercial data processing, disk space is a relatively low priority item. On the average, disk storage costs are dropping at the rate of approximately 30% per year. Programmer time is much more important.

Programming Problem   **17-1**   This problem is an expansion of the case study involving the do-it-yourself kits. For each order received from customers the management wishes to produce a summary. It is to be a parts explosion for each kit ordered by the customer (see the explosion example earlier in this chapter). Also, a summary is required for the total number of raw components required by this order. In preparing this summary remember that many of the raw components will be used by two or more kits.

     Input to the program (via the keyboard) is to be the kit number and the quantity ordered for each entry in the order.

     Note: For further random access file programming problems see the following section.

Random Access File Programming Problems

Note: The following problems may be programmed using either virtual array or record I/O files.

F-1. Figures 15-10 and 15-11 illustrate processing a randomly arranged virtual array file sequentially through use of a pointer table. This problem, using the file of Example 15-2, involves creating that pointer table, then printing a listing of the student number, name, and current units attempted in sequence based on student number. One simple approach to building the pointer table is to use the sort algorithm of Problem 9-4. However, it is important to recognize that the desired end result is a table of record numbers, not a table of sorted student numbers. This concept is illustrated in Figure F-1.

Figure F-1

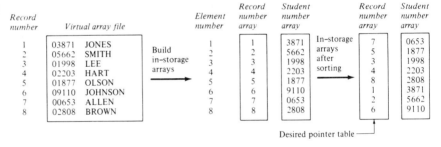

F-2. One method of handling the pointer table of Problem 15-2 is to store it as a separate file (as described in this chapter). Another is to include it within the original file in a slightly different form. For this purpose, let us assume that the last 5 bytes of each

Figure F-2

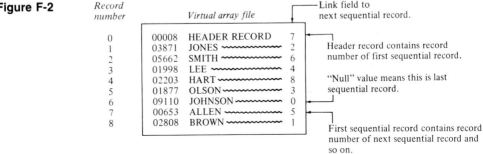

record in the file (bytes 509–512) contain the *record* number of the next sequential record. Thus this field in each record will point to the next sequential record as is illustrated in Figure F-2. This is commonly referred to as a *linked list* and involves a powerful programming tool. Write a program to build these links. Probably the simplest approach when beginning with an existing file is to build a pointer table as in Problem F-1, then use that table to build the links. Print the contents of each record (in ascending sequence) to verify your links.

F-3. The process of adding records to and deleting them from a linked list while maintaining the sequence is relatively simple. For instance, assume that a record with the student number 02115 is to be added to the file illustrated by Figure F-2. The easy approach is merely to add it to the end of the file as illustrated in Figure F-3(a). As we can see, the links must be adjusted. This is done by scanning the records of the file (using the link fields) until we find the record which it must follow (the largest student number which does not exceed the new one). By inspecting, in order, records 7, 5, 3, and 4, we see that the new record must "follow" record 3. Thus the link field in record 3 is changed to point to the new record, and the new record is given the previous link field from record 3. Note that none of the other records in the file are affected by this insertion.

Write a program which will allow records to be inserted into the file with appropriate adjustments to the link fields.

Figure F-3

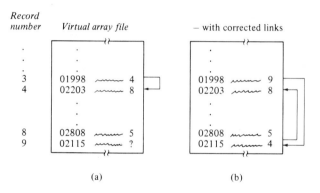

(a)   (b)

F-4. A company stocks approximately 2,000 different items for distribution to its sales representatives. Each part includes a 5-position ID code. A decision has been made to computerize the inventory system. In the interest of simplifying file-handling aspects of the computer system, each item in the inventory will be given a unique 4-digit number which will identify the record number of that part in the file. These will be assigned sequentially beginning with 0001. This is illustrated for the first three items in the inventory by the following table.

ID CODE	BECOMES	PART NUMBER
3792A		3792A0001
771PB		771PB0002
1311C		1311C0003

Thus the item identified by ID Code 3792A (part number 3792A0001) will be the first logical record in the file, ID Code 771PB will be the second logical record in the file, and so on. Each record is to include the following fields.

POSITIONS	DESCRIPTION
1–5	Part ID code
6–25	Part description
26–29	Quantity on hand
30–33	Quantity on order
34–37	Reorder level
38–256	Other data

Note that only the ID code portion of the part number is stored in each record.

This problem involves writing three separate programs for handling this file.

1. *File creation and record entry program.* For testing purposes, assume that the maximum number of logical records in the file will be 20. First create the file and preextend it to its full disk size by writing to the last record. Then the program must allow the user to enter up to 20 data records. Remember to provide some means for identifying which record is the last active logical record in the file.

2. *File dump program.* In order to verify file contents, a dump program is required which will print a listing of each record in the file from the first through the last.

3. *User inquiry program.* This program will allow the user to enter the full 9-character part number to obtain current information on any item. The logical record whose number is the last 4 digits of the entered part number should be read. Check the first 5 characters of the entered part number against the ID code of the record obtained. If they are different display an error message. If the same, then display the individual fields on the screen.

If record I/O is used, this system may be programmed using either unblocked or blocked (two per block) records. Check with your instructor which to use.

F-5. This is a further expansion of Problem F-4. A generalized reporting system is required that will print a listing of the file as follows:
    (a)   For every record in the file (same as part 2 of Problem F-4).
    (b)   For only those records where the quantity on hand plus the quantity on order is less then the reorder level.
For convenience, the user must have the option of having the report printed with the records in any of the following sequences.
    (a)   In file sequence (same as the file dump in part 2 of Problem F-4).
    (b)   Sorted on the first 10 characters of the part description field.
    (c)   Sorted on the ID code.
One method for handling the sorting requirements of this problem is to build one or more indexes (or index files) to the data file. Then the index(es) can be sorted using the sort algorithm suggested in Problem 9-4.

F-6. *Note*: This problem as stated requires use of principles described in Chapter 16.

A producer of a seasonal line of products, ships to customers from March through September. Orders for each new season are accepted beginning the preceding December. A typical order might appear as follows:

3 ea.	Free safety	Delivery: May 1
6 ea.	Cornerback	Delivery: May 1
5 ea.	Tight end	Delivery: June 15

As each order is received, the quantity and items ordered are tabulated by month of requested delivery. The result of this tabulation is a worksheet which summarizes scheduled shipments by the month as follows.

ITEM	MAR	APR	MAY	JUNE	JULY	AUG	SEPT	TOTAL
Tight end	3	15	137	48	8	4	0	215
Loose end	0	20	121	61	12	3	3	220
Free safety	0	20	97	39	6	2	5	169
Bargain safety	4	16	161	40	13	8	1	243

The company has decided to computerize this system in order to provide more efficient planning. The computerized system will be based upon a random access data file in which there will be a record for each product in their line. The data record will consist of the following information.

FIELD	DESCRIPTION
Stock number	5-digits, between 00001 and 50000.
Description	Alphanumeric, up to 20 characters in length.
Monthly sales	Seven monthly numeric fields, each less than 200.
March	
.	
.	
September	
Other data	73 positions

The systems analyst has determined that, with some ingenuity, the stock number can be stored in 2 bytes as an integer. Furthermore, monthly sales quantities, being less than 200, can be stored in a single byte. The record size can thus be reduced to 102 bytes, and five logical records can be written to each sector. This file will be named PROD.DAT. In addition, two directory files will be required for this file. PROD.DRS will be the stock number directory. For each record in PROD.DAT, there must be one entry in PROD.DRS consisting of two integer quantities: the first is the stock number and the second is the block (physical record) number of the disk block in PROD.DAT which contains the corresponding record. The first two bytes of the directory must contain an integer which is the number of records in the directory and, hence, in the main file. For testing purposes, assume that the file will never contain more than 50 records. PROD.DRD will be the product description directory. This directory will be similar to PROD.DRS except the first eight letters of each product description will be used as the directory entry. With these two directories, it will be possible to randomly access the file by either product stock number or description.

This programming problem consists of the following three major components.

1. *Build the master file and directories*. All needed files must first be created. Then the master file can be loaded from the sequential file PROD.RAW which contains one record for each product in the line as follows.

POSITIONS	FIELD
1–5	Stock number
5–	Description

Use the **INPUT LINE** statement to read this file; if a description is longer than 20 bytes, truncate to the right. As each record in PROD.DAT is built, all monthly accumulators must be set to zero. Directory tables may be built concurrently. When the end-of-file is detected in PROD.RAW, the file build is complete. At this time sort the two directory tables then write the sorted directories to disk.

2. *Update sales quantities*. As each order is received, the quantity ordered for each item must be entered into the appropriate monthly accumulator. Input shall be from the keyboard and will include the stock number, quantity and requested month of delivery.

3. *File inquiry capability*. Management wishes the capability to inquire via the keyboard for information on any given product. When run, this program is to ask the user which record is desired. The user can enter *either* the item stock number *or* the item description. If the first character entered is a digit, the program is to interpret it as the stock number and the stock number directory (PROD.DRS) is to be used. If it is a letter, then it is to be interpreted as the description and the first eight letters are to be used in conjunction with the description directory (PROD.DRD). In either case, when the desired entry is found, display the stock number, description, monthly figures, and total on order (sum of monthly values). If no table entry is found corresponding to the inquiry, display an appropriate error message. If there are two or more table entries for a description inquiry, then display each corresponding record.

F-7. A large organization with multiple buildings and many rooms in each (such as a university) will usually have a substantial task in keeping track of keys to rooms and buildings. For instance, there will be master keys which open all rooms in one or more buildings, and area keys which open all rooms in a given area (for example, the chemistry department). Furthermore, there will also be keys which open only a few selected rooms and even keys which open only one room. Some rooms will be opened by only a single given key but others by several or more different keys. For instance, we might have a room-key combination such as the following.

ROOM	OPENED BY KEY
100	A only
200	A, B, C, and D
300	C, X, and Y

The significance of this is that there is no logical (from a programming point of view) grouping or subsetting which can be used. Key and room assignments are made on the basis of needs of the organization. (This is often diametrically opposed to simplicity of program design.) Keys are issued to individuals of the organization based on their needs. Some people might be issued but one key and others may be issued many.

This problem involves a file system which will maintain an inventory of which rooms each key opens and to whom each key has been issued. Conceptually, a file would include a record for each key including an indication of all the rooms which it opens and all of the people to whom the key has been issued. This is illustrated in Figure F-4. The problem which arises here relates to how many rooms and people each key record should accommodate. For instance, some keys might open 40–50 different rooms, whereas most might open fewer than 10–12. Similarly, the restroom

Figure F-4

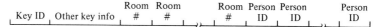

| Key ID | Other key info | Room # | Room # | | Room # | Person ID | Person ID | | Person ID |

keys might be issued to hundreds of people where many others are issued to but a few people. If the record is large enough to handle the maximum values, then a tremendous amount of storage will be wasted. Actually, we need the variable-length-record capabilities as described in the case study of Chapter 17 (Figure 17-17). However, the important difference between the case study and this problem is that keys are continually being issued and returned so that the variable length portion of the record continually changes.

Another approach, that which is to be used in this problem, is to define three separate files: (1) the *key master* file (KEY.MAS), (2) *key-room* file (KEY.RM), and (3) *key-issue* file (KEY.ISS). Information to be stored in these files is as follows.

KEY.MAS

FIELD	DESCRIPTION
Key ID	5-digit number between 00001 and 20000
Keying code	7-digit number
Creation date	4-digit date field *mmyy* format
Security level	1 character alphabetic field
Authorization code	5 character alphanumeric field
Room pointer	4-digit record number of record in KEY.RM containing list of rooms open by this key.
Person pointer	4-digit record number of record in KEY.ISS containing list of people holding this key.

KEY.RM

FIELD	DESCRIPTION
Key ID	5-digit number to which this record belongs.
Room number	Composed of 2-letter building number and 3-letter room number (e.g., QT162). The record is to contain space for room numbers of 12 rooms related to this key.
Pointer	4-digit record number of next record in this file containing room numbers of rooms opened by this key.

KEY.ISS

FIELD	DESCRIPTION
Key ID	5-digit key number to which this record belongs.
Social Security number	Social Security number of person to whom this key has been issued. The record is to contain space for 8 Social Security numbers of people issued the key.
Pointer	4-digit record number of next record in this file containing Social Security numbers of persons issued this key.

Since some records in KEY.MAS will require two or more records in KEY.RM and/or KEY.ISS, it will not, in general, be possible to use corresponding record numbers in each of the three files for a given key. For instance, let us assume that a new key is added to the file and, at the time it is added, the last logical records in use in each of the three files is as follows.

KEY.MAS—421
KEY.RM—537
KEY.ISS—586

The sequence of what occurs from the creation of a new master record through the designation of rooms and issuance of keys is illustrated in Figure F-5. Note that all pointers, room number, and Social Security number fields are initialized to nulls.

This problem consists of two programs.

1. *Data entry program*. This program must allow the user to enter new key information to KEY.MAS and corresponding room numbers to KEY.RM. It must also provide the user with the option for recording issuance of keys in KEY.ISS.

2. *Inquiry program*. This program must allow the user to request from the keyboard a list of all the rooms which can be opened by a given key or a list of people (Social Security numbers) to whom the key has been issued.

F-8. Problem F-7 can be further expanded to include a room master file (ROOM.MAS) which contains one record for each room. Within this record is the room number and

Figure F-5 KEY.MAS – Record 422

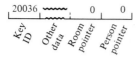

(a) The new master record is created. Nulls are entered into pointers since corresponding records not yet created.

KEY.RM – Record 538

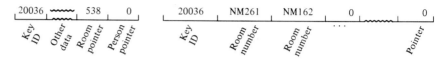

(b) Two corresponding room numbers have been entered. This triggered assigning the next available record in KEY.RM to this KEY.MAS record.

KEY.ISS – Record 586

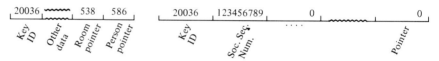

(c) The first issuance of a key to a person triggers assigning the next available record in KEY.ISS to this KEY.MAS record.

KEY.ISS – Record 586

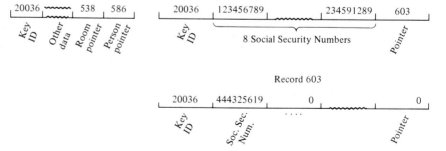

Record 603

(d) After a period of time further issuances of this key have been made. Upon issuing for the ninth person, another KEY.ISS record is assigned. The assumption here is that the next available one at the time was 603.

descriptive data. There is also a pointer to the corresponding record in the room-key file (ROOM.KEY) which contains the key numbers of all keys which open the room. In other words ROOM.MAS and ROOM.KEY have the same relationship as KEY.MAS and KEY.RM (or KEY.ISS).

Similarly, a third set of files can be defined to include an employees master file (EMPLOY.MAS) with the employee's Social Security number, name, and so on, and a corresponding keys-issued file (EMPLOY.KEY). Each master record would "point to" the record in EMPLOY.KEY which contained the list of keys issued to that person.

Although this expansion may sound somewhat confusing, it is actually relatively simple once the basic techniques for Problem F-7 are defined. Now the inquiry portion of F-7 can be modified to require printing the names (rather than Social Security numbers) of all employees who have been issued a particular key. An inquiry of a more complex nature might involve displaying a list of the names of all people who have a key to a given room.

Appendix I
Basic-Plus Reserved Words

In EXTEND mode keywords, including predefined function names, cannot be used as variable names. Following is a list of these *reserved words*.

ABS	EQV	MODE	RIGHT
AND	ERL	MOUNT	RND
APPEND	ERR	NAME	RSET
AS	EXP	NEW	RUN
ASCII	EXTEND	NEXT	RUNNH
AS FILE	FIELD	NO EXTEND	SAVE
ASSIGN	FILE SIZE	NOT	SCALE
ATN	FIX	NUM	SGN
BLOCK	FNEND	NUM$	SIN
BUFSIZ	FOR	NUM1$	SLEEP
BYE	FOR INPUT AS FILE	NUM2	SPACE$
CAT	FOR OUTPUT AS FILE	OLD	SPEC%
CATALOG	GET	ON	SQR
CCONT	GOSUB	ON ERROR GOTO	STATUS
CHAIN	GOTO	OPEN	STEP
CHANGE	HELLO	OR	STOP
CHR$	IDN	PEEK	STRING$
CLOSE	IF	PI	SUM$
CLUSTER SIZE	IFOR	PIF	SWAP%
COMPILE	IMP	PIFOR	SYS
COMP%	INPUT	PLACE$	TAB
CON	INPUT LINE	POS	TAN
CONT	INSTR	PRINT	TAND
COS	INT	PROD$	TAPE
COUNT	INV	PUT	THEN
CVTF$	KEY	QUO$	TIME
CVT$F	KILL	RAD$	TIME$
CVT$%	LEFT	RANDOM	TO
CVT%$	LEN	RANDOMIZE	TRN
CVT$$	LENGTH	READ	UNLESS
DATA	LET	REASSIGN	UNLOCK
DATE$	LINE	RECORD	UNSAVE
DEASSIGN	LIST	RECORD SIZE	UNTIL
DEF	LISTNH	RECOUNT	USING
DELETE	LOG	REM	VAL
DET	LOG10	RENAME	WAIT
DIF$	LSET	REPLACE	WHILE
DIM	MAGTAPE	RESTORE	XLATE
ELSE	MAT	RESUME	XOR
END	MID	RETURN	ZER

Appendix II
The ASCII Character Set

The following table summarizes the 7-bit ASCII character set and includes the decimal equivalent of each character.

Decimal Value	ASCII Character	RSTS Usage	Decimal Value	ASCII Character	RSTS Usage	Decimal Value	ASCII Character	RSTS Usage
0	NUL	FILL character	27	ESC	ESCAPE[1]	54	6	
1	SOH		28	FS		55	7	
2	STX		29	GS		56	8	
3	ETX	CTRL/C	30	RS		57	9	
4	EOT	CTRL/D	31	US		58	:	
5	ENQ		32	SP	SPACE	59	;	
6	ACK		33	!		60	<	
7	BEL	BELL(CTRL/G)	34	"		61	=	
8	BS	BACKSPACE	35	#		62	>	
9	HT	HORIZONTAL TAB	36	$		63	?	
10	LF	LINE FEED	37	%		64	@	
11	VT	VERTICAL TAB	38	&		65	A	
12	FF	FORM FEED (CTRL/L)	39	"		66	B	
13	CR	CARRIAGE RETURN	40	(		67	C	
14	SO		41	)		68	D	
15	SI	CTRL/O	42	*		69	E	
16	DLE		43	+		70	F	
17	DC1	XON (CTRL/Q)	44	,		71	G	
18	DC2		45	-		72	H	
19	DC3	X OFF (CTRL/S)	46	.		73	I	
20	DC4		47	/		74	J	
21	NAK	CTRL/U	48	0		75	K	
22	SYN		49	1		76	L	
23	ETB		50	2		77	M	
24	CAN		51	3		78	N	
25	EM		52	4		79	O	
26	SUB	CTRL/Z	53	5		80	P	

Decimal Value	ASCII Character	RSTS Usage	Decimal Value	ASCII Character	RSTS Usage	Decimal Value	ASCII Character	RSTS Usage
81	Q		97	a		113	q	
82	R		98	b		114	r	
83	S		99	c		115	s	
84	T		100	d		116	t	
85	U		101	e		117	u	
86	V		102	f		118	v	
87	W		103	g		119	w	
88	X		104	h		120	x	
89	Y		105	i		121	y	
90	Z		106	j		122	z	
91	[		107	k		123	{	
92	\		108	l		124	| Vertical Line	
93	]		109	m		125	}	
94	^ OR ↑		110	n		126	~ Tilde	
95	— OR ←		111	o		127	DEL RUBOUT	
96	` Grave accent		112	p				

Appendix III
Summary of Basic-Plus Statements

CONVENTIONS USED IN THIS APPENDIX

In the interest of standardizing, certain conventions are used to represent general statement forms.

1. Items in lowercase are supplied by the programmer. The abbreviations used in this book are as follows:

   arg—argument or arguments used in a function call
   cond—conditional that may be true or false
   const—numeric or string constant
   dim—dimension required in defining an array
   expr—arithmetic expression; may be a simple constant or variable
   list—list of variables, expressions, or constants
   ln—line number
   string—string variable or constant (enclosed in quotes)
   string var—string variable
   var—numeric variable

2. Items in capital letters (LET, DATA, etc.) must appear exactly as shown because they represent Basic keywords.

3. Angle brackets <> indicate required elements that are to be supplied by the programmer. For instance,

   ln LET <*var*> = <*expr*>

   Note: Each statement is shown with a line number. If multiple statements per line are used, statements following the first statement will not have line numbers.

4. Square brackets [ ] indicate a required choice of one element among two or more possibilities. For example:

$$\text{IF } <expr> \left[\begin{array}{l} \text{THEN } <statement> \\ \text{THEN } <ln> \\ \text{GOTO } <ln> \end{array} \right]$$

5. Braces { } indicate an optional element (or choice of elements as in rule 4):

   ln {LET} <*var*> = <*expr*>

6. An element repeated twice followed by ellipses (periods) implies that one or more such elements may be included:

DATA <*const*>, <*const*>, . . .

SUMMARY OF STATEMENTS

The following statement general forms each includes one or more example statements. For simplicity of reference they are listed alphabetically rather than grouped by function.

CHAIN

ln CHAIN <*string*> {<*expr*>}

```
100   CHAIN "CHECK"        ! CHAIN TO PROGRAM CHECK
110   CHAIN PROG$  100     ! CHAIN TO LINE 100, PROGRAM NAME IS PROG$
```

CLOSE

ln CLOSE <*expr*>, <*expr*>, . . .

```
100   CLOSE #1%, #2%
120   CLOSE I%
```

DATA

ln DATA <*const*>, <*const*>, . . .

```
920   DATA 25.3, 64, "STRING DATA"
```

DEF

ln DEF FN<*var(arg)*> = <*expr(arg)*> single-line function
ln DEF FN<*var(arg)*>   multiple-line function

```
200   DEF FNC(R) = 2.0*3.14*R*R     (single line)
300   DEF FNCNT$(A,B,C)             (multiple line)
```

DIM

ln DIM <*var(dim)*>, <*var(dim)*>, . . .
ln DIM #<*const*>, <*var(dim)*>, . . . <*string var(dim)*> = <*const*>

```
150   DIM A(20), B%(10%, 15%), C$(15%)
160   DIM #4%, X%(500%), Z$(100%) = 128%   (virtual array)
```

END

ln **END**

```
32767  END
```

EXTEND

ln **EXTEND**

```
10  EXTEND    ! Switch to EXTEND mode
```

FIELD

ln **FIELD #**<*expr*>, <*expr*> AS <*string var*>, <*expr*> AS <*string var*>, . . .

```
470  FIELD #3%, N% AS D$, 24% AS DESCR$
```

FNEND

ln **FNEND**

```
920 FNEND   ! END OF MULTIPLE LINE FUNCTION
```

FOR

ln **FOR** <*var*> = <*expr*> **TO** <*expr*> {**STEP** <*exp*>}

```
370  FOR I% = 1% TO 20%
980  FOR J% = N% TO 0% STEP -1%
```

FOR-UNTIL, FOR-WHILE

ln **FOR** <*var*> = <*expr*> {**STEP** <*expr*>} $\begin{bmatrix} \textbf{UNTIL} \\ \textbf{WHILE} \end{bmatrix}$ <*cond*>

```
650  FOR A% = 1%   WHILE X>0.0
790  FOR B% = 3% STEP 4%   UNTIL FINISHED%
```

GET

ln **GET #**<*expr*> {**,RECORD** <*expr*>}

```
470  GET #5%
500  GET #6%, RECORD N%
```

GOSUB

ln **GOSUB** <*ln*>

```
280  GOSUB 750
```

GOTO

ln **GOTO** *<ln>*

```
370   GOTO 260
370   GO TO 260
```

IF-THEN

$$ln \text{ IF } <cond> \left[\begin{array}{l} \text{THEN } <statement> \\ \text{THEN } <ln> \\ \text{GOTO } <ln> \end{array} \right]$$

```
750   IF A=B THEN PRINT "VARIABLES CHECK"
800   IF X<0 THEN 270
850   IF X<0 GOTO 270
900   IF X>0 OR Y=2*P GOTO 990
```

IF-THEN-ELSE

$$ln \text{ IF } <cond> \left[\begin{array}{l} \text{THEN } <statement> \\ \text{THEN } <ln> \end{array} \right] \left[\begin{array}{l} \text{ELSE } <statement> \\ \text{ELSE } <ln> \end{array} \right]$$

```
640   IF A=B THEN PRINT "CHECK" ELSE PRINT "NO CHECK"
690   IF X<0 THEN 720 ELSE 780
```

INPUT

ln **INPUT** *{#<expr>,} <list>*
ln **INPUT** *{literal,} <list>*

```
120   INPUT #1%, A,B,C
130   INPUT P,Q$
140   INPUT "WHAT IS THE MAXIMUM", M%
```

INPUT LINE

ln **INPUT LINE** *{#<expr>,} <string>*

```
460   INPUT LINE Q$
470   INPUT LINE #4%, L$
```

KILL

ln **KILL** *<string>*

```
500 KILL "ABC.DAT"    ! Delete the file ABC.DAT
```

LET

ln **LET** *<var>, <var>, . . . = <expr>*

```
220   LET A = B*C + 25.0
240   A = B*C + 25.0
300   X%, Y%, Z% = 0%      ! SET all 3 variables to zero
```

LSET

ln **LSET** *<string var>*, *<string var>*, . . . = *<string>*

```
370   LSET D$ = Q$ + "OVERDUE"
```

MAT INPUT

ln **MAT INPUT** {#*<expr>*,} *<list of matrices>*

```
460   MAT INPUT #1%, A%, B%
```

MAT PRINT

ln **MAT PRINT** {#*<expr>*,} *<matrix name>*

```
500   MAT PRINT A
510   MAT PRINT #3%, B%
```

MAT READ

ln **MAT READ** *<list of matrices>*

```
180   MAT READ A,B
```

MAT ZER

ln **MAT** *<matrix name>* = **ZER** {(dim)}

```
200   MAT A% = ZER
250   MAT B% = ZER (15%, 10%)      ! REDIMENSIONS MATRIX
```

NAME-AS

ln **NAME** *<string>* **AS** *<string>*

```
410   NAME "TEST.FLE" AS "PERM.FLE"      ! RENAMES FILE ON DISK
```

NEXT

ln **NEXT** *<var>*

```
490   NEXT J%
```

NO EXTEND

ln **NO EXTEND**

```
10  NO EXTEND    ! SWITCHES TO NO EXTEND MODE
```

ON ERROR

ln **ON ERROR GOTO** {*<ln>*}

```
20  ON ERROR GOTO 30000
```

ON-GOSUB

ln **ON** *<expr>* **GOSUB** *<list of line numbers>*

```
400  ON N% GOSUB 500, 620, 700, 850
```

ON GOTO

ln **ON** *<expr>* **GOTO** *<list of line numbers>*

```
500  ON L% GOTO 600, 700, 920
```

OPEN

ln **OPEN** *<string>* $\left\{ \text{FOR} \begin{bmatrix} \text{INPUT} \\ \text{OUTPUT} \end{bmatrix} \right\}$ **AS FILE** *<expr>* {**,RECORDSIZE** *<expr>*}

```
100  OPEN "ABC.XYZ" FOR INPUT AS FILE #1%
110  OPEN F$ FOR OUTPUT AS FILE #2%
120  OPEN "WORK.FLE" AS FILE #3%
130  OPEN "NL:" AS FILE #4%, RECORDSIZE 64%
```

PRINT

ln **PRINT** {**#**<expr>,} {*<list>*}

```
250  PRINT A,B$,C%
260  PRINT #1%,X,Y,Z
270  PRINT
```

PRINT-USING

ln **PRINT** {**#**<expr>,} **USING** *<string>* {**,**<list>}

```
330  PRINT USING M$
390  PRINT #4%, USING "###.##     ###", A,I%
```

PUT

ln **PUT #**<expr> {**,RECORD** *<expr>*}

```
480  PUT #5%
490  PUT #4%, RECORD 20%
```

RANDOMIZE

ln **RANDOMIZE**

```
20 RANDOMIZE
```

READ

ln **READ** *<var>*, *<var>*, . . .

```
210  READ A,B$
```

REM

ln **REM** *<message>*
ln **!** *<message>*
ln *<statement>* **!** *<message>*

```
100  REM   EXAMPLE
110  !     EXAMPLE
200  I% = 0%  ! INITIALIZE COUNTER
```

RESTORE

ln **RESTORE**

```
100  RESTORE
```

RESUME

ln **RESUME** {*<ln>*}

```
300  RESUME        ! RESUME PROCESSING AT ERROR LINE
350  RESUME 600    ! RESUME AT LINE 600
```

RETURN

ln **RETURN**

```
900  RETURN     ! RETURN TO STATEMENT FOLLOWING GOSUB
```

RSET

ln **RSET** *<string var>*, *<string var>*, . . . = *<string>*

```
750  RSET X$ = B$ + Q$ + R$
```

SLEEP

ln **SLEEP** *<expr>*

```
800   SLEEP 20%    ! SUSPEND PROCESSING FOR 20 SECONDS
```

STOP

ln **STOP**

```
900 STOP
```

Appendix IV
Summary of Basic-Plus Commands

This appendix briefly summarizes the Basic-Plus commands that most commonly will be encountered by the student.

COMMAND	EXPLANATION
APPEND	Used to include contents of a previously saved source program in current program.
BYE	Indicates to RSTS/E that a user wishes to leave the terminal. Closes and saves any files remaining open for that user.

After the user types BYE the system responds:

Confirm:

At this point the user has five options:

?   Requests information on valid responses to the "Confirm" prompt.
Y   Requests normal log-out.
N   Requests no log-out; effectively negates the **BYE** command.
I   Requests an opportunity to delete files individually prior to log-out.
F   Fast log-out.

If BYE is followed immediately by one of the valid responses, the "Confirm" prompt is not printed.

COMMAND	EXPLANATION
CAT **CATALOG**	Returns the user's file directory. Unless another device is specified following the term **CAT** or **CATALOG**, the disk is the assumed device.
COMPILE	Allows the user to store a compiled version of the user's BASIC program. The file is stored on disk with the current name and the extension .BAC. Or a new file-name can be indicated and the extension .BAC will still be appended.

COMMAND	EXPLANATION
CONT	Allows the user to continue execution of the program currently in memory following the execution of a **STOP** statement or use of a control c.
DELETE	Allows the user to remove one or more lines from the program currently in memory. Following the word **DELETE** the user types the line number of the single line to be deleted or two line numbers separated by a dash (—) indicating the first and last line of the section of code to be removed. Several single lines or line sections can be indicated by separating the line numbers, or line number pairs, with a comma.
EXTEND	Allows the user to include Extend Mode features in programs and to execute programs that include Extend Mode features. This is necessary if the system default is No Extend Mode following log-in. Either mode condition can be overridden at the program level.
HELLO	Indicates to RSTS/E that a user wishes to log onto the system. Allows the user to enter the project-programmer number and password.
LIST	Allows the user to obtain a printed listing at the user terminal of the program currently in memory, or one or more lines of that program. The word **LIST** by itself will cause the listing of the entire user program. **LIST** followed by one line number will list that line; and **LIST** followed by two line numbers separated by a dash (—) will list the lines between and including the lines indicated. Several single lines or line sections can be indicated by separating the line numbers, or line number pairs, with a comma.
LISTNH	Same as **LIST**, but does not print header containing the program name and current data.
NEW	Clears the user's area in memory and allows the user to enter a new program from the terminal. A program name can be indicated following word **NEW** or when the system requests it.
NO EXTEND	Negates any previous **EXTEND** command, placing the system default in No Extend Mode. Extend Mode features are no longer

COMMAND	EXPLANATION
	available unless the program includes an **EXTEND** statement to override system default.
OLD	Clears the user's area in memory and allows the user to recall a saved program from a storage device. The user can indicate a program name following the word **OLD** or when the system requests it.
RENAME	Causes the name of the program currently in memory to be changed to the name specified after the word **RENAME**.
REPLACE	Same as **SAVE**, but allows the user to substitute a new program for an old program with the same name, erasing the old program.
RUN	Allows the user to begin execution of the program currently in memory. The word **RUN** can be followed by a file-name, in which case the file is loaded from the disk, compiled (if necessary), and run. The default file-name extension is **.BAS**.
RUNNH	Causes execution of the program currently in memory but header information containing program name and current data is not printed. If a file-name is used, the command is executed as if no file-name were given. The default file-name extension is .BAS.
SAVE	Causes the program currently in memory to be saved on disk under its current file-name with the extension .BAS. Where the word **SAVE** is followed by a file-name or a device and a file-name, the program in memory is saved under the name given and on the device specified.
UNSAVE	The word UNSAVE is followed by the file-name, and, optionally, the extension of the file to be removed. The **UNSAVE** command cannot remove files without an extension. If no extension is specified, the source (.BAS) file is deleted.

Special Control Character Summary

COMMAND	EXPLANATION
CTRL/C	Causes the system to return to Basic command mode to allow for issuing of further commands or editing. Echoes on terminal as ^C.
CTRL/O	Used as a switch to suppress/enable output of a program on the user terminal. Echoes as ^O.
CTRL/Q	When generated by a device on which a CTRL/S has interrupted output, causes computer to resume output at the next character.
CTRL/S	When generated by a device for which STALL characteristics are set, interrupts computer output on the device until either CTRL/Q or another character is generated.
CTRL/U	Deletes the current typed line, echoes as ^U, and performs a carriage return/line feed.
CTRL/Z	Used as an end-of-file character.
ESCape or ALT MODE Key	Enters a typed line to the system, echoes on the user terminal as a $ character, and does not cause a carriage return/line feed.
RETURN Key	Enters a typed line to the system, results in a carriage return/line feed operation at the user terminal.
RUBOUT or DELETE Key	Deletes the last character typed on that physical line. Erased characters are shown on the teleprinter between backslashes.
TAB or CTRL/I	Performs a tabulation to the next tab stop (eight spaces apart) of the terminal printing line.

Appendix V
Summary of Basic-Plus Functions

This appendix briefly summarizes the Basic-Plus functions that will most commonly be encountered by the student.

TYPE	FUNCTION	EXPLANATION
MATHEMATICAL	Y=ABS(X)	Returns the absolute value of **X**.
	Y=ATN(X)	Returns the arctangent (in radians) of **X**.
	Y=COS(X)	Returns the cosine of **X** where **X** is in radians.
	Y=EXP(X)	Returns the value of e^X, where $e = 2.71828...$
	Y=FIX(X)	Returns the truncated value of **X**, SGN(X)*INT(ABS(X)).
	Y=INT(X)	Returns the greatest integer in **X** that is less than or equal to **X**.
	Y=LOG(X)	Returns the natural logarithm of **X**, $\log_e$ **X**.
	Y=LOG10(X)	Returns the common logarithm of **X**, $\log_{10}$ **X**.
	Y=PI	Returns the constant 3.14159...
	Y=RND	Returns a random number between 0 and 1.
	Y=RND(X)	Returns a random number between 0 and 1.
	Y=SGN(X)	Returns the sign function of **X**; + 1 if positive, 0 if zero, − 1 if negative.
	Y=SIN(X)	Returns the sine of **X** where **X** is in radians.
	Y=SQR(X)	Returns the square root of **X**.
	Y=TAN(X)	Returns the tangent of **X** where **X** is in radians.

TYPE	FUNCTION	EXPLANATION
PRINT	Y%=POS(X%)	Returns the current position of the print head for I/O channel X%, 0 is the user's terminal.
	Y$=TAB(X%)	Moves print head to position X% in the current print record, or is disregarded if the current position is beyond X%. (The first position is counted as 0.)
STRING	Y%=ASCII(A$)	Returns the ASCII value of the first character in the string A$.
	Y$=CHR$(X%)	Returns a character string having the ASCII value of X. Only one character is generated.
	Y$=CVT%$(K%)	Maps integer into two-character string.
	Y$=CVTF$(X)	Maps floating-point number into 4- or 8-character string.
	Y%=CVT$%(A$)	Maps first two characters of string A$ into an integer.
	Y=CVT$F(A$)	Maps first four or eight characters of string A$ into a floating-point number.
	T$=CVT$$(S$,M%)	Converts the source character string S$ to the string referenced by the variable T$. The conversion is performed according to the decimal value of the integer represented by M% as follows. These digits may be summed to produce any combination of these conversions. 1% Trim the parity bit. 2% Discard all spaces and tabs. 4% Discard excess characters: CR, LF, FF, ESC, RUBOUT, and NULL. 8% Discard leading spaces and tabs.

(continued on next page)

TYPE	FUNCTION	EXPLANATION
STRING		16% Reduce spaces and tabs to one space.
		32% Convert lowercase to uppercase.
		64% Convert [to (and] to).
		128% Discard trailing spaces and tabs.
		256% Do not alter characters inside quotes.
	Y$=LEN(A$)	Returns the number of characters in A$
	Y$=STRING$(N1%,N2%)	Creates string Y$ of length N1%, composed of characters whose ASCII decimal value is N2%.
	Y$=LEFT(A$,N%)	Returns a substring of the string A$ from the first character to the Nth character (the left-most N% characters).
	Y$=RIGHT(A$,N%)	Returns a substring of the string A$ from the Nth to the last character (the right-most characters of the string starting with the Nth character).
	Y$=MID(A$,N1%,N2%)	Returns a substring of the string A$ starting with the N1% and being N2% characters long (the characters between and including the N1% to N1%+N2%–1 characters). in the string A$, including trailing blanks.
	Y%=INSTR(N1%,A$,B$)	Indicates a search for the substring B$ within the string A$ beginning at character position N1. Returns a value 0 if B$ is not in A$, and the character position of B$ if B$ is found to be in A$ (character position is measured from the start of the string).

TYPE	FUNCTION	EXPLANATION
STRING	Y$=SPACE$(N%)	Indicates a string of **N** spaces, used to insert spaces within a character string.
	Y$=NUM$(N)	Indicates a string of numeric characters representing the value of **N** as it would be output by a **PRINT** statement. For example: **NUM$(1.0000)** = b1b and **NUM$(−1.0000)** = −1b.
	Y$=NUM1$(N)	Returns a string of characters representing the value of **N**. This is similar to the function **NUM$**, except that it does not return spaces.
	Y=VAL(A$)	Computes the numeric value of the string of numeric characters **A$**. If **A$** contains any character not acceptable as numeric input with the **INPUT** statement, an error results. For example: VAL("15")=15
MATRIX	MAT Y=TRN(X)	Returns the transpose of the matrix **X**.
	MAT Y=INV(X)	Returns the inverse of the matrix **X**.
	Y=DET	Following an **INV(X)** function evaluation, the variable **DET** is equivalent to the determinant of **X**.
	Y%=NUM	Following input of a matrix, **NUM** contains the number of rows entered, or in the case of a one-dimensional matrix, the number of elements entered.
	Y%=NUM2	Following input of a matrix, **NUM2** contains the number of elements entered in that row.
SYSTEM	Y$=DATE$(0%)	Returns the current date in the following format: 02-Mar-81
	Y$=TIME$(0%)	Returns the current time of day as a character string as follows: TIME$(0)="05:30 PM" or"17:30"

Appendix VI
Summary of Basic-Plus —
RSTS/E Error Messages

Because a Basic-Plus program can recover from certain errors, this appendix lists errors in two categories—recoverable and nonrecoverable. The recoverable error messages are listed in ascending order of their related error numbers. A program can use these error numbers to differentiate errors. Nonrecoverable errors are in alphabetical order without error numbers, because a program cannot use the numbers in an error-handling routine. The first character position of each message indicates the severity of the error.

%   Execution of the program can continue but might not generate the expected results.

?   Execution cannot continue unless the user removes the cause of the error.

A message beginning with neither a question mark nor a percent sign is for information only.

ERR	MESSAGE PRINTED	MEANING
		User Recoverable
0	(system installation name)	The error code 0 is associated with the system installation name and is used by system programs to print identification lines.
1	?Bad directory for device	The directory of the device referenced is in an unreadable format. The magtape label format on tape differs from the systemwide default format, the current job default format, or the format specified in the **OPEN** statement. Use the **ASSIGN** command to set the correct format default or change the format specification in the **MODE** option of the **OPEN** statement.
2	?Illegal file-name	The file-name specified is not acceptable. It contains unacceptable characters or the

ERR	MESSAGE PRINTED	MEANING
		file-name specification format has been violated. The **CCL** command to be added begins with a number or contains a character other than A through Z, 0 through 9, and commercial at (@).
3	?Account or device in use	Reassigning or dismounting of the device cannot be done because the device is open or has one or more open files. The account to be deleted has one or more files and must be zeroed before being deleted. The run time system to be deleted is currently loaded in memory and in use. Output to a pseudo keyboard cannot be done unless the device is in KB wait state. An echo control field cannot be declared while another field is currently active. The **CCL** command to be added already exists.
4	?No room for user on device	Storage space allowed for the current user on the device specified has been used or the device as a whole is too full to accept further data.
5	?Can't find file or account	The file or account number specified was not found on the device specified. The **CCL** command to be deleted does not exist.
6	?Not a valid device	The device specification supplied is not valid for one of the following reasons. The unit number or its type is not configured on the system. The specification is logical and untranslatable because a physical device is not associated with it.
7	?I/O channel already open	An attempt was made to open one of the 12 I/O channels that had already been opened by the program.
8	?Device not available	The specified device exists on the system but a user's attempt to **ASSIGN** or **OPEN** it

ERR	MESSAGE PRINTED	MEANING
		is prohibited for one of the following reasons. The device is currently reserved by another job. The device requires privileges for ownership and the user does not have privilege. The device or its controller has been disabled by the system manager. The device is a keyboard line for pseudo-keyboard use only.
9	?I/O channel not open	Attempt to perform I/O on one of the 12 channels that has not been previously opened in the program.
10	?Protection violation	The user was prohibited from performing the requested operation because the kind of operation was illegal (such as input from a line printer) or because the user did not have the privileges necessary (such as deleting a protected file).
11	?End of file on device	Attempt to perform input beyond the end of a data file; or a Basic source file is called into memory and is found to contain no **END** statement.
12	?Fatal system I/O failure	An I/O error has occurred on the system level. The user has no guarantee that the last operation has been performed. This error is caused by hardware condition. Report such occurrences to the system manager.
13	?User data error on device	One or more characters may have been transmitted incorrectly due to a parity error, bad punch combination on a card, or similar error.
14	?Device hung or write locked	User should check hardware condition of device requested. Possible causes of this

ERR	MESSAGE PRINTED	MEANING
		error include a line printer out of paper or high-speed reader being offline.
15	?Keyboard **WAIT** exhausted	Time requested by **WAIT** statement has been exhausted with no input received from the specified keyboard.
16	?Name or account now exists	An attempt was made to rename a file with the name of a file that already exists, or an attempt was made by the system manager to insert an account number that is already within the system.
17	?Too many open files on unit	Only one open DECtape output file is permitted per DECtape drive. Only one open file per magtape drive is permitted.
18	?Illegal SYS( ) usage	Illegal use of the SYS system function.
19	?Disk block is interlocked	The requested disk block segment is already in use (locked) by some other user.
20	?Pack IDs don't match	The identification code for the specified disk pack does not match the identification code already on the pack.
21	?Disk pack is not mounted	No disk pack is mounted on the specified disk drive.
22	?Disk pack is locked out.	The disk pack specified is mounted but temporarily disabled.
23	?Illegal cluster size	The specified cluster size is unacceptable. The cluster size must be a power of 2. For a file cluster, the size must be equal to or greater than the pack cluster size and must not be greater than 256. For a pack cluster the size must be equal to or greater than the device cluster size and must not be

ERR	MESSAGE PRINTED	MEANING
		greater than 16. The device cluster size is fixed by type.
24	?Disk pack is private	The current user does not have access to the specified private disk pack.
25	?Disk pack needs 'CLEANing'	Nonfatal disk mounting error; use the **CLEAN** operation in UTILITY.
26	?Fatal disk pack mount error	Fatal disk mounting error. Disk cannot be successfully mounted.
27	?I/O to detached keyboard	I/O was attempted to a hung up dataset or to the previous, but now detached, console keyboard for the job.
28	?Programmable ↑ C trap	A CTRL/C combination was typed while an **ON ERROR GOTO** statement was in effect and programmable CTRL/C trapping was enabled.
29	?Corrupted file structure	Fatal error in **CLEAN** operation.
30	?Device not file structured	An attempt is made to access a device, other than a disk, DECtape, or magtape device, as a file-structured device. This error occurs, for example, when the user attempts to gain a directory listing of a nondirectory device.
31	?Illegal byte count for I/O	The buffer size specified in the **RECORD-SIZE** option of the **OPEN** statement or in the **COUNT** option of the **PUT** statement is not a multiple of the block size of the device being used for I/O, or is illegal for the device. An attempt is made to run a compiled file that has improper size as a result of incorrect transfer procedure.
32	?No buffer space available	The user accesses a file and the monitor

ERR	MESSAGE PRINTED	MEANING
		requires one small buffer to complete the request but one is not currently available. If the program is sending messages, two conditions are possible. The first occurs when a program sends a message and the receiving program has exceeded the pending message limit. The second occurs when a sending program attempts to send a message and a small buffer is not available for the operation.
39	?Magtape select error	When access to a magtape drive was attempted, the selected unit was found to be off-line.
40	?Magtape record length error	When performing input from magtape, the record on magtape was found to be longer than the buffer designated to handle the record.
41	?Non-res run-time system	The run-time system referenced has not been loaded into memory and is therefore nonresident.
42	?Virtual buffer too large	Virtual core buffers must be 512 bytes long.
43	?Virtual array not on disk	A nondisk device is open on the channel upon which the virtual array is referenced.
44	?Matrix or array too big	In-core array size is too large.
45	?Virtual array not yet open	An attempt was made to use a virtual array before opening the corresponding disk file.
46	?Illegal I/O channel	Attempt was made to open a file on an I/O channel outside the range of the integer numbers 1 to 12.

ERR	MESSAGE PRINTED	MEANING
47	?Line too long	Attempt to input a line longer than 255 characters (which includes any line terminator). Buffer overflows.
48	%Floating-point error	Attempt to use a computed floating-point number outside the range $1E-38 < n < 1E38$, excluding zero. If no transfer to an error-handling routine is made, zero is returned as the floating-point value. (C)
49	%Argument too large in EXP	Acceptable arguments are within the approximate range $-89 < arg < +88$. The value returned is zero. (C)
50	%Data format error	A **READ** or **INPUT** statement detected data in an illegal format. For example, 1..2 is an improperly formed number, 1.3 is an improperly formed integer, and X" is an illegal string. (C)
51	%Integer error	Attempt to use a computed integer outside the range $-32768 < n < 32767$. For example, an attempt is made to assign to an integer variable a floating-point number outside the integer range. If no transfer to an error-handling routine is made, zero is returned as the integer value. (C)
52	?Illegal number	Integer overflow or underflow or floating-point overflow. The range for integers is -32768 to $+32767$; for floating-point numbers the upper limit is 1E38. (For floating-point underflow the FLOATING POINT ERROR (**ERR** = 48) is generated.)
53	%Illegal argument in LOG	Negative or zero argument to **LOG** function. Value returned is the argument as passed to the function. (C)
54	%Imaginary square roots	Attempt to take square root of a number

ERR	MESSAGE PRINTED	MEANING
		less than zero. The value returned is the square root of the absolute value of the argument. (C)
55	?Subscript out of range	Attempt to reference an array element beyond the number of elements created for the array when it was dimensioned.
56	?Can't invert matrix	Attempt to invert a singular or nearly singular matrix.
57	?Out of data	The **DATA** list was exhausted and a **READ** requested additional data.
58	?ON statement out of range	The index value in an **ON-GOTO** or **ON-GOSUB** statement is less than one or greater than the number of line numbers in the list.
59	?Not enough data in record	An **INPUT** statement did not find enough data in one line to satisfy all the specified variables.
60	?Integer overflow, FOR loop	The integer index in a **FOR** loop attempted to go beyond 32766 or below −32767.
61	%Division by 0	Attempt by the user program to divide some quantity by zero. If no transfer is made to an error-handler routine, a 0 is returned as the result. (C)
62	?No run-time system	The run-time system referenced has not been added to the system list of run-time systems.
63	?FIELD overflows buffer	Attempt to use **FIELD** to allocate more space than exists in the specified buffer.
64	?Not a random access device	Attempt to perform random access I/O to a nonrandom access device.

ERR	MESSAGE PRINTED	MEANING
65	?Illegal MAGTAPE ( ) usage	Improper use of the **MAGTAPE** function.
66	?Missing special feature	User program employs a Basic-Plus feature not present on the given installation.
67	?Illegal switch usage	A **CCL** command contains an error in an otherwise valid CCL switch. (For example, the /SI:n switch was used without a value for *n* or a colon; or more than one of the same type of CCL switch was specified.) A file specification switch is not the last element in a file specification or is missing a colon or an argument.

MESSAGE PRINTED	MEANING
	Nonrecoverable
?Arguments don't match	Arguments in a function call do not match, in number or in type, the arguments defined for the function.
?Bad line number pair	Line numbers specified in a **LIST** or **DELETE** command were formatted incorrectly.
?Bad number in PRINT-USING	Format specified in the **PRINT-USING** string cannot be used to print one or more values.
?Can't CONTinue	Program was stopped or ended at a spot from which execution cannot be resumed.
?Data type error	Incorrect usage of floating-point, integer, or character string format variable or constant where some other data type was necessary.
?DEF without FNEND	A second **DEF** statement was encountered in the processing of a user function without an **FNEND**

MESSAGE PRINTED	MEANING
	statement terminating the first user function definition.
?End of statement not seen	Statement contains too many elements to be processed correctly.
?Execute only file	Attempt was made to add, delete, or list a statement in a compiled (.BAC) format file.
?Expression too complicated	This error usually occurs when parentheses have been nested too deeply. The depth allowable depends on the individual expression.
?File exists-RENAME/REPLACE	A file of the name specified in a **SAVE** command already exists. In order to save the current program under the name specified, use **REPLACE**, or use **RENAME** followed by **SAVE**.
?FNEND without DEF	An **FNEND** statement was encountered in the user program without a previous function call having been executed.
?FNEND without function call	A **FNEND** statement was encountered in the user program without a previous **DEF** statement being seen.
?FOR without NEXT	A **FOR** statement was encountered in the user program without a corresponding **NEXT** statement to terminate the loop.
?Illegal conditional clause	Incorrectly formatted conditional expression.
?Illegal DEF nesting	The range of one function definition crosses the range of another function definition.
?Illegal dummy variable	One of the variables in the dummy variable list of user-defined function is not a legal variable name.
?Illegal expression	Double operators, missing operators, mis-

MESSAGE PRINTED	MEANING
	matched parentheses, or some similar error has been found in an expression.
?Illegal FIELD variable	The **FIELD** variable specified is unacceptable.
?Illegal FN redefinition	Attempt was made to redefine a user function.
?Illegal function name	Attempt was made to define a function with a function name not subscribing to the established format.
?Illegal IF statement	Incorrectly formatted **IF** statement.
?Illegal in immediate mode	User issued a statement for execution in immediate mode that can only be performed as part of a program.
?Illegal line number(s)	Line number reference outside the range $1<n<32767$.
?Illegal mode mixing	String and numeric operations cannot be mixed.
?Illegal statement	Attempt was made to execute a statement that did not compile without errors.
?Illegal symbol	An unrecognizable character was encountered; for example, a line consisting of a # character.
?Illegal verb	The Basic verb portion of the statement cannot be recognized.
%Inconsistent function usage	A function is defined with a certain number of arguments but is elsewhere referenced with a different number of arguments. Fix the reference to match the definition and reload the program to reset the function definition.
%Inconsistent subscript use	A subscripted variable is being used with a number of dimensions different from the number with which it was originally defined.

MESSAGE PRINTED	MEANING
x(y)K of memory used	Message printed by the **LENGTH** command. The value for x is the current size, to the nearest 1k-word increment, of the program in memory. The value for y is the size to which the program can expand, given the run-time system being used and the job's private memory size maximum set by the system manager.
?Literal string needed	A variable name was used where a numeric or character string was necessary.
?Matrix dimension error	Attempt was made to dimension a matrix to more than two dimensions, or an error was made in the syntax of a **DIM** statement.
?Matrix or array without DIM	A matrix or array element was referenced beyond the range of an implicitly dimensioned matrix.
?Maximum memory exceeded	During an **OLD** operation, the job's private memory size maximum was reached. While running a program the system required more memory for string or I/O buffer space and the job's private memory size maximum or the system maximum (16k words for Basic-Plus) was reached.
?Modifier error	Attempt to use one of the statement modifiers (**FOR**, **WHILE**, **UNTIL**, **IF**, or **UNLESS**) incorrectly. An **OPEN** statement modifier, such as a **RECORDSIZE**, **CLUSTERSIZE**, **FILESIZE**, or **MODE** option, is not in the correct order.
?NEXT without FOR	A **NEXT** statement was encountered in the user program without a previous **FOR** statement having been seen.
?No logins	Message printed if the system is full and cannot accept additional users or if further log-ins are disabled by the system manager.
?Not enough available memory	An attempt is made to load a nonprivileged com-

MESSAGE PRINTED	MEANING
	piled program that is too large to run, given the job's private memory size maximum. The program must be made privileged to allow it to expand above a private memory size maximum; or the system manager must increase the job's private memory size maximum to accommodate the program.
?Number is needed	A character string or variable name was used where a number was necessary.
?1 or 2 dimensions only	Attempt was made to dimension a matrix to more than two dimensions.
?ON statement needs GOTO	A statement beginning with **ON** does not contain a **GOTO** or **GOSUB** clause.
Please say HELLO	Message printed by the **LOGIN** system program. User not logged into the system has typed something other than a legal, logged-out command to the system.
?Please use the RUN command	A transfer of control (as in a **GOTO**, **GOSUB**, or **IF-GOTO** statement) cannot be performed from immediate mode.
?PRINT-USING buffer overflow	Format specified contains a field too large to be manipulated by the **PRINT-USING** statement.
?PRINT-USING format error	An error was made in the construction of the string used to supply the output format in a **PRINT-USING** statement.
?Program lost-Sorry	A fatal system error has occurred that caused the user program to be lost. This error can indicate hardware problems or use of an improperly compiled program. Consult the system manager or the discussion of such errors in the *RSTS/E System Manager's Guide*.

MESSAGE PRINTED	MEANING
?Redimensioned array	Usage of an array or matrix within the user program has caused Basic-Plus to redimension the array implicitly.
?RESUME and no error	A **RESUME** statement was encountered where no error had occurred to cause a transfer into an error-handling routine via the **ON ERROR GOTO** statement.
?RETURN without GOSUB	**RETURN** statement encountered in user program without a previous **GOSUB** statement having been executed.
%SCALE factor interlock	An attempt was made to execute a program or source statement with the current scale factor. The program runs but the system uses the scale factor of the program in memory rather than the current scale factor. Use **REPLACE** and **OLD** or recompile the program to run with the current scale factor. (C)
?Statement not found	Reference is made within the program to a line number that is not within the program.
Stop	**STOP** statement was executed. The user can usually continue program execution by typing **CONT** and striking the RETURN key.
?String is needed	A number or variable name was used where a character string was necessary.
?Syntax error	Basic-Plus statement was incorrectly formatted.
?Too few arguments	The function has been called with a number of arguments not equal to the number defined for the function.
?Too many arguments	A user-defined function may have up to five arguments.

MESSAGE PRINTED	MEANING
?Undefined function called	Basic-Plus interpreted some statement component as a function call for which there is no defined function (system or user).
?What?	Command or immediate mode statement entered to Basic-Plus could not be processed. Illegal verb or improper format error most likely.
?Wrong math package	Program was compiled on a system with either the two-word or four-word math package and an attempt is made to run the program on a system with the opposite math package. Recompile the program using the math package of the system on which it will be run.

Appendix VII
Sample Errors and Their Diagnosis

Syntax errors: Those which occur upon entering an incorrect statement. Each of these statements should immediately be corrected and reentered.

1. `100 Y = SQR(A,25)`

    `?Arguments don't match at line 100`

Explanation: This function calls for only one argument. Since two are used in this example, it is interpreted as an error.

2. `130    Q = (P+1)(R-5)`
    `130    A = 2*B*((C-5)/(B+2)`

    `?Illegal expression at line 130`

Explanation: These represent errors in forming the expression. In the first, the operator is omitted between parentheses. In the second, the close parenthesis is missing on the right.

3. `100    C = A + '123'`
    `100    A = MID(X$,5,3)`

    `?Illegal mode mixing at line 100`

Explanation: In the first statement, A (a numeric quantity) and the literal '123' (a string quantity) are included in an addition operation; this is not possible. In the second, an attempt is made to place a string value into a numeric variable. Corrected versions might appear as:

    `100    C = A + 123`
    `100    A$ = MID(X$,5,3)`

4. `100    SUBROUTINE EXAMPLE`
    `.`
    `.`
    `.`
    `150    GOSUB 500`
    `.`
    `.`
    `.`

```
340     PRINT A,B,C
500     !SUBROUTINE
  .
  .
  .
620     RETURN
```

?RETURN without a GOSUB at line 620

Explanation: At first consideration, this appears as it should be since the subroutine is executed via a GOSUB at statement 500. However, the main program will "fall through" into the subroutine after statement 340. A GOTO should be included prior to statement 500.

```
5.  200     GOTO 405
      .
      .
      .
    400     ...
    410     ...
```

?Statement not found at line 200

Explanation: This is obvious: the GOTO refers to statement 405 which does not exist in the program.

```
6.  100     ON ERROR GOTO 810
      .
      .
      .
    200     INPUT #1,A,B,C
      .
      .
      .
    800     ...
    820     ...
```

?Statement not found at line 200

Explanation: This is a very subtle error and anything but obvious: How can we have a "statement not found" when an INPUT operation is being executed? This happens when an error condition occurs (such as ERR 11—end of file) which should cause a branch, in this case, to statement 810 (via statement 100). However, statement 810 does not exist, hence the error message which refers to the GOTO of statement 100.

```
7.  100     IF A<0 PRINT 'LESS' ELSE PRINT 'NOT LESS'
```

?Illegal IF statement at line 100

This form of the IF statement requires use of the word **THEN** following the condition.

Errors which result from commands or immediate mode statements that cannot be carried out.

8. NEW ABC
    100 !DEMO
      .
      .
      .
    32767 END

    SAVE

    ?File exists - RENAME/REPLACE

Explanation: A file named ABC.BAS is already stored in this account. The user should either select a new name for the current file (**RENAME**) then **SAVE** it, or replace the presently stored file with the current one (**REPLACE**).

9. OLD TEST

    ?Please say HELLO

Explanation: The user has not signed on to an account; must sign on and respond to the password request—for example:

    HELLO 25,20

    Password: (enter password)

10. OLD EXAMPL

    ?End of file on device

    LIST
    100 !NO END STATEMENT
    110 INPUT A,B,C
    120 D = A+B-C
    130 PRINT D,A,B,C
    140 GOTO 110

Explanation: The END statement is omitted; hence the error "End of file on device." Enter the statement **32767 END**, then **REPLACE** the program.

11. DIM A(30)

    ?Illegal in immediate mode

Some Basic statements (such as FOR, ON GOTO, etc.) can be executed only as part of a program.

Error messages which occur during execution of a program. Note that these can be trapped using the ON ERROR *statement. The error number is shown to the right of the error message.*

12. 100   OPEN 'ABC.XYZ' FOR INPUT AS FILE #1

?Can't find file or account at line 100 (ERR 5)

Explanation: The file ABC.XYZ does not exist on the user's account. The user should check to make certain that this is the proper file name.

13. 100   OPEN 'A.A' FOR INPUT AS FILE #4
      .
      .
      .
200   INPUT #5, A,B,C

?I/O channel not open at line 200 (ERR 9)

Explanation: The file A.A has been opened on channel 4 (line 100), but the INPUT statement refers to channel 5. They should both refer to the same channel number.

14. 100   OPEN 'A.A' FOR INPUT AS FILE #1
110   INPUT 1, A,B,C
120   D = A+B-C
130   PRINT A,B,C
140   GOTO 110
32767 END

?End of file on device at 120 (ERR 11)

Explanation: Execution of statement 110 has continued until the program attempted to ready beyond the last data record. Detection of end of file is described in Chapter 3.

15. 140   NAME 'EX2.BAS' AS 'EXAMPL.BAS'

?Name or account now exists at line 140 (ERR 16)

Explanation: The file currently named EX2.BAS is to have its name changed to EXAMPL.BAS. However, another file already exists named EXAMPL.BAS. Either select another name or first kill EXAMPL.BAS.

16. 100   DIM #1, A%(1000)
110   S% = A%(1)

?Virtual array not yet open at line 110 (ERR 45)

Explanation: A% has been defined as being associated with a virtual array file in statement 100. Then an element is read from the array without opening the file. The file must first be opened before it can be processed.

17. `100    READ A,B,C`

`     .`
`     .`
`     .`

`300    DATA 25,-378,XYZ`

`%Data format error at line 100`

Explanation: Statement 100 attempts to read three numeric quantities (A, B, and C). However, the third field of the input data (statement 300) contains nonnumeric data. This can also occur with the INPUT statement.

18. `100    A = 10000`
`120    B% = 20*A`

`%Integer error at line 120` (ERR 51)

Explanation: The computed result in statement 120 is 200,000. This is too large to be stored in the integer quantity B%. This may be corrected by using B in place of B%.

19. `100    FOR I = 1 TO 15`
`110        READ C`
`120        S = C(I+5)        !INTENDED TO BE C*(I+5)`
`     .`
`     .`
`     .`
`200    NEXT I`

`?Subscript out of range at line 120` (ERR 55)

Explanation: In statement 120, the simple variable C is interpreted by the Basic system as a subscripted variable because of the parentheses. Since Basic automatically dimensions to 10 in a case such as this, the program will execute until I+5 reaches 11.

20. `100    READ A,B`

`     .`
`     .`
`     .`

`200    GOTO 100`

`?Out of data at line 100` (ERR 57)

Explanation: Statement 100 has already read all of the values in the DATA statement.

21.   3 (3)

```
100    INPUT A,B
110    C = 0
120    D = A/C
```

%Division by 0 at line 120   (ERR 61)

Explanation: The value of **C** is zero and division by zero is impossible. However, execution will continue (unless the **ON ERROR** has been set) and this message will be repeated each time the zero division occurs.

22.
```
100    ON ERROR GOTO 500
120    OPEN 'X.X' FOR INPUT AS FILE #1
130    OPEN 'Y.Y' FOR OUTPUT AS FILE #2
        .
        .
        .
210 READ A
        .
        .
        .
500    !GENERAL ERROR TRAP
510    IF ERR = 5 GOTO 600
520    IF ERR = 57 GOTO 700
        .
        .
        .
600    !FILE OPEN ERROR
        .
        .
        .
670    PRINT 'FILE "X.X" DOES NOT EXIST -
       CORRECTIVE ACTION TAKEN.'
680    GOTO 130
700    !DATA STATEMENT EXHAUSTED
710    PRINT 'NO MORE DATA -
       WILL USE RANDOM GENERATION'
```

FILE   "X.X" DOES NOT EXIST -
       CORRECTIVE ACTION TAKEN.

?Out of data at line 210

Explanation: The file X.X does not exist in the account so the **ON ERROR** statement caused a branch to statement **500**; the ERR 5 in turn caused the **600** error sequence to be executed and a branch back to statement **130** (line **680**). Statement **210** attempted to **READ** when there were no more data fields in the **DATA** statement. This error (57) should cause statement **710** to be executed. However, the system responded as if the **ON ERROR** statement never existed. The reason lies with the previous error recovery. In order to "re-enable" the ON ERROR, the statement 680 should be 680 RESUME 130. Then the output would have been:

```
FILE "X.X" DOES NOT EXIST -
     CORRECTIVE ACTION TAKEN.

NO MORE DATA - WILL USE RANDOM GENERATION.
```

Index